SENTENCED

A True Story

ANDREW HAWKE   VICTORIA OAK

Grosvenor House
Publishing Limited

The right of Andrew Hawke and Victoria Oak
to be identified as the author of this
work has been asserted in accordance with Section 78
of the Copyright, Designs and Patents Act 1988

The book cover is copyright to
Barbara Borko hello@barbaraborko.com

This book is published by
Grosvenor House Publishing Ltd
Link House
140 The Broadway, Tolworth, Surrey, KT6 7HT.
www.grosvenorhousepublishing.co.uk

A CIP record for this book
is available from the British Library

ISBN 978-1-83975-390-9

DEDICATION

To Quinlan, Samantha, Emma, Tom and William
and to BBC Radio 4 (our favourite station)
for giving us good times
and getting us through the rest.

CONTENTS

Some names have been changed to protect
peoples identities.

ACKNOWLEDGEMENTS

Andy and I are indebted to Becky Banning and all at Grosvenor House Publishing for painstakingly turning an idea into a reality; our gratitude to Marie Estrella, Jasmin Jagger and my daughter Emma, for taking up the editing baton with enthusiasm and sensitivity. Thank you to Louise my daughter-in-law, Sandy Lee and Maureen Rollo-Walker, for doing the lion's share of the typing. We are grateful to Charles Watson, Paul Malvey, Jenny Burt, my son-in-law Ben, Isabelle Craner, Anu Patel, Barbara Roberts, Amanda Browne, Lucinda Snowden and all who both read and advised. Thank you to Debbie Simmons, Maria Wesson and Sally Gaunt, who provided the encouragement necessary to keep going whatever the cost, and finally to my other children Samantha, Tom and William for whose computer know-how and emotional support throughout this book's journey I will forever be grateful.

To my beautiful, sainted mama, who sadly was unable to see the publication of this book RIP.

ACKNOWLEDGMENTS

FOREWORD

In the course of my business career, I have been lucky enough to meet hundreds of talented and admirable people, but I can honestly say, I have only met one who would do what Vicky Oak did. She gave shelter to a convicted drug trafficker; opened up her home, shared meals and gave support to a man everyone else would have considered to be a danger. Vicky's unshakable faith in humanity led a true friendship to develop between her and Andy, which may ultimately have saved his life. Vicky has the capacity to look beyond the obvious and see patterns and solutions that evade most other people. She is blessed with a deep wisdom which comes from her inquiring mind and a truly creative vision of the world. We often say to our friends, your life reads like a book but in Vicky's case it's actually true. That Vicky and Andy should write a book about their friendship comes as no surprise. It's a true story that only they can tell. Enjoy the read: it will leave you believing you can become a better person.

Debbie Simmons

I am Vicky's daughter and was privileged to have been part of the "blood, sweat and tears" editing process or more accurately, therapy sessions. Andy has become the "cool" uncle for me and my siblings. He spends Christmas with us and will be at all our weddings; he is family and we are very lucky for that. Vicky was a life line for Andy but over time Andy became Vicky's "Rock". Whatever mountainous struggles we face, angels can appear just when we need them.

Their unconventional friendship has restored my faith in the importance of felt human connection rather than adhering to society's safe conventions. Mavericks to their core!

Thank you Andy and Vicky for giving us that,

Emma

PREFACE

Samantha

It was June 2005 and my girlfriends Alex, Alice and I had been travelling for five months. By now wizened veterans of the backpacker trail, we arrived in Bangkok and hauled our moth-eaten and musky gear into what felt like the hundredth hostel dormitory. After subtly assessing our roommates and dumping our backpacks on our beds, we went to find the nearest internet cafe as we always did, to let our parents know we had arrived safely. We got chatting to two English girls who showed us the way. We were intrigued to find out that they were heading for the local prison. A nineteen-year-old Brit called Michael had been caught trying to smuggle 3000 pills out of Bangkok. He'd been given a life sentence. His parents couldn't afford to fly out from England to visit him and had asked them to go instead. I had heard of Bang Kwang gaol from reading a book a few months before called *The Damage Done* by an ex-inmate. It was notorious for its brutality and my heart went out to this teenager.

The next day we decided to visit Michael ourselves and naively turned up at the prison in the suburbs, only to discover that thousands of prisoners were housed in several blocks and his block had had their visiting day the day before. We were told it was Block 6's visiting day but without names of prisoners we would not be allowed in. On a hunch, I rang the British Consulate. The receptionist was very helpful and immediately gave us three names. I'm not sure how we decided who visited who. I think it was a lottery based on who sat on which chair in the visitors room. When I say room, it was actually a dilapidated concrete corridor with a foot gap between the inmates and the visitors, these areas separated by two walls of bars. The perspex screen and phone were introduced a year later when my sister Emma visited, but for now we had to shout to each other above the din of the other voices.

After all the rigmarole of finding prisoners and getting through security with around thirty others, mostly Thai mothers, wives and girlfriends, we were left with only an hour to chat. I'm not sure what I was expecting when Andy came and sat down in front of me. He'll kill me for saying this but I had imagined someone younger. However I got on with him immediately. He was a great listener which couldn't have been better as I had a multitude of stories to tell from my travels. He asked a lot of questions and was clearly very bright. I told him I was going to be studying Drama and English at Uni which led us to discussing literature. He had read way more than I had. Much to my surprise, the hour was suddenly up and we girls were being ushered out. I hadn't even asked Andy about his own situation. He had shown no self-pity. I did ask him if he wanted anything from the visitor's shop in the way of food or cigarettes and put in an order on my way out.

Despite resolving to write to Andy, as I left the prison I never for a moment imagined the possible repercussions of this chance encounter.

INTRODUCTION

Vicky

All sorts of questions are rising to the surface this morning. What is it Andy and I are embarking on? A memoir, biography, autobiography, critiques on each other, to each other, to ourselves? Andy has a story to tell of his time in Thailand's Bang Kwang prison. I know something of his early life, but I know very little about what happened to him between leaving school and being arrested. 'Bikes and pubs', he says. Three little words to cover twenty-three years. His life is his story and he can tell it (or not tell it) anyway he chooses. But then I wonder, do those aspects of his life, that he puts to the back of his drawer, make for a more interesting story, a more authentic book?

And what about my part in all of this, 'Mrs Oak, South-West London housewife'. Who wants to read about me, except as it relates to Andy? He is a rarity. I was told that a person of his high intelligence and wit only enters through Bang Kwang's gates once in twenty-five years.

I belonged to a book club for two years and, in almost every book selected, the wife hardly featured except as a worn-out, bitter non-event. That's not how I see myself, although there were times when that description did come close to the mark. I will try and convey the truth of my story as I see it but, before you read this book, will it have been censored or sanitised? Will fear have got in the way of honesty?

I was born a year after Andy in 1958. As a teenager I would only have needed to take the District Line to Earl's Court, then jump on another train to Ealing, to be at his door.

I first heard of Andy when my daughter, Samantha, visited him in prison on her 'Gap year.' [1] *On her return, she began to exchange letters with Andy and allowed me to read them. Eloquent, loquacious, wry and angry by turns, I realised that his exquisite writing was a dying art. None of the sloppy email punctuation and syntax common nowadays. He was painting in minute detail, in the manner of Henry James, his thoughts and feelings, coloured by the frustrating penal system he was having to endure. His letters often told more by what they left unsaid.*

A year after Samantha my other daughter, Emma, went to visit Andy. She said the smile he gave her through the perspex glass lit up the whole visitors' area. The only painful moment came at the end of the call – there was no warning that the session was coming to an end, and Andy was in the middle of a sentence when the phones were cut off. He tried to mouth what he wanted to say, and looked grief-stricken at her uncomprehending face.

A few months later, Samantha sent a photo of me taken about seventeen years earlier, telling Andy that I would love a letter. My reply to Andy began by putting him firmly in the picture as to my age and status – middle-class and middle-aged. So began seven years of letters.

Andy

I've never really thought, despite the exhortations of kith and kin, that I would, or even should, write some kind of memoir of my time as a prisoner in the 'Land of Smiles'. Even now, I have misgivings. To put down on paper my own experience, internal and external, subjective and objective, clashes with my most basic, most instinctive nature, the default setting of my being. This is hard to overcome. Silence has always been golden to me. It gives nothing away – no utterances to be misinterpreted, no levers to be used against one.

This is even truer if we are at the mercy of a prison regime. A careless word can cause havoc. Consequence spread out in a series of ripples, some of which then rebound off the metaphorical walls of our existence to come right back and bite us on the arse.

Six months after my physical release from gaol, I am still hemmed in by the walls erected in my noggin and it's time to start knocking a few of them down. Not *all* of these, of course, since some of them have foundations that go deep, deep back in time. They may be all that is holding the construction which is 'me' together. I have no wish to, well, deconstruct that person entirely and start from scratch. Just de-programming the gaol-house mentality would be a major achievement, since the habits of discretion, already in my make-up, were magnified many fold by living for over fourteen years amongst people that the state deemed fit to put within the walls of Bang Kwang.

It is humbling to know how large I figured in Vicky's thoughts in those seven or eight years, and embarrassing to admit that this degree of focus was not immediately reciprocated, at least not in full. Only when I actually met this extraordinary 'Putney housewife'[2] did I come to realise how much she meant to me.

"Society, as we have constituted it, will have no place for me, has none to offer; but nature, whose sweet rain falls on unjust and just alike, will have clefts in the rocks where I may hide, and secret valleys in whose silence I may weep undisturbed. She will hang the night with stars so that I may walk abroad in the darkness without stumbling, and send the wind over my footprints so that none may track me to my hurt: she will cleanse me in great waters, and with bitter herbs make me whole".

Oscar Wilde, *'De Profundis'*

PRISON

"The most terrible thing about it is not that it breaks one's heart – hearts are made to be broken – but that it turns one's heart to stone".

Oscar Wilde, *De Profundis*

ANDY

1998 Bangkok

Wednesday 9 December

I am smoking a last cigarette in Don Muang Airport. Two dozen other people are also puffing away and the ashtrays are overflowing. The air quality in this designated smoking room is no better than downtown Bangkok in the rush hour. The haze of smoke is suddenly yanked to one side as yet another fellow leper opens the door. I put down my book and raise my head to look and see behind the newcomer a clock. Buggeration, it's almost midnight!

I hustle out of there smartish, heading for the gents clutching my carry-on bag. Once in, I take out the smuggler's belt I'd been given by the couriers the day before. It's flexible plastic with a Velcro fastener on the flap. Inside lie three bricks of double UO Globe weighing in at 350 grams each, still in the original wrappers from the manufacturer up in the Golden Triangle over the border in Burma. Velcro attaches the two ends in front.

I put on the belt in the cubicle, the over-size trousers I've had made accommodating it nicely. It would be ill-advised to bend at the waist, the damn thing adds at least two and a half inches back there.

The 00.40 flight was called at midnight and I was supposed to be first up at the gate, though I wasn't told why. I'm late.

There are fifteen or so people ahead of me, queuing up for the scanners.

I shuffle forward, running a mental checklist; wristwatch in carry-on check, belt, with metal buckle, ditto check, spectacles, in hand ready for the X-ray, check, jewellery, not wearing any, check. Damn, I forgot to tell the tailor to put a plastic zip on these trousers. Oh well, can't be helped, plus I'm sure that many of these people must be going through the metal detector wearing similar and they aren't setting it off. So onwards I go, wearing the blank, stoic look of late-night plane passengers the world over. It's now my turn.

00.20, Thursday 10 December

I step through the arch and the alarm beeps immediately. 'Oh shit, oh shit, oh shit' and 'what the fuck' race through my brain, while out of my mouth comes, "but I have no metal on me". The tiny little Thai woman, in her twenties, in some sort of airport uniform, tells me to step through and to one side as she apologetically starts to pat me down. Soon enough she comes upon the unyielding thick mass on the small of my back.

"What is, pleez?"

"It's a back support," I say feebly.

"Wait pleez."

I stand there like a div while she goes off to consult someone. I watch as other passengers go through the machine, wearing belt buckles of metal without it making a beep. I don't get it. She didn't touch the machine in any way to activate the alarm, so it MUST have been something on me – but what? Could my zipper have set it off after all? No

– ludicrous! I cannot believe that all these other passengers streaming through didn't have a metal zipper on between them. My fillings? Even more ridiculous. My heart has been pounding like a jackhammer since the alarm triggered, and my breathing is fast and shallow. The ancient fight/flight reflex is battering away at me. I can see airport security numbering almost a dozen from where I'm standing. Flight then? No, trying to get into the plane is pointless and in the other direction is the whole damned airport. Even were I an Olympic track medallist, I would never make it.

A middle-aged Thai fellow in black trousers, white shirt, collar undone, ambles up to me. "This way please," he says motioning me to a door. I take one last look at the Jet bound for Copenhagen knowing I'll never get there now.

I am ushered into a bare room, cheap carpet tiles, plaster board walls and a dark hole above where the ceiling should be. Three bog-standard tables, steel legs and ersatz Formica tops are all that is in it. The Thai chap motions that I should lift my shirt. I do so. He signals that I should remove the belt. Again I comply. He frowns, starts to speak, thinks better of it and moves to the table, opening the flap, with the unmistakeable rasp of tearing Velcro filling the small space. The three blocks are there, bound in black electrical tape. He is motionless for a few seconds, then it's "You wait" and he's off out of the door. I note that the word "pleez" has vanished from the conversation.

After what feels like an eternity, two men enter and I am led to a room and plonked down in front of a very large, low table. It has various inlaid detail, some mother-of-pearl, other stuff. Right in front of me, under the clear lacquer surface are the words, in English,

"May this table groan under the weight of seized heroin."

I lean back into the long low sofa. I know I'll be in here for a while.

Men are walking in and out, some with the purpose, I note, of taking a look at the newest witless 'farang' to get reeled in. It's a good twenty to thirty minutes before someone approaches me directly and it is to ask if I want something to drink. I am parched, unsurprisingly, and he reels off a list, "tea, coffee, Pepsi, Sprite, maybe beer? You want whiskey?" I've not had a drink in over a day and I'm for damned sure not about to get liquored up just prior to the inevitable interrogation which I can see coming. I ask for water and get it after a few minutes.

Finally my Samsonite suitcase gets brought in and given a good rummage. There is nothing in it to warrant further attention. A uniform sits next to me and starts the ball rolling. He asks my full name and date of birth.

"Are you sure this your passport?"

"Absolutely sure." There is about a kilo of China White sitting on that table and he's concerned about the possibility that I'm travelling on a dodgy book?

"Where then are you going?" a half smile.

"What?"

"After you go to Copenhagen, then what you do?"

"Oh, I go to SAS Hotel and book into a room, wait for a phone call."

"Whose call?"

"I'm not sure, I'm only the courier".

"Who gives you drug?"

"A guy in the car park at Robinsons".

"Who the man?"

"I don't know. I've never seen him before but he knew me by name so he must have had the correct information. He, or maybe someone else, called me by phone in the Honey Hotel."

I learn much later that this was a well-known haunt of dope dealers and smugglers, so much so that it was already going out of fashion.

Amsterdam

26 November (two weeks earlier)

It was 2am and I was sitting at a bar having a drink with my funds visibly dwindling in front of me. I was homeless, jobless and potless, and was feeling lower than a snake's belly. The love of my life had left me without reason. She had taken our son with her and cut all ties with me. Hitting rock-bottom, I had decided to go to Amsterdam to blow all my cash, intending to throw myself off the ferry on the way back. I was talking to a chap in a bar there about the desperate state I was in, in the way one can with a chance-met stranger, when another voice said, "I might be able to help with at least part of that." A tall chap, who I assumed to be Dutch, then pitched me the smuggling job, all expenses up front. Five grand total fee for one carry to Denmark. I had nothing to lose.

Until that moment, other than selling the odd bit of weed and road-traffic offences, I've never considered myself a criminal. At any other time I would have said no, possibly quite forcefully, perhaps taking time to explain that I'd always had an abhorrence of smack and anyone using it. But this was now, and my highfalutin moral, ethical and practical objections vanished faster than a politician's manifesto promises. I accepted on the spot.

In twenty-four hours I was on the flight to Bangkok. Looking out of the plane's window on that late November afternoon in 1998, I saw frost on the grass by the runway. I would not see frost or snow again for more than fourteen years.

Bangkok

27 November

The Taiwanese airliner disgorges its passengers into Arrivals at Don Muang Airport. It's mid-morning. I pick up my luggage and make for the exit and a cab. As I go through the doors, I'm hit with a wall of heat and humidity, stopping me dead in my tracks. I start sweating immediately. I grab the first available taxi with a meter and say "Sukhumvit Soi II" as per verbal instructions in the 'Dam.

I check into the little hotel: it is clean, utilitarian. I shower off the travel grime and lie down, listening to the humming of the air-conditioning. I doze off.

Near sunset I wake, groggy and disorientated. I venture out to remedy my hunger. After bowl of chicken in peanut sauce over rice which I get from a roadside vendor, I step over to what looks like a makeshift bar set against the wall of a building. While downing my second Singha beer, I find myself tapped on the shoulder by the trunk of a young elephant. A smiling Thai boy stands beside him with an upturned palm.

The traffic is mayhem, I watch three lanes of cars interspersed with a number of pick-up trucks, larger goods vehicles, blue city buses, taxis, motorcycle taxis and tuk-tuks or samlors as they are known in Thailand. There seems to be a fourth lane by the sidewalk and I am duly surprised by a motorcyclist with a girl sitting side-saddle behind him, going the wrong way down it. Behind them I see a moped with five family members somehow hanging on. No one bats an eyelid. It is chaos, loud and full of petrochemical fumes and it is already giving me a headache, not to mention a hint of nausea.

The first bar I wander into, I'm accosted by half-a-dozen girls at once. "Me love you long time. You buy me lady drink." I look at the Mamasan behind the bar imploringly as a five foot, bikini-clad Isaarn girl slides her hand between my thighs. Mamasan nods and growls something in a low voice, and the would-be seductress backs off pouting a little. I nod back gratefully and slowly sip my beer as I take in the room. I'm in this country for one reason only and I'm loath to part with cash which I'm going to need once back in Blighty, or so I think. I will later wonder whether I'd have done the same if I'd known what the future held for me,

For the next two days I wander from bar to bar. I make friends with an East Midlands bloke, called Jim – very impressive belly: think circumference, think equator. He takes me to the infamous Pat Pong area. In the first bar we enter, girls are gyrating round poles, strutting bikini-clad, in high heels between tables and he seems to know them all. He drags me away before I am accosted by a lady boy, a 'katoy'.

We move on to yet another girlie bar, and I'm getting déjà vu. This time a naked girl is squatting in front of a German tourist, writing his name with big magic markers wielded in a most novel manner. I cannot help but grin at the sheer inventiveness of these women in devising ways of getting their Marks to part with their, well, in his case marks – or was it euros? By now though, I cannot take much more, and resolve to get out of Bangkok and make for the coast.

Apart from Phuket I don't know any of the other resorts by name, so I get a map from reception. The helpful lady identifies a couple of well-known resorts; one is near enough to reach easily. So I'm off to Pattaya. Yes, I am that green.

A couple of hours on an express coach and I'm there. The place has a slight air of Benidorm about it, at least in daylight. I begin to notice that yet again I'm surrounded by girlie bars, with a sprinkling of restaurants and hotels but I'm thinking, "Jesus, it can't all be like this can it?" Here, English signs are everywhere; 'Hard Wok Cafe', 'Monica's', 'Pussy Galore' and 'Pink Tulip'.

I meet an American couple and we go for dinner at a beachfront restaurant. The husband, Oliver, tells me how the presence of the US Navy during the Vietnam War turned Pattaya into Sodom-by-the-Sea. An entire carrier group of horny sailors attracts thousands of hookers, pimps, shills and associated trades. The US Air Force contributed too, as did the Army, but it was mainly the Navy. From fishing village to sex tourist mecca in a few years.

Phyllis, his wife, points out that despite the 'official' cultural picture of modest and demure womanhood which permeates the society, an army of women engage in prostitution on a casual, part-time or full-time basis. It's that or starve and their families with them. Almost all of the women lucky enough to be working the foreign tourist trade send substantial sums home to support their families. In the hinterland, away from bulging foreign or 'farang' wallets, a far larger number of women and girls unfortunately work for much smaller rewards. I say, she seems remarkably well-informed. She giggles.

Thus educated, I try to make like I'm having a holiday by the seaside but the vibe of ersatz eroticism and frenetic fornication is overpowering. At the suggestion of a Belgian bar owner, Bruno, I fly to the island of Koh Samui. After a short, low hop across the Gulf, the plane turns, wing angling sharply down to what I see looks like a strip of tarmac the size of a postage stamp. A bounce or two on touchdown and the plane pulls up a couple of yards from the perimeter fence, swinging away with rotors still spinning. I disembark shaking with relief.

I take a cab to Lamai, the main town on the island's eastern side but I'm looking for something on a beach, a hut, or chalet or something. An agent directs me, again in a cab, to a little place a couple of miles or so down the coast.

There I find the idyllic spot I have been hoping for, a simple beach hut, bathroom and bedroom with ceiling fan. A cove with a little reef protecting it, the tide currently receding. Five yards to the left a beachfront bar and restaurant, very small, perhaps four people there apart from the English barman and his German wife in the kitchen. I plonk myself down at a table with an ice-cold Tiger beer, put my book, *The Sleepwalkers* by Arthur Koestler, down by my side and look out at the horizon. I'm shaded by palms, there's a pleasant little breeze, and I think: "Now this is more like it."

I settle down and do the lotus-eater thing for a week or so. When I look out at night between whiskey and games of chess with the restaurant owner, pinpricks of light bob around far offshore, the lanterns of small fishing boats, far outnumbered by the glittering diamond dust of stars above. Damn, I could get used to this.

These few halcyon days are wonderful but I am coming up to my deadline. I leave behind my copy of *The Sleepwalkers* as I leave the tranquillity of the little cove, with a pang of regret that both are over for me.

On the ferry to the mainland, I get into conversation with a chap called Fred from Rochdale. He offers to give me a lift to Bangkok in return for splitting the petrol money, which suits me fine.

We end up taking three days, partly because, on the second day, in torrential rain, the car aquaplanes, spins 180 degrees and narrowly misses ending up in a deep ditch. Shaken by this experience, we decide to spend a night in Hua Hin, a resort kept dignified and refined from its days as the seaside retreat of choice for the then young king Bhumipol in the 1950s.

Arriving in Bangkok, Fred drops me as promised at the beginning of Sukhumvit Road and I grab a tuk-tuk to the Honey Hotel on Soi 17. I am back in the city and now I have to get ready to do the job I've been trying to avoid thinking about for the last two weeks. There's a lump in my stomach as heavy as lead. I square my shoulders, trying to shrug off the tension, the apprehension; alright, the fear.

"Time to roll the dice," I say to myself as I check in.

The next day, after a surprising hotel breakfast of bacon and eggs, I search the street vendors for a digital watch and at the same time purchase a sharkskin wallet I take a fancy to.

On to a 24-hour tailors. I get measured up for a jacket and two pairs of trousers; the latter I order with an extra two inches or so of give at the waistline. I'm going to have to fit the carry belt in there. Last, a pair of black leather moccasins to complete the get-up for the flight out of Bangkok. I've already bought a shirt but draw the line at a tie. I hate the damned things. And now I have to do one last thing, something I was told was absolutely imperative. I've been putting it off as long as possible.

I walk into the barbers as though to my own funeral. I've not had a haircut in over a decade and my thinning barnet hangs almost to the belt of my jeans. The beard I take care of myself, trimming it about once a month, or whenever I can be bothered and it looks neat enough now to pass muster. I sink into the chair and, having established that the chap speaks English, ask him to, "make me look like a businessman."

I watch in dismay as the scissors in the hands of the tonsorial torturer send long hanks of hair dropping to the floor.

I leave the place rubbing my neck and feeling light-headed. I go back to the hotel and wait for the call. It comes just after 6pm. Out of the hotel again to meet someone – "He'll know you" – in the McDonald's round the corner on the main drag. I am to give him my passport, so he can make the airline ticket purchase, something I'm none too happy about, but what the hell.

A guy, Thai or Chinese, shows up while I'm listlessly munching a chicken burger. "Mr Andrew?"

"Yes", say I.

"I go get for you ticket."

I sigh and hand over my passport. "I call you tomorrow after ten o'clock," he says. "Morning?" I ask – best to make sure.

"Yes, morning time," he says smiling and he turns and leaves. Another night to kill in the City of Angels.

On the dot of 10am next day, the call comes. I'm to meet what I have realised is the cut-out man, in the carpark of Robinson's department store, a literal stone's throw away.

I am there a minute or so early and as I walk between the cars I see him standing by a Japanese pick-up truck. He reaches in and hands me a plastic carrier bag. Inside is a ticket wallet, with my passport, thank God. Curses, the flight isn't until 00.40hrs on 10 December. I will be leaving and arriving in the dark, with a whole day ahead of me.

I take a peek in the bag. The belt is in there, curled up like a black mamba. I feel sick. I prod it and feel a smooth curve, solid.

"You go back hotel now, goodbye," and he is into the pick-up and gone from sight before I get to the stairs. Now I have twenty-four hours to get through, with a weight I daren't take the chance of either carrying around or leaving in the hotel.

I pick up the clobber from the tailors, leaving the cargo in a locked hotel closet. On my return, I rig myself out in what I'll be wearing for the trip, which in my head I'm calling my disguise. I look in the full-length mirror. Damn, I barely recognise myself. Whether or not I look like anyone's idea of a businessman is debatable, but it'll have to do.

The day is a blur. I pack my kit and try one more time to make the damned belt appear not to be there. I think I'll be OK if I don't bend over. For now, I stuff it into my hand luggage and order a cab for 9pm. I don't want to spend too much time in the airport but in the circumstances it's better to be early, rather than chance missing the flight.

I check out, tipping the receptionist a hundred baht and the bellboy fifty. I tell the cabbie to take the toll road and we're off out of the city and heading for the airport. The cabbie is silent, for which I am grateful.

Through the doors of the airport into another air-conditioned space, this one huge. I look at the board; it is a while yet before I can check in my main luggage. I sit in a café on the mezzanine, eat a sandwich, drink some coffee. I am looking, without being obvious, to see if anyone is paying any attention to me, but no-one seems to be.

I roll the suitcase through the scanner and now, carrying only my hand luggage with its cargo, now seemingly red hot and weighing a ton, head off for the leper's room – that is, the designated smoking area. The dense blue-grey fug in here is so thick it looks as though some film crew has left a dry ice-blower on. I sit next to an ashtray that's already full, put my bag between my knees, fish out a copy of *Time* magazine and read. The irony of that title passes me by.

*

I re-focus my eyes and I'm back in the room with the huge coffee table in front of me. A cop walks up with a 'farang' in tow. This fellow, in shirt and slacks, says he's representing Her Majesty's government.

I sigh and give him an even more abbreviated version of the events of the past half a month or so than I gave the Thai guy. I have realised that there's nothing that could lead them to anyone else, because that's the way it was organised. I was in an exterior loop of the whole operation, in the most vulnerable and dangerous position, and ultimately expendable. Even if I'd been inclined to turn King's evidence, or its equivalent, I'd have nothing to offer. You have to admire that sort of attention to detail.

Another cop appears wearing latex gloves, cuts open one of the three bricks from inside the belt. A little white powder spills out.

"Maybe milk powder?" says the cop to my left. I let out the breath I've been unconscious that I'm holding in.

A few seconds later, the be-gloved individual looks up from his testing and nods. A complete change comes over all the cops; gone are the smiles, the solicitous inquiries as to what I might want to drink.

He stands abruptly, saying, "You are under arrest for smuggling heroin," while unhooking a set of cuffs from his belt.

I continue to sit for what seems an age while the uniforms bustle in and out. A big whiteboard stands to one side with about three dozen photos on it. They are all men that have been nabbed here at the airport in the last few months. The last in the series is a 'farang', a date underneath is only a few days old. I will meet him soon and my own ugly mug will be there for the next poor sod getting busted to see.

Finally activity seems to wind down. I stand, expecting to be taken to a lock-up somewhere here at the airport or in town, but no, it's, "You stay here," pointing at the long sofa. Confused, I sit. He pulls out an odd-looking set of cuffs. They are slightly bigger and more oval, with about two feet of chain. I look and he points to my ankle and to the steel tubular frame of the sofa. Then he pauses and considers; "You want toilet?" I suddenly realise they mean to leave me here until morning: half the lights in this big room having already been turned off. "Definitely," I say. He follows me out as far as the door of the WC – there are no windows – and going back to the sofa I'm chained ankle to frame and within a couple of minutes I am alone in the room with one light on. Most peculiar.

I am woken about 6.30, stiff as a board, knees, hip and back protesting. I ask for coffee and I get it, which surprises me a little. I'm hustled out through the already thickening mass of people in the airport's public spaces. My jacket is draped over my cuffed wrists. I'm squeezed into the back seat of an unmarked vehicle, with a cop either side of me.

After miles of traffic, we swing in off the road and pull up abruptly before a government building. This is the narcotics squad's own police station.

Up the stairs and into an office furnished with ancient, scarred and tatty desks, chairs and filing cabinets. I see to my right, floor-to-ceiling bars with a four-foot gap and, beyond, two fair-sized cells. A large pile of footwear in front of the right-hand cell indicates multiple occupancy. A pile of smaller shoes says that the left-hand cell is probably for women.

A cop takes me by the arm to do the booking-in thing, take prints etc. I indicate by dumb show my need to take a leak. Still cuffed, I go where directed. Having extracted myself with difficulty and just let go, a cop walks in and says, "Gimme 200 baht."

I shake my head, astounded, as he sticks his hand into my right front trouser pocket, looking for moolah. I knock his hand away and make an outraged noise, unmistakable in any language. He backs away; this 'farang' isn't sufficiently frightened to let him get away with it.

This is the earliest indication of several truths about the environment that I've already accepted I will be spending a very long time in. Notions of personal space are now history. Standards of probity amongst custodians of the law are moveable feasts, dependant on what can be safely extorted/

nicked/agreed as a fee. Above all, my status as a 'foreign guest' has altered to 'dumb farang who got caught'. A whole new world is opening up before me. I doubt whether it will be an improvement on the one I have just left behind me, but it should be... interesting.

Then I am led by the arm to the cell, my cuffs finally removed, my footwear as well. They bundle me inside and I see it's about fifteen feet square, ten feet high, with squat toilet and water troughs at the back by the barred and netted window. Ancient lino, or similar, covers the wooden floor. Two big ceiling fans slowly stir the air. There is no furniture of any kind, a feature of cells throughout the country, in police stations and prisons alike, as I will eventually discover.

In the cell are nine locals, four Chinese and one Brit. I recognise Steve from his mug shot, the latest on the whiteboard back in the airport room. We exchange names. Steve's in for a couple of kilos of hashish of all things. "Oh, there's a market all right," he says. "The farang punters love a bit of hash. It makes a change from Thai grass."

I notice a 5ft 4inch Chinaman listening. I nod companionably and ask his name. "Patrick," says he, "from Singapore. This is Ken." He indicates a Chinese beanpole with long, straight-back hair who is being massaged by a large slab of a Chinaman. "This is Ah-Hong. He's from China, only speaks Chinese."

Ken lifts his head listlessly and says "Hi" in a weak voice. He's clearly going through withdrawal. Ah-hong says nothing and his expression doesn't change at all, even at the mention of his name.

An elderly cop comes to the bars. "And-oo How-keh?" he sings out, mangling my name. Still barefoot, but thankfully not cuffed, I'm led to an office in which sits one cop at a computer screen and another, obviously higher-ranking cop, at a desk. I'm told to sit.

After the now familiar recitation of name, age, place of birth etc., I'm made to go through the fifteen days yet again. Then he says, "please repeat all that, slowly, so that I can translate into Thai and the Sergeant, can type up the statement."

I try not to show my exasperation. "Patience," I tell myself. "You've got nothing but time now" and I do as I am told. On completion I'm asked to sign the statement. I've absolutely no idea what I'm reading. I'll just have to accept it's a reasonable facsimile of what I've said, so I sign it anyway. The major takes it and leaves the office.

The sergeant is sitting with his back to me. My suitcase, hand luggage and my duty-frees are eighteen inches from my knees. I reach into the carton of Rothmans, take a pack and offer one to the cop. He smiles, accepts and goes back to his keyboard, puffing away. Stuffing two more packs into my waistband, I then contemplate the bottle of Tequila. *Carpe Diem*, I think, sliding it out noiselessly, uncapping it as I cough on my cigarette. I glug away and I'm making a decent headway when he turns and grins. I offer him a swig but he says, "No, cannot," indicating that I should put it back, unable to stop grinning. I burp theatrically and chance another three or four glugs and replace the now considerably depleted bottle of Cuervo Gold.

The boss comes back and looks surprised to see me. He shouts down the corridor and the old turnkey comes to take me back to the cell. I'm feeling the burn of approximately six or so double tequilas in the space of a very few minutes. I sit talking with the lads for a while, leaving one pack of smokes with Steve, when I announce that I'm done for the day. It's been dark for two or three hours and I'm bushed. I try to settle on the hard floor, jacket for a pillow. I'm asleep in less than a minute.

The next day, I am taken to a large, open-plan office and introduced to two 'farang' female consular officers. I groan inwardly as they begin to ask pretty much the same sort of questions as the various cops have done so far, but they veer off quickly into family details.

"Now not everyone in your sort of situation necessarily wants their family informed, so this is entirely your decision. Is there anyone you'd like us to contact?" It hadn't even occurred to me that sooner or later my mother (whose 74th birthday it was only two days ago I realise with dismay), is going to have to be told. I bite the bullet and give them her full name and contact details. I know she's going to take this hard.

The rest is an attempt to familiarise me with the legal process and since I'm pleading guilty from the outset, the likely consequences. Then comes, "Would you like a lawyer?" I say that I've not enough money for that. They suggest that perhaps my family might help and that it really would be a good move. "I don't know where to start," I mutter, at which they pull out a shortlist, half a dozen firms who, "have lawyers who speak English. We can't advise you as to which to pick, but these are supposed to be good," indicating the second name on the list. So I indicate that, given some financial help from the family, they'll do nicely. Getting up to leave, they tell me that as soon as I'm remanded into custody, they'll visit me at Bambat Prison. It is the first time that I hear the name.

The following day I am told to grab all my stuff and I am taken to the nine-storey courthouse. I am led to the rear of the building and put in a holding cell for the morning. Eventually my name is called and I am led cuffed and barefoot to the lift and we go up to the 9th floor. My own matter takes only a quarter of an hour. A cop gives the details of my arrest and requests that I be denied bail. The judge bangs the gavel and I am led back to the cells.

Relatively quickly, I and nineteen others, are bundled into the back of a very small bus. I've been handcuffed to a female prisoner. The windows have both bars and mesh but no glass, and the traffic exhaust fumes of the twenty-minute ride leave me feeling queasy and green about the gills. We pull into the open main entrance of Bambat Narcotics Remand and Rehabilitation Centre. This is one of several prisons on an extended site, housing well over 20,000 people. I am going to be here until I am tried and sentenced in a hundred and ten days time.

VICKY

1998 Surrey

5.20, Wednesday 9 December

I am driving down the A3 with my son Tom and his friends, Luke and Piers in the car, doing the school run. Luckily Luke hasn't thrown up as he did last week, opening the window with the car going at fifty miles an hour so that the vomit spattered over everything and everyone. I took three days with detergent and a toothbrush to get rid of the smell. They are completely hyper and, in the driving rain, disorientated by the headlights of the oncoming cars in the darkness, it is all I can do to stay focused.

I drop Piers off in Barnes and having got to Putney, we drop Luke at his house. My boys are silent as we turn into the small driveway of our house. It looks like a giant doll's house. I always tell people we bought a façade – if you trip through the front door you will find yourself falling through the back window into a 120ft garden.

Nick, my husband, and I had bought it ten years earlier at a bargain price, when the owner had just received a posting to Paris and wanted shot of it. Even in a buoyant market they couldn't shift it and it was easy to see why. The hall was pokey with an initial view of a frosted glass door open to reveal an ancient WC. The electric blue bathrooms and orange loos had last been painted in the 1960's as had the chocolate brown dining room and pale green kitchen. The garden was completely overgrown. I wanted to sing for joy but Nick told me to put on a poker face. The next day he bought the house for considerably less than the asking price. Our avenue is tree-lined, unmade up and one of the few private streets in Putney. Turning into the gravel road is to turn back in time. Residents are encouraged to park in their driveways to preserve this illusion.

I bundle the boys into the house. They've had tea in the car. Now it's only homework, supper, bath and story.

Nick is away but should be back from one of his business trips abroad. He is the owner and director of a family holiday company. He tends to be in the office for Monday and the rest of the week focuses on renewing leases or looking for new sites. That's when he isn't dealing with the dramas that arise on a day-to-day basis. A disastrous week, I recall, was when a few members of staff on their day off in Greece, had a fatal car accident. The driver of the other car was also killed and was one of Greece's top footballers. A few days later a parasol was blown out of its stand and one of the metal spokes speared the eye of a female guest. The next day, a chef tried to commit suicide. I have never seen Nick panic. He is the perfect man in a crisis.

Tom takes ten minutes to do his homework. William takes an hour and there are tears because Tom is yet again in front of the TV without his little brother.

I am reading them Roald Dahl's, 'The Twits'. I realise that I had given the characters Yorkshire accents yesterday but now they are decidedly Somerset. The boys haven't noticed. Tom takes over the reading as I run downstairs to answer the phone. It's Nick. He asks how things are going. We discuss the car's MOT and a golf match I had narrowly won.

"How are you?" I ask.

He tells me some stuff about business that goes right over my head and then says,"I've got to go to Paris and then Albertville this weekend on business."

"Oh. Why the weekend?"

"Hoteliers don't take weekends off," he reminds me.

My voice goes flat. I put down the phone and brace myself for juggling all four children over the weekend with their sports matches, extras, homework and meals. I had signed up to this life, after all – "for better or worse". The "better" is that I never have to worry about bills – I'm a member of both a golf and tennis club, and we go on holiday all over the world. The "worse" is that, at forty years old, I'm beginning to feel like I'm in this marriage on my own.

*

It's Saturday. My patience is at an all-time low. The children seem to be at each other's throats.

"Tom. Come here. All of you in the kitchen. Tom, 'Fuck' seems to be your favourite word at the moment. Do you know what it means?"

A pause and then, *"The woman touches the man's willie and the man rubs the woman's boobs."*

"Anything else?" Cold steel in my voice. Tom shakes his head.

"OK, girls, what does 'Fuck' mean?"

"Oh really!" says Samantha, going red and flouncing off. She's almost a teenager and this is clearly way too embarrassing. Emma, 15 months younger on the other hand, has been doing this very subject in Biology.

"Sexual intercourse is when the penis is inserted into the vagina," she says matter- of-factly.

"The penis is inserted into the vagina, the penis is inserted into the vagina" Tom chants as he marches round the kitchen, until *"the penis....Oh Fuck! No! No! No!"*

36

There is a silent pause before the horrible reality sinks in. "Oh my God, not you and Daddy!"

Now he is gagging over the sink and trying to wash out his mouth with soap. I feel sad that one more layer of innocence has gone.

"I'm sorry Tom but now do you see why I get so upset when you keep saying that F word? Anyway," as I see he is calming down, "when two people love each other, it is not disgusting."

Ten minutes later he comes up to me. "When I marry, can I say fuck to my wife?"

"Yes, Tom." I give this darling eight-year-old boy a big hug, "when you marry you can say fuck to your wife."

Two weeks later, my mother is doing the school run. She has filled her gin and vodka bottles with orange juice and Ribena. Tom, Luke and Piers have the windows down on the A3 and are pretending to be drunk to passing cars. Tom is sitting in the front passenger seat. He leans over to her (and will never know that his next remark nearly causes both a fatal accident and guffaws at the Bridge Club), "Grandma, have you ever had sexual intercourse?"

ANDY

Bambat Narcotics Remand and Rehabilitation Centre

I arrive at the prison in the afternoon, the only 'farang' amongst the day's intake of about eighteen newly remanded prisoners. First order of business, the strip search, accompanied by my first, and thankfully last, cavity search. My clothes and possessions are systematically rifled, anything saleable within the prison being set aside. An unworn pair of flip-flops, which everyone else I see is wearing, is taken from me. The sharkskin wallet and a silver necklace go too, though not my silver crucifix on its chain. They know better than to mess with religious items.

I am led to a low, open-sided lean-to and made to sit on a tiny stool. Now clad only in T-shirt and shorts, my leg is stretched out by one of the blue shirts, a class of prisoner roughly equivalent to a trusty, and he reaches out for a length of elephant chain with an open iron hoop at each end. Placing my left foot on an iron block with a shallow groove in it, he slips on a hoop. He picks up a four-pound sledgehammer and before I can utter a sound of protest starts to beat the hoop into shape around my ankle. I realise that any movement, any distraction of his concentration, may result in said sledgehammer smashing my foot, ankle or both beyond repair. I keep shtum and offer up a prayer to any deity that maybe listening. The process is then repeated on the other leg.

As I stand up, somewhat shaken, the grinning blue shirt magnanimously gives me a length of plastic twine. Uncomprehending, I raise my eyebrows, so he indicates, with the sign language reserved for use with idiot foreigners, that I should tie it to the centre of the chain and hold the other end so it doesn't drag on the concrete.

I notice that I'm the only one of the new guys with such a heavy chain. About half the others have chains fitted, that are a tiny fraction of the weight of my one, which I estimate to be 10-12 pounds. The rest have no chain at all. I resolve to discover why.

We've missed dinner but they've kept back some food for us. I put some dog-rice onto an aluminium plate with a flat-bottomed metal spoon. It is odd stuff, vari-coloured and gritty. Another pot proves to contain a sort of soup made of some unidentified vegetable matter and a third has in it what I shall only describe as fish head soup. I dislike fish at the best of times, but I haven't eaten more than a few mouthfuls in the last three days so I am feeling distinctly peckish.

Bits of fishbone stab into my palate and shreds of fish skin stick into my teeth as I prod the stuff looking for something that might have once been part of the edible section of a fish. I soon give up and concentrate on the rice and veg.

I am then shown to a 20-yard concrete trough, a yard or so wide and about as deep. I've managed to retain a small towel and am given a flat-bottomed plastic bowl. I have in my washbag some soap, a toothbrush and a small, clear plastic bag which contains toothpaste, squeezed out during the search.

A new problem arises, how to take off my thin shorts when I'm in leg-irons? It takes me several minutes of head-scratching, stretching the material and cursing before I manage it. Then I dip the bowl in the water-trough, dowse myself thoroughly, apply shampoo (also in a plastic bag) ditto, towel down. Now do the shorts thing again, in reverse, find it only slightly easier than removing them.

The sun is now half-way back down the sky and we realise that all the other prisoners, of whom there seemed to be several hundred, are no longer about. The concrete cell block is on stout pillars. Wide stairs lead up to the cells, ten of them, five a side. During the strip search I was told to keep only those clothes – T-shirts and shorts – and items such as toiletries, plus a book or two. The rest of my baggage was taken into 'storage'. I wonder if I'm ever going to see it again. So up the stairs I shlep, carrying my meagre possessions precariously in one hand, the string fixed to the leg chains in the other.

I am bundled into Room Two. On either side are six-foot wide wooden platforms, thirty inches high. They are packed with men, some chained, some not, sitting in small groups around metal snap-tins. The ubiquitous flat-bottomed spoons are the only eating utensils being used. Some have poured coconut milk into their plastic bowls and are dipping slices of white bread into it. A few large red Chinese flasks have hot water to make coffee and I see the only African in the room looking at me and smiling.

I weave towards him, through the chaps sitting on the floor in the three-foot wide gangway, between the sleeping platforms.

"I hope you speak English," I say.

"Of course," says he and I have my first proper conversation since the big cell in the Chinatown nick. He is Didi, Nigerian, and like the great majority of those found abroad, an Ibo. I tell him I'm from London. We discuss our respective case details. I've held my hands up, having had little option, but he is going with "not guilty."

"I run a travel business and I was taking the suitcase to the airport for a customer who'd forgotten it," he tells me, looking at my eyes, my expression, to see how this plays. Even then, I know enough about Thailand to understand that this was a thousand, a million-to-one shot at acquittal.

We fall to speculating on likely sentences. It is only now that I discover the full mind-blowing range of bad news on offer.

"50 years?" I gasp.

"Maybe 40," he grudges. "Maybe only 33. But minimum 25 years, up to 50, or life, or death."

"Gulp" from me. My own case is "attempting to export without licence" – damn, sunk by a missing bit of paperwork – "897 grams of pure heroin." Any amount over 20 grams leaves the defendant open, theoretically, to the death penalty. In practice this is usually passed only on those with large amounts and usually, only if they've had the brass neck to plead "not guilty" to the charge.

At 6pm one of the prisoners strikes a short length of thick bamboo against another stick six times, an audible, sharp sound that resonates round the prison block. The national anthem is sung at this time by all the Thais, to my genuine amazement, followed by another number hailing the King and Queen personally. I ask Didi when lights out is. He looks at me strangely. "The lights never go out my friend, but after 9 o'clock everyone goes quiet, they roll out their beds and most try to sleep." He indicates his own bedroll, an affair of a number of coarse blankets folded in half lengthways and stitched together. I glance around, seeing nowhere for me to lie down.

The room is full, men having marked their part of the platform by the width of their bedrolls, usually eighteen or twenty inches, each bed touching its neighbour. Those with no bedding makeshift without. Those not fortunate enough to be in a spot up top, sleep cheek-by-jowl in the gangway. In the end a Laotian, who has bagged the doorway to the cell, offers to share with me, giving me a few bits of cardboard to cushion me from the unyielding concrete floor. I've managed to hang on to a battered and worn, thin leather jacket – the pockets and lining are shot – and together with my towel for a blanket and my possessions all wrapped in clothes for a pillow, I finally bed down at about 10pm. I wake at 11pm to the sound of two strikes on the bamboo. Our room is number two, I hear three strikes from the next room, then four, then five, all the way up to ten. "Not every hour, surely?" I whisper to Didi, across four or five dozing Thais. "I'm afraid so" he says. "Do not worry, in a day or two you will not even notice it." What with starting off in a police cell in Chinatown, a few hours in a holding cell in the courthouse, a lightning remand hearing and then an induction into prison proper, it has been a long day. It was to be the forerunner of many more.

The next few days are spent acclimatising. Coming downstairs out of the block with some 570 odd prisoners at about 6.30am, it doesn't take long for me to realise that I'm the only 'Farang' in this building. An Arab, about 5'll", with skin lying in folds over his body as though from major weight loss over a concentrated period, introduces himself as Adel. A 5'5" Nepali, Andre, shakes my hand. I'm given coffee, a couple of pieces of white sliced bread and a brief rundown of how the place works.

Adel says he's half-and-half Kuwaiti and Egyptian, 25-years old – he looks older – and that he's fighting a heroin case. No surprise there – most foreigners in here, at least for now, are doing the same. Andre has already been sentenced to two years for four kilos of hashish. He was in transit for Bali and its tourist custom, but fell foul of the law at Don Maung Airport while changing planes. He has less than a year to serve.

I ask Adel why quite a few Thai guys have thin, light chains. Small cases, he says. My own chain has twenty-three links and weighs about five kilos; apparently this is to be expected. I see one shaven-headed Thai, very muscular and heavily tattooed with a chain so thick, so heavy, that it has only seven links, each as wide as my hand. It must weigh ten kilos or more. Adel sees where I'm looking.

"Yaba; big case, millions of tablets," he says.

At 8am we are all chivvied into a small concrete yard in ten ranks of fifty. A flag is hoisted up a flagpole by two prisoners while the National Anthem is playing. The Thais all sing with some fervour. Everyone then sits, oriental style on the ground. I sit with my arms round my knees; I can no more sit cross-legged than I can fly to the moon. A Thai, middle-aged, with steel-grey hair cut military fashion, stands before the group and starts talking. He has the voice and manner of a sergeant-major, and no-one, certainly no Thai, is ignoring him. I ask the guy next to me, "What's he saying?"

"I don't know" he replies slowly. "I'm Chinese."

My ears start to pick up at least one constantly repeated word, 'Krap'[3] I know, I know!

As this is going on, a screw (prison warden) appears at the end of the rows of men. He's carrying a hardwood baton three feet long. All of a sudden he goes between the rows and fetches one guy a thwack across the shoulders, then the chap next to him who is cringing away. "The Terminator," as both Adel and Andre later call him, has a penchant for delivering such violence, and not a day passes without his doling out at least his minimum ration.

Indeed he isn't the only one, though he seems to like it the most. Over the next fifteen weeks or so, scarcely a day will pass without someone getting a hiding from the guards. Occasionally extra punishment is deemed necessary, such as being made to lie on the dirty concrete floor of the yard, full length, and then rolling like a log first to one end, then the other, a dozen times. A lot of skin gets left behind.[4]

The corporal punishment seems to be restricted to the younger Thais, and they do seem to be very young, despite this being an adult institution. A rough estimate would put at least half in the 18–24 bracket. Mehmet, an Iranian doing fifteen months for possession of a tiny amount of heroin, says, "They are like children, they think they are playing a game." It's true, even after a standard thumping from the Terminator, they go straight to their little cabal of chums, to brag how it wasn't so bad and that they've had worse from their sisters.

That very afternoon two are brought out to be beaten, one for getting tattooed behind the stairwell, and the other for doing the tattooing. Each receives special attention on their right arm, the one because that's where the tattoo is, the other because he's right-handed. They are not laughing now.

Adel asks if I have any cash. I explain that the senior cop, who interrogated me at the Chinatown police station, took the cash and had it changed into Thai Baht for me. This brings cries of amazement from those listening.

"He didn't steal ANY of it?" demands Adel in utter disbelief.

"No, he gave it to me and said I would be needing it. I thought it was good of him to do that," I replied. Much head shaking and muttering follows.

"Anyway they took it off me here and said they would put it on my book. How long will that take?" I ask a bit anxiously. It's clear that, without access to funds, my diet will be abysmal, and other necessities will be unavailable. "Well, you'll have some credit with the cash salesmen," Adel says, indicating various emporia arranged at the end of the dining tables. "But for the fresh food that we cook, we'll have to cover you until your money comes through. You can only spend 200 baht per day from your book and we have to order two days in advance. "Also if you have visitors, they can buy you stuff from the visitor shop outside."

I file this away. I'm due a visit from the consulate any day now and I've a shopping list to make. For now I'm going to be eating halal if I stick with this mess group.

Andre pulls out an electric wok which seems to be operated on a time-share arrangement with the Chinese at the next table. He quickly fries up some small fish, serving them up after democratically dividing them amongst the group. I chew the white meat methodically, slowly. It won't kill me but I'll never get to like it.

Adel then goes about finding me two lockers for my stuff. They cost me 400 baht from the Thai prisoner, who seems to have bagged the concession.

In the early afternoon, a pair of small carts enter through the only gate. The first is piled with cooked food in clear plastic bags; rice, chicken, pork, fish and vegetables. The other has several cases of Pepsi, cigarettes, canned tuna, canned coconut milk, soya milk, toothpaste and soap. They'd been purchased outside the gate by this morning's visitors and their recipients crowd eagerly round. Most they will use, the rest are bartered or sold for cash. Once I have had a consular visit, I will also be able to purchase these items.

When we go up to be locked in our cage for the night, at just after 3.30pm, I now have a borrowed thin blanket, and a plastic bag with a cup, bowl and flat-bottomed spoon, a tin of coconut milk and half a loaf of sliced white. Didi brings a thermos of hot water and a small container of ready mixed coffee, sugar and coffee mate. Supper is coffee and bread dunked into a bowl of coconut milk, and so to bed, still in the doorway with the Laotian guy.

The next morning, the Tannoy mangles my name. I look at Andre who says', "Embassy visit." Off I scuttle out of the gate, down the wide path between the fenced, walled building compounds, and eventually I get to the visit area. I sit facing a Perspex window behind which sits a good-looking forty-something woman. The Perspex has numerous vertical slits in it, so we can hear each other. It also has a larger opening, above a metal tray at the bottom, as in a post office or bank.

The lady says her name is Kate and I'm mildly surprised to hear an Australian accent. I ask if she's mistaken me for some new Aussie prisoner. But no, she works for the Brits and asks how I am etc. She has brought me some basic toiletries and pushes them through the lower slot onto the tray. "Embassies are allowed to give stuff directly to prisoners here, though not in other prisons," she says. She then pushes through some envelopes, stamps, writing paper, a couple of pens and a dozen Aerogrammes and I thank her profusely.

I then tell Kate about the 20,000 baht I'm proposing to have transferred to the Embassy. Her eyebrows go up. "Well, you make a change. Normally we have to lend a new bloke a small amount."

"Er actually, I wondered if you could spring for some stuff from the shop? I really need some blankets to be sewn into a bedroll plus about five or six cartons of Krong Thip to use as currency." She thinks a bit. "Well, I'm going to see if your request has been approved. If it has, then I'll do as you ask. I'll be back shortly anyway, to see all the Brits in here for their Christmas visit. I'll be bringing over some Xmas goodies." This is the first time I've heard of other Brits in here but there are seven other blocks like mine in the prison.

Then she says my mum has been informed and will be writing to me, and would I write to her. Of course I will. I've let her down as badly as one could imagine. It's the least I can do, let her know that I'm OK and that I will get through this, and I'll come back, eventually.

With this, Kate says goodbye and I return to the building. It's Friday afternoon, so even in the unlikely event that she can access my funds, I'd not get any goods until Monday. Weekends and holidays in the prison system are dead zones; no visits, no mail, no hospital call unless it's a genuine emergency. Only pre-ordered fresh food and the daily delivery of ice in three-litre blocks comes through the gate then.

On Monday afternoon, Patrick, from the Chinatown nick arrives. Ken has gone next door, to Building Five, as have his impassive Chinese friends, Ah-Hong and English Steve. I arrange to get Patrick into Room Two with me and we both natter for a few minutes before lock-down through the chicken-wire fence across the narrow roadway to Ken and Steve.

47

I'm able to donate a pair of shorts to Patrick and, as four or five men were moved to Klong Prem prison next door, we both go up on to the wooden sleeping platform, as does Lao. Unfortunately, one of those moved was Didi: I will not see him again for six or seven years, but it is his spot I get, a decent one, away from the squat khazi.

The next morning it's prison haircut time. When my turn comes, I protest that I'd had it cut just a few days before, to no avail. I've hated the process ever since I was little, in the days when I had to sit on a plank placed across the arms of a barber's chair. As the remains of my hair join all the dark locks already on the floor, I look at the ring of grinning faces and wonder just how little entertainment there is, if this is so gripping. The guy with the clippers asks me to tip up my chin and keep still. I groan. I feel like a newly shorn sheep, naked and defenceless. Note to self: get a hat or cap, smartish, or your scalp will burn and peel like a dumb tourist.

I find a mirror and, once again, almost don't recognise myself. The buzz cut on top and white-wall sides look like a rookie in boot-camp, with only the millimetre or so of facial stubble spoiling the effect. I look five years younger than my actual age of 41. With a beakier nose I'd look like Magwitch from the 1940's version of *Great Expectations*. On second thoughts, perhaps that's appropriate, though I can't see myself escaping.

As I lie back that night, I think about this business of escape. Not from this prison, or the one I'll be sent to when sentenced; that's just a wish fulfilment fantasy. But have I not actually escaped, albeit in the most perverse way possible, my original predicament? Homeless: check, roof now provided, though mod cons are noticeably absent. Jobless: check, am now a prisoner, soon to be a convict (not much of a job, but certainly one with long-term prospects. Potless:

check (some funds to my name, now worth considerably more than previously). Needs: minimal (a little will go a long way). And all my personal problems, distressing as they were, are now completely beyond my ability to engage with effectively. If I were inclined to worry about things I cannot change, I would now be in terminal emotional decline, but I am not. It is an oddly liberating thing to realise that I can surrender the control I sought to exercise over my life. I no longer have any. I am, in a way, free.

December 1998

A few days before Christmas, I and a few other Brits are called out on an embassy visit.

We are taken to a small room. Inside is Kate, the pro-consul, sitting on one of half-a-dozen plastic chairs at a cheap, metal-framed deal-topped table, on which are some carrier bags. This is called a 'contact visit', informal and unobstructed by any barriers.

As we sit, she says, "Merry Christmas," to which we raggedly reply in similar vein. A couple of mince pies each follow some sandwiches with roast chicken slices inside. A green plastic cup proves to contain a selection of individually wrapped sweets and chocolates. She says we should consume it all on the spot, as we won't be allowed to take back anything from this visit. I want to save some of the candy, so chance it. I go on to use that plastic cup, first as a coffee-cup, then as a toothbrush and paste mug until the day I'm sprung.

As we amble back from the visit, I discover Filipino Ted is in Building Eight awaiting trial, even though he's charged with 140 grams of crystal meth, attempted export. "Their paperwork said 14 grams. Well, I wasn't going to tell them, was I?" The result, a low category building and no bloody leg-irons, a real stroke of luck on which I congratulate him.

Haydn, a fellow Brit, turns out to be serving a one year nine-month sentence for ganja. "Thai grass it was, see," he says in his sing-song Welsh accent. "It's a bit on the smelly side, no matter how many layers of plastic you wrap it in, on account of its being so fresh. And I didn't want to just pack it in my luggage. I thought it would be bound to get spotted. So I had a bit of an idea, see? I'm grinning away, the voice and delivery are such that I can't help myself. "So what I done, see, I wore a wetsuit under my clothes with the weed inside, next to my skin. But by the time I got to the airport, I was struggling, and when I got to security I was almost fainting away. Andy, I was so-o-o hot in that suit! I thought I was going to collapse and of course all the staff was looking to give me medical attention, and that's when they found the wetsuit. I must have sweated pints man," he says, shaking his head ruefully.

By this time, I'm almost doubled over with laughter, tears brimming, and the sounds of my wheezing, snorting merriment have finally attracted the attention of the gate screws. With shouts in Thai echoing in our ears, we wave goodbye. He's due for release in a month but I hope to see him again soon; the next consular visit is only four weeks away.

There is always a hiatus of fifteen or twenty minutes between half-past three in the afternoon when the gates to the stairs of the cellblock are opened, and the point when the cells themselves are all locked and the guards walk down doing the headcount. Being amongst the first up that day, I wander down the corridor to see into the other cells. I belatedly notice that there is a second stairwell at the far end, padlocked and unused, with what looks like a set of royal blue filing cabinets about 6ft high parked in front of them.

Next day I ask Adel about these. He says that the blue boxes are for punishment; that, if an offence is bad enough, the prisoner stays inside all day, with almost no light and with one break of half-an-hour to eat and use the latrine. Sometimes the offender would go into his normal cell overnight. Other times he might be sentenced to a week, or even a month, of continuous near darkness inside these stifling boxes. There are about five, six-inch slits punched into the sheet metal at eye-level at each end, constituting the only entry for light and air.

Then he tells of an escape attempt some time before. Five of the suspects were kept in those boxes for eight months, having received a thorough beating with hardwood clubs.

"When they finally let them out, they were like skeletons. Their skin was grey and they were covered in sores," he says. "They almost forgot how to speak, they could hardly walk, hardly stand even."

I will later learn that they were lucky to survive. In Thailand, nine out of ten would-be escapees end up dead. The fury of the screws who have lost face, because of such an attempt, should not be underestimated.

News Year's Eve, 2541 according to the Thai calendar (apparently they count from the death of the Buddha), and we are in our cells as usual. I've nodded off to sleep but am woken by an almighty racket of fireworks. Amazingly about half the guys in the cell haven't even stirred through this cacophony. I shake my head, muttering, and try to get back to sleep.

1999

The New Year begins much as the old one ended. My diet has become monotonous. I quite like rice but I'm longing for something with potato in it. And, like Ben Gunn[5], I dream of cheese, mostly. Grilled cheese on toast, cheese omelette, grated parmesan on pasta, rubbery mozzarella on pizza, cottage cheese on rye bread with a dollop of honey on it, cheddar cheese and onion rolls, a cracker with a morsel of mousetrap on it even. But there's no cheese to be had in this place and such drooling daydreams are getting me nowhere.

The next day I'm called to the gate. In response to the list I'd given Kate, she has come up trumps. I've got a whole cart of stuff just for me. A dozen thin blankets, nine to be stitched into a bedroll, two for a pillow and one to cover me. Three cases of Pepsi, five cartons of Krong Thip cigarettes, for use or barter. Some canned tuna for Nepali Andre. Also four bags each of coffee and Coffee-Mate.

First thing next morning, I collar the lean, greying type whom I call 'The Sailmaker.' He seems to be the go-to guy for stitching blankets into a bedroll. Didi had a thick one made, sixteen blankets. I'll make do with nine, and two sewn up into a pillow. We agree on four packs of smokes for the job and he starts straight away.

I arrange with a guy that I'll part with two packs and four Pepsi's in exchange for a pair of custom-fitted knee garters. I discard the twine and walk for the first time without the damned chain either being held by hand or dragging on the concrete floor. It feels a lot easier, and certainly worth it.

I take delivery of my new bedroll in the late afternoon. A couple of smokes for the Lao chap to haul it upstairs. I roll it out immediately and lie down on it with the little pillow under my head. It feels like luxury. The blankets have been folded in half, increasing the thickness, with the ninth one wrapped around the whole to conceal the folds. The stitching job is thorough throughout, and even the sound of my leg-irons clanking when I move is muffled a little, which is a bonus.

I'm feeling pretty pleased with myself when I notice something which had previously escaped me. The other bedrolls in the room are all lying on a cover made of three or four large sugar sacks. These have straps, with which to tie up the rolled bedding each morning. Something to take care of tomorrow then. But that night I drop off to sleep feeling as though I'm sinking into a down mattress, and for the first time in nearly four weeks, my joints aren't being bruised by an unforgiving cold, hard, floor. I sleep like the dead.

*

I hear my name mangled over the Tannoy, followed by 'Lawyer's visit.' I stroll down – alright, hobble down – to the separate section for a legal visit and find a Thai chap, in his late 40's, black shoes and trousers, and open-necked white shirt, sitting with a notebook on the other side of the mesh. My advocate's name is Vorathum, from the firm of Putri & Co.

After our hellos, his first question is, "What is your offence?" which I find odd – didn't anyone tell him anything? But I tell him anyway. His response is, "Pity it's not murder, I could have maybe helped you there." On seeing my jaw drop, he adds, "If you plead guilty I can represent you for 50,000 baht." Just about £900 at the time. "If you need to appeal sentence, maybe another 25,000 baht." I can see that he is planning ahead.

"You know I cannot pay you myself?" I say, and he nods, saying "Your mother contacted us already but I still need your signature." He pushes a form under the mesh, "to confirm that you authorise us to act for you." I shrug, and sign. He then says briskly, "OK, now I will get the police report and your statement, then I will come back and we can decide what to do."

"I'll see you soon then," I say as we both stand and turn to leave. "Oh, by the way," I add, "I've not had any visits and I need some cigarettes. Could you possibly get me a couple of cartons from the visitor shop?" He freezes for a second, then with a half-smile, says, "Of course." These will eventually show up in the itemised account presented for payment. Of course.

Just after New Year comes a sudden wave of Nigerians. All of them were pinched in the same street, at different times, having just left the same supplier's flat. It had been a set-up by the cops, the bag with the dope returned each time to the apartment, to be passed to the next unsuspecting buyer. Only the seventh man, suspecting intuitively that something was amiss, dropped the bag and escaped. One had to wonder how the cops were going to manage to get the same drugs and bag, registered as principal physical evidence, with six different reference numbers in six separate cases.

Early February and my eldest brother Pete pitches up at Bambat to visit me. I've not seen him for two years since he got married to Agata in the summer of '97. He's been living in Warsaw since '95 and has flown here to see me. He's my first visitor other than the consular staff.

Pete is teaching English and the loss of a week or so is significant in terms of income, never mind the cost of the trip, so I'm touched that he made the effort.

The fraternal greetings completed, he begins to ask about, well, just what the hell did I think I was playing at, was I out of my mind and more in this vein. I can hardly complain; it is a legitimate line of enquiry, so I tell him.

"Do you think you were set up?" he asks. I raise an eyebrow. "Only your lawyer says that the authorities received a phoned-in tip and that's why you were stopped." I tell him it is news to me and that he should ask my lawyers to come see me forthwith. The visit ends with Pete taking down a somewhat lengthy list of stuff to get for me from the visitors shop. He says he'll be back in a couple of days and that he'll be sure to speak to the brief.

The day after his next visit, the lawyer does indeed show up as requested. I ask him what the hell this phone tip business is all about.

"According to the airport police authorities, they received a phone call from a secret informant, as a result of which they made the arrest." Then a thought occurs to me. "What time did they get the call?"

"Erm, it says here 00.35 hrs." "Then it's rubbish," I say with certainty. "I'd already set the metal detector off some fifteen minutes before that. The flight was due to depart at 00.40 hours for God's sake. What is this crap?"

"I can only tell you what they wrote here," he says.

My pleas in mitigation, since I'm pleading guilty, come next. When my legal eagle hears that, although I've never used heroin, I <u>have</u> been prescribed dihydrocodeine tartrate (for my Perthé's Disease)[6] for some time, he tries to portray this as an addiction, a drug habit that is the cause of my offence. It's a form of victim psychology – something of a bugbear of mine. I look at him and say, "But that's not true."

He drops the notion immediately. Frankly, I doubt that such an approach would have cut much ice with a judge come sentencing anyway but being painted for the court as some kind of opiate addict is a prospect I cannot regard with equanimity. I resist taking those pills far more often than I actually use them, and I'd rather suffer some pain than slip into the habit of topping up daily from the medicine bottle. I am not, and never will be, a junkie.

The entire panoply of the Thai legal system, from enforcement through the judicial process to the penal institutions, is governed first and foremost by economic considerations. A given case is dealt with in a way which reflects its income potential. A murder investigation might have a nominal budget of only £20 or so: if the victim was poor and no immediate suspect was to hand, a written report on the body might be the entirety of the file. If, on the other hand, the victim was from a wealthy family, or better yet, a suspect was to hand with a healthy bank balance, the cops swing into high gear in an effort to increase their own bank deposits still further. In my case, the scam is simple. The regulations provide that in the event that a 'secret informant' provides information leading to an arrest and conviction, particularly in a drug case, the said informant is entitled to a reward. Since the informant is <u>secret</u>, no information about them, no name, no bank details, nothing at all, need be revealed. And thus, since there IS no informant, the reward is claimed for a fictitious, unnamed and untraceable individual and the money shared out amongst the cops.

Another consular visit and more news. My mother is coming out to see me, and she'll be here in less than two weeks. I soak this up and am slightly aggrieved. It'll be a damned sight more embarrassing than my brother's visit and I'm squirming already, even before she's here. But her ticket is already booked so all I can do is wait.

She arrives during the first week in March. The 'cool' dry season is hotting up, the temperatures are around 35°C, or even higher. My mother arrives, looking as graceful and elegant as ever, but the long flight, the heat and humidity, are obviously bothering her. We go through the same sort of thing as I did with brother Pete, but I'd already written to my mother a few times and she knows that too many redundant questions are going to be counterproductive. She wants to see the leg-irons she's been told I have to wear and I stand and show them, albeit reluctantly.

She says she's already paid the lawyers' fees in full. I groan, you **NEVER** pay lawyers before they've done the work; it's **ALWAYS** afterwards. If you pay a Thai lawyer in advance, he may well simply bugger off with the cash without so much as a backward glance. But I say nothing; she thinks she's doing the right thing.

There is pain in her eyes that her son is in such a terrible place, and compassion, empathy even. But she is, above all, a practical soul and deals with what IS before thinking about how it might, or should, be. She says I look well, indeed that I appear younger. What she means, I think, is that minus the thinning hair and the big, bushy, grey/white beard, I now look my age, rather than five years older. I reply in kind, saying how well she looks and it's the simple truth. She looks ten years, or more, younger than her actual age of seventy-four. She really does look good.

She says she'll stay for four weeks but in the event the punishing sun, the relentless heat and the humidity will change her mind. When the temperature starts to hit 40°C and higher, she returns to London. So, after two weeks and six visits, we say our goodbyes. She tells me that all will be well; that we will be re-united back in England; that I am not to worry. That last should have been my line, I felt, but I agree with her and she leaves, turning once to wave. I'm left to wonder whether I'll ever see her again.

April Fool

Towards the end of March I'm summoned to court again. The courtroom is identical to the one I was first taken to, but two floors lower down. There is a translator on hand, but on this occasion no jury. My brief makes a plea of leniency, having nothing else to work with. And so it's over in an hour or so and I'm led back to the ground level holding cell. There are not many men in it, but it's a filthy hole, the worst aspect of which is missing the mozzie net over one of the windows. The place is crawling with a plethora of insects of all types, and the noise of them frying on the lights keeps me awake most of the night.

I only have to wait two days to be called back to court. This time when I enter the courtroom, there is only the interpreter, the lawyer and myself. A single judge comes in and begins to read from a sheet of paper. The lawyer's face looks a picture when my sentence is read. He's surprised but pulls himself together enough to assume a look of satisfaction at a job well done. The judge repeats, in halting English for my benefit, my prison term: "Fifty years".

The penalty is death cut to fifty years, I assume for not wasting the court's time with a not guilty plea. All I feel is mild surprise, not exactly elation. It is after all a life sentence. I'd had three months to adjust to the enormity of the sentence which, I admit had shocked me when I first heard of it at the time of my arrest.

Back at the prison, I'm being congratulated on my 'good fortune' by screws and prisoners alike. It is the next bit I'm not looking forward to. The prison has a rule that anyone who is sentenced to more than 20 years, has his chain attached to a brass rail in the cell when everyone is locked in for the night. This leaves the newly sentenced desperado just about able to piss in the toilet facility but shit-out-of-luck when it comes to taking a dump. I wonder how long I'll have to put up with this nonsense.

The answer turns out to be just one night. Next morning I'm told to get myself together by 10.30am, as I am off to Bang Kwang. I pack my stuff, and Nepali Andre reminds me that the bulk of my belongings are still in 'storage', and not to forget about them. I thank him and give him all the food in my lockers; only the cigarettes are coming with me. A short while later, I'm ushered out, after brief farewells with the guys I've lived with for three and a half months. I've learned the ropes here but now I'll have to do it all over again in what is perhaps the most infamous penal institution in Thailand. I settle in the back seat for the drive up-river to Bang Kwang prison.

Bang Kwang

Andy's prison ID 290/42 April 1999

The main gate slams shut behind me. The lone screw from Bambat Remand gaol follows me. Somehow I have managed to get him to carry half my stuff, a major achievement and minor miracle, since screws normally carry nothing except a little light paperwork or a hardwood club. I then emerge through the inner steel doors of the gatehouse to see a long tree-lined avenue with the visit areas either side and the entrance to the prison proper at the end. Atop sits a high tower with all sorts of aerials and speakers on it from which vantage all parts of the nick are visible.

Through another gate and round a corner to a workshop and the reason for this screw's continued presence becomes immediately apparent. A widget with a long lever lies next to a big chest full of lengths of elephant chain. A trusty indicates that I put my shackled ankles up on the block. He then pries apart the hoops around them. I stand up as my chains are handed to my escort, but I'm only unchained for the time it takes to pick out new ones before I'm clapped in irons again.[7]

Finally, I come to the double gates set in a crenelated block house; the entrance to the compound of Block Six. I recognise the Thai numeral; it's almost a mirror image of the Western one.

The last steel door swings open to space, green, and lots of people. An open-sided structure, easily large enough to park two or three old DC3 'Dakota' aircraft, is on my left. A very long path, flanked on the right by a riot of greenery under which are tiled concrete tables and benches, is to my right. This place is much bigger than Bambat, and though more populated, seems less congested. I can smell dried chillies being crushed, so strong I am almost choking. Chemical fumes are wafting from a local factory which I later find out makes balloons. There is a constant hum of noise, machinery from the factories, numerous fans, the constant sound of chatter, mostly Thai and Chinese, with a smattering of French and English, louder than the rest the Nigerian contingent. And as I try to get a handle on this cacophony of sound, a flight of military helicopters appears overhead and in my head I hear 'The Flight of the Valkyries'. Its straight out of *Apocalypse Now*.

New faces, new circumstances. A crash course on the ins and outs, the do's and don'ts, is in order. It has long been the last word in penal servitude amongst Thai convicts: the only legal place of execution in the country. By long custom and practice, all convicts within the multiple walls have at least thirty years left to serve and if, after a few years, their remaining sentence stands below thirty years, they can be transferred. If this did not happen, the place would be even more ridiculously over-crowded than it already is, more than six thousand men being held here. In the future I will look back fondly on the days when there were 'only' nine hundred and sixty in our block, but for now it seems a huge number.

Only a handful of the men are 'farang' or European in origin. One such, with a crewcut of blonde hair, detaches himself from the curious throng of prisoners. It's Johan, a Swede whom I briefly met as I arrived at Bambat, he being then freshly sentenced and due to be shipped here the next day. He greets me with, "Welcome to Hell" but grinning as he says it. He starts to talk nineteen to the dozen, and I can hardly get a word in edgeways. He is acting as if we were bosom buddies, and while I am happy to have an English speaker as a tour guide, something seems off. Sure enough, within minutes, he's asking if I've brought any money with me. I tell him that the bulk of my funds are either with the consulate or now in the process of being credited to my Bwang Kwang prison account, but that I've managed to slip a small amount of cash through. He immediately asks if he can borrow 1,500 baht, about £27 at the time. I say that I'll think about it, but inwardly I'm sighing.

There are NO good reasons to be trying to borrow cash from a newly arrived prisoner. I can expect to get credit because all here know that it takes time, about three weeks, to process money transfers from one prison to another. For Johan to be trying to tap me before I've even met any of the other 'farangs' in the block can only mean that he is already in debt up to his eyeballs with everyone else. Such indeed proves to be the case. Johan's bonhomie is an act. He was an amphetamine user, or abuser, when a free man. Now he has decided that he's a victim, that everything is hopeless, and he has swapped his drug of choice for a heroin habit[8].

I meet some foreign or more colloquially 'farang' prisoners, tucked away under a long hangar with a low corrugated metal roof. Around them are aisles of lockers made of concrete. An empty one is immediately found for me, a snip at 400 baht, no payment required until my cash comes through. Dieter, a six-foot, shaven-headed thirty-something German, and Hans, a moustachioed five foot six, sixtyish Canadian citizen, stack my stuff into my new locker. A tall Burmese (a Karen tribesman I think) who goes by the name of Ken, then rustles up some 'maa-maa' (or instant noodles), chopping up a few hot-dogs, breaking a few eggs and adding these in. A bowl of this, along with coffee, sets me up nicely, and Dieter makes me a couple of peanut butter sandwiches to take up to the room. An ice-cold Pepsi and a bottle of water for the 15-hour lock-up completes the preparations – a 'boy' has already put my bedroll, painstakingly hauled from the last prison, by the gates of the cell block itself.

I am assigned to Room 28, on the upper floor of the two-storey block. The lighting is dim. The barred but unglazed window is above eye-level, and the sky blocked by overhanging eaves. The bottom third of the walls are red-brown gloss and the rest extremely worn green. It's a rectangular space about 24ft long and 13ft wide. There is a raised, tiled cubicle in the far corner that is the extent of the 'facilities.' Not a stick of furniture on the floor, only the bedrolls of the twenty prisoners already in the cell. A TV in a bracket, clipped over the bars that separate the front of the cell from the corridor, completes the description of the room.

It is soon clear that not one of the twenty men squeezed in here speak English. I'm put under the window, opposite the toilet cubicle. An oil drum of spare water, filled during the day, lies in-between me and it. A smiling Thai helps me squeeze my bedroll in, the cell door is slammed shut and padlocked, and the headcount starts. I'm number 12: 'sib-song' in Thai. The TV has been on since before the door was locked (though muted during the headcount) and, after the screw disappears with his clipboard, the volume is turned up again. It's the first of the month, so at 4pm the twice monthly Thai National Lottery draw is being broadcast. I see that several of the men in the cell have bits of paper in their hands and are groaning, nodding, or smiling as the numbers are drawn. The old cliché of gambling-mad Asians seems confirmed.

As the natural light fades, the interior lights feel brighter. Again, they are never switched off. This is principally because the guards don't patrol the insides of the cellblocks at night and they want to see the windows backlit to expose any would-be escape artist sawing through the bars, something that had happened a year or two before. Even looking through those high windows was technically forbidden. I eat my peanut butter sandwiches, washed down with the Pepsi. As the hubbub subsides, I snuggle down into my bedroll and am asleep in minutes. So ends my first day in Bang Kwang.

VICKY

Parentage

left to right, Sarah and Vicky 1959

I've heard it said that a person's first memory provides the key to his or her nature, whether pessimistic or optimistic. Mine was sitting in an old-fashioned twin perambulator, the two navy-blue hoods pulled up so they were almost touching. Through the crack I could see the gate, tessellated path and pale yellow front door of our Fulham house. The rain was falling and I remember sharing a look with my twin-sister sitting opposite. We were both thinking the same thing. Mummy was in a bad mood so we'd better watch out.

To understand why, we would need to go back two generations and cross to the other side of the planet. Our mother, Sonia, or Chick to her friends, was born and bred in Australia. She was the first girl in the Booth family for fifty years and doted on, particularly by her father. However, she never saw eye-to-eye with my intellectual and artistic British grandmother Kathy d'Abreu, rebelling against her English refinement, loving sport and the great outdoors instead.

This grandmother was one of seven remarkable siblings. They were raised in Birmingham, well-to-do, until my Indian great-grandfather, a doctor, died suddenly age 49, infected by a patient he was treating, leaving my Irish great-grandmother in straightened circumstances. She couldn't turn to her parents or in-laws for help as she and her husband had both been disowned by their families when they married. The three eldest daughters were recalled from finishing school in Switzerland. Doris, the eldest, had been worshipped from afar by Bert, a local Brummie. Now, as a result of Doris's change of fortune, Bert felt he could ask for her hand in marriage. He was accepted. Theirs was a wonderful union. When Doris died at age 84, Bert died forty-eight hours later and they were buried together. The next two sisters, Jo and Maggie, following the First World War, remained spinsters, becoming Head Teachers and Lady Captains of their golf clubs. John, the oldest boy, was an epileptic, who died in his early twenties. My grandmother, the fifth child, was reluctantly kept on by the nuns for free. Being poorly treated, she developed TB and so from the age of fourteen, stayed at home. However she sailed into Birmingham University, reading English, and there met and later married Eric Booth, reading Mechanical Engineering. Her two younger brothers, Pon and Frank, were at Stonyhurst College, a Jesuit boarding school, and the monks agreed to keep them on for free. They returned the kindness when they became top surgeons, setting up a trust for the Jesuit monks at the Hospital of Saint John and Saint Elizabeth. Both married into the royal family.

It was Frank my great uncle, who stepped in when my Australian grandfather died after a long illness, also at the age of 49. He bought my grandmother a flat in Montague Square and so my *mother, age 18, and grandmother, emigrated from Melbourne to London. Her elder brother John, a doctor, stayed behind and her younger brother Mickey emigrated to America.*

I am not sure mum ever truly recovered from this traumatic experience. She loathed the English weather, was teased because of her Aussie accent and dark skin, was still grieving for the loss of her adored father and beloved country and, in having four girls, the patriarchal environment she had thrived in was well and truly over.

My mother and father met on a tennis court at Hurlingham. My father, Guy, was fanatic about tennis and found this beautiful Aussie with a decent game and quick wit, very attractive. However she refused his offer of marriage three times before finally accepting. She got pregnant while engaged, so the wedding was brought forward. My parents never celebrated or told us when they were married. Only when we were nineteen did my godmother tell my twin sister and I the truth.

Pregnancy should have given my mother time to adjust to motherhood, but three weeks before our due date, she tried to move a heavy wardrobe on her own and went into labour. I was born first and then she was told to push again because she was having twins. No one had picked up on this, so my parents having no money, with my father still studying and my mother clearly unable to go back to work, were in complete shock. She told me that my father's first response to our birth was to blurt out "cataclysmic". She mistook this to mean "catastrophic" and instead of feeling the elation of a new mother, was filled with misgiving. I was born 3lb 11oz and Sarah 4lb 2oz. My grandmother didn't help matters by saying she thought it would be better for everyone if we died as we'd probably be sickly for the rest of our lives.

We did not leave the incubator and start suckling until nearly a month after we were born. Sarah, my twin, refused, as she sensibly realised a bottle was far easier to drink from than the breast. I, however, tried and nearly died in the process. My mother never forgot this. As far as she was concerned, she had been rejected by my sister, whom she had not been expecting anyway. Looking back, I cannot remember ever seeing my mother spontaneously hug, kiss or praise Sarah. Worse still, as Sarah got older, she started to take on the mannerisms of my other grandmother, Babs, whom my mother found intensely irritating. As the favoured twin, I carried a huge sense of guilt and as the oldest, a huge sense of responsibility, both of which so irked me, I would take it out on Sarah herself. Although we fought throughout our childhood, I don't have any memory of Sarah starting these quarrels. In fact, when we were too small to sit up, our cots were placed side by side. Every morning my father would come in to find Sarah lying next to me. Mystified, he decided, like the 'Elves and the shoe-maker', to keep watch through a crack in the door. Astonished, he watched as Sarah hauled herself up the bars of her cot, leaned over, dropped into my cot and snuggled up next to me.

Left to right, Sarah and Vicky on our doorstep 1962

Mum found it hard to show affection generally unless we fell ill. And we really did have to be ill. When I was four years old, Sarah and I were playing in the shallow end of the Hurlingham swimming pool when I developed a splitting headache and felt nauseous. Arriving home I was sick on the doorstep. Mum, irritated at the mess, sent me straight to bed. My grandmother Cathy was visiting that afternoon. Seeing me limp and drowsy, she persuaded Mummy to get our local doctor to come and examine me. She had only read about meningitis, but acting on a hunch, called for an ambulance and in doing so saved my life. Mummy tells me that the attendant yelled at the driver to step on it. I remember bits of the journey but blacked out as the ambulance dived down a ramp to the hospital entrance. My next memory is of lying in a hospital bed and Mummy spooning gravy into my mouth, from a beef stew she had made. I also remember Daddy carrying me up the stairs to my bedroom on coming home as I was too weak to walk.

At thirteen, the family went on a Club Mediterranee holiday abroad, to Livigno in the Italian Alps. I remember one summer's day trekking with Mum to a summit, something I'd never done before. I think that instilled in me a lifelong thirst for mountains. One night Sarah and I had a massive fight over who had the right to the one chair between our beds. Before the manager came to shut us up due to complaints from guests, I had given her a massive scratch down her arm and she had screamed, "I hope you die!" The next morning I woke with a stomach pain which persisted all week. On the day we were leaving, climbing the steps to the hotel entrance, I fainted. My mother told me to stop making an unnecessary scene in front of the other guests and go and have a shower. I felt revived but when she saw my white face, for the first time I saw a look of fear on her face. She told me to lie down. She collared a guest who she knew was a doctor and asked him to examine me. He said it was almost certainly appendicitis and needed to be operated on immediately. Mum rang Uncle Frank who booked me in for an operation in Westminster Children's Hospital, as long as we made the afternoon flight from Milan.

Despite my father's best efforts, we missed the plane. I was taken into the airport medical centre and on being examined, the doctors were horrified. They said that if I'd made the plane I would have been dead on arrival. I had peritonitis. Next thing I was racing in an ambulance to Milan's general hospital with my father following behind at breakneck speed, narrowly missing cars and trams. The next day after the operation, Sarah came to visit, with tears streaming down her face, "I didn't mean it, I didn't mean it!"

In making sure we were well-fed and clean, my mother could not be faulted. I think it was her way of being maternal but I can count on one hand the times I saw her truly happy. I remember when my younger sister Boozy, (yes, that's her nickname!) was three and we twins were seven, jumping into a huge pile of leaves, trying our hardest to make Mum laugh and feeling sad at her sadness. She didn't even smile.

She was never diagnosed, but I think she was bi-polar or manic-depressive as it was then known. When she wasn't screaming and shouting at us, she would be cleaning the house with an obsession bordering on madness. The carpet had lost its pile because we were dutifully expected to Hoover it three times a day. I can still hear her bashing each tread and riser on the stairs. My sisters and I were each given cleaning chores. All clothes had to be colour-coordinated, pre-soaked and rubbed individually in the bath and rinsed three times BEFORE they made it to the washing machine. EVERYTHING had to be ironed. We girls were all assigned different pieces of antique furniture to polish. Mine was the grand piano. Meals were a tense affair. My father, with three scholarships to Cambridge, only opened his mouth to tell us not to slurp our food or hit our utensils on any part of our teeth. My mother sat at the purpose-built Formica kitchen table with a sponge cloth next to her plate, eyes darting around the room, particularly the floor, for any sign of a germ which she would pounce on triumphantly. Strangely, she never saw the cobwebs on the ceiling. Exhausted, she would take to her bed, curtains drawn, for a few days and then the cycle would begin all over again. A bang on the bedroom floor was the signal for one of us little girls to bring her up a cup of tea. It had to be in her favourite floral china cup. Woe betide if we slopped any into the saucer.

In my teens, I once and only once, brought a potential boyfriend back for tea after a game of tennis. I felt sick as we approached the house. I rang the bell. My mother parted the curtains, saw who was with me and proceeded to unravel the Hoover, plug it in, Hoover the whole hall, banging against the front door and shaking the rug. By the time she'd opened the front door, the boy had, quite rightly, decided this was a nuthouse. He stayed ten minutes and I never set eyes on him again. Generally she Hoovered in the nude, so I should have counted my blessings that this time she was dressed!

Eventually, Mum, in a cry for help, threw herself out of the second-floor window of our house, but only sprained her ankle. This was followed by psychotherapy and a short period of happiness which ushered in the birth of my youngest sister, Itsy. (This time my mother so wanted a boy she hadn't chosen any girls names.) She was the livewire, wild-child and captivating beauty who woke us all up.

My mother once travelled to India to meet Mother Theresa in person and offer her help. She was told to go back to England. "The needy are on your own doorstep," was this remarkable nun's reply. Mum took this to heart, and like the Good Samaritan, she never walked by on the other side. When people were afraid to breathe the same air as anyone with Aids, she was helping a young lad to die with dignity. She got him a council flat, sorted out all his benefits, begged furniture, kitchen appliances, bedding etc. from all her friends. Waifs and strays were always in our kitchen having tea, Battenburg cake and malt loaf.

My parents had been scrimping and saving from the beginning of their marriage. For the first six months of our life, they lived with Babs, now a widow, in my father's draughty childhood home in

Hillingdon. Then Uncle Frank generously secured the freehold for them on a Fulham house. My other grandmother Cathy, gave them her car when we were born and never drove again. My parents could only move into the ground floor as sitting tenants occupied the rest. We had a small garden with sunflowers in it. I remember drying my hair near a three-bar heater, the only one we had. We couldn't afford meat so mum plied us with kidneys, liver, even brains, as well as mackerel and sardines. With her Australian upbringing, she under-cooked the vegetables and never bothered making cakes or pastries, so I think our diet, while limited, was healthy. In the ensuing years, my father became a stockbroker with Hoare Govett, eventually becoming a partner. By the time I was eight years old, my parents had bought the tenants out and now we lived on all three floors.

From age four to 11 we girls went to the local convent. Mum used to give a lift to a young widow and her three children she had seen walking to and from school. This remarkable woman, Kathleen, one of the kindest and wisest women I ever knew, sewed uniforms all night and took in alterations by day, in order to give her three children a private Catholic education. When she was about to be evicted from her house, my mother persuaded our father not to invest in the dream weekend cottage for which they had been saving, but to buy Kathleen's house for her instead. Kathleen would pay my father back at regular intervals, with cash in brown envelopes. He got back every penny within ten years. Her children all ended up being successful. The eldest daughter, Zakia, and her husband together rose up the ranks of radio advertising, winning international awards and buying a huge house in Richmond. Her second daughter, Safia, an accountant, managed millions of pounds for the council; and her son, Baboo, was a designer for Smallbone Kitchens.

My mother always called us 'wet London girls' and was forever trying to toughen us up. For two weeks of our summer holidays, we stayed on a farm in Devon, where the farmer's wife, Mrs Hallett, ran a B&B. Our days were spent swimming miles out to sea, scaling cliff-faces, climbing over rocks, and diving into ice-cold streams and dams. My father rarely joined in, preferring to read the Financial Times on the beach.

My father could not have been more opposite to my mother. He was all reason, she all intuition. While he would be arguing that if A=B, B=C, then C=A, she would say, "I just know I'm right". His upbringing was solitary. His father, a Yorkshireman, joined the Navy and became an Admiral by merit and determination rather than connections but he was away during the war and his much older brother Derek, was at boarding school. By the time he was seven years old, my father realized his mother, who immersed herself in the world of amateur dramatics, couldn't be relied upon to say a single truthful word. This resulted in my father becoming in his own scientific way a 'free-thinker'; for him, there was a 'God,' but all religion was man-made and therefore dispensable. However, he encouraged us to kneel and pray beside our beds every night, something I have never lost. He taught me to question everything, in marked contrast to my mother whose Catechism was learnt by rote.

Luckily, Sarah and I were sent to a convent boarding school at eleven years old. We loved it. Sarah was captain of every sport and I excelled academically. The nightmares I regularly had at home, stopped. We arrived just after the changes brought about by Vatican II. The nuns had thrown off their habits, grabbed their guitars, and we sang songs about peace and reconciliation. They told us to question our faith. If we didn't like a certain rule, we could complain, but we were then given the responsibility of finding and implementing a working alternative. There were not many complaints.

I lived in the same house until I was 23, when my parents separated and my father bought us three older girls a place in another part of Fulham, three roads away from my future husband.

Nick

I had witnessed my parents' unhappy marriage and my father's unrequited love so, as a young girl, I prayed to God for, "a man who would love me and who I would love." I asked to be given a sign when I'd met the right person.

I felt comfortable being a practising Catholic. I once heard an Italian nun on the radio explaining why she had taken her vows, "If the dress fits, wear it." The Catholic dress did indeed fit me. I couldn't see the point of sleeping with someone if it wasn't going to go anywhere. I was an avid reader and, having devoured every fairy tale I could lay my hands on as a child and later the novels of Jane Austen, I was secretly hoping a Mr Darcy or Prince Charming would whisk me away. What then followed were a string of suitors, including a professional comedian and tennis player. My reputation vacillated from blue stocking lesbian to princess on top of the glass mountain as I refused to sleep with any of them.

One summer day in 1981, Boozy asked me to make up a mixed doubles on the Friday with her two bosses, Nick and Alex on one of the grass courts at The Hurlingham Club. These two young men were joint owners of their own holiday company and my sister worked for them.

"I can't think of anything more boring!" I retorted. "They probably can't even play tennis, and don't expect me to stay afterwards for a drink or dinner, because I'm already fixed to go out with Ian," who was suitor number three, a Spanish banker.

A few days later, I set eyes on Nick for the first time. Just under 6 feet, tanned, fit, he had dark blonde hair in a halo of curls round his head. Nick's look as we walked on court – 'I've got better things to do' – mirrored mine. Determined to wipe that expression off his face, I aimed every ball straight at him as hard as I could. Nick told me since, that he never saw me play better. Apparently he walked off court, saying to Alex that he'd be going out with me within six months.

I cancelled on the banker and we went for drinks and dinner as a foursome. That night, I asked Boozy if I was imagining that Nick appeared to 'undress' me with his eyes each time we changed ends.

"Oh, he does that with all the attractive girls," she replied. Right, he's the last person I'd be seen dead with, I thought. I then spent six months making sure I was out when he arrived for dinner with my sisters.

As a result I hardly saw Nick – despite the fact we lived three roads away from each other in Fulham – until that life-changing weekend the following year when he turned up in Klosters, Switzerland, where I was 'repping' for the Ski Club of Great Britain. I remember having butterflies in my stomach as I came down the stairs of the hotel to meet him and wondering why. No man had ever crossed borders expressly to see me, and I felt the same attraction for him as I had on the tennis court. Ten years later, Nick burst that bubble by telling me he was in the next valley anyway on business.

That evening I took Nick to see the hotel's disused ballroom. The floor was subsiding, the bulbs had long gone and the moonlight filtered through translucent curtains. Next thing, he had me in an embrace and was declaring undying love. I heard a voice near me, loud and clear, saying, "This is your husband." I remember my shoulders dropping with relief. I had finally been given a clear sign. I would never have to fend off men again. A few days later, he asked me to come to bed with him and I didn't hesitate. As I saw it, I was married in the eyes of God. A year later, to the day, he got down on one knee and proposed to me in the same ballroom. Call me a romantic but in that setting he had me at "Will you?"

Vicky on honeymoon September 1984

After a fairy-tale wedding, Nick whisked me away on a surprise honeymoon to India. We spent the first ten days relaxing in Goa, Salman Rushdie's 'Portuguese pimple on the face of Mother India' [9], *at the beautiful Fort Aguada Hotel. I was particularly touched at Nick's thoughtfulness, as my great grandfather came from there. We borrowed a moped from a waiter called Jesus and, while exploring the jungle, by chance passed the medical school where, in all likelihood, my Indian ancestor would have trained.*

One morning, as the waves were big, Nick decided to body surf. I was lying on the sand in a demure, black swimming costume, which was obligatory for all female guests, when I found myself surrounded by four men. They asked if they could take a photo with me. Mistaking them for the hotel staff on a break, I naïvely said yes. Before I knew what was happening, two had their arms round me and one was putting his hand inside my costume, cupping my breasts. I yelled and Nick turned round. In seconds he was out of the water, had grabbed a paddle and was chasing the men down the beach with it. My hero!

A few days later, I'm lying on my bed having a siesta when the internal phone goes. "Excuse me madam, but could we bring you your laundry now?" Confused, I told housekeeping that we hadn't sent any laundry. "Oh no, no, Madam! We have it here." A pause and then, "Nick, you devil! What a brilliant Indian accent! You had me fooled!"

I loved Nick's energy. Every second of his day was filled and when he turned out the light at night, he was asleep in moments. If he woke at 5am, he would be off to the office. If he woke at 6am he'd be off to the pool. If he woke early at weekends, he'd be off for a cycle. With all this activity came an air of purposefulness, of being his own man, which I found immensely attractive. He was an entrepreneur who had built his travel business from scratch. He was organised. Like me, he was an all-round sportsman. It was wonderful to have a skiing, running and tennis partner. We were compatible physically. We generally liked the same books, films and theatre, but what impressed me was his insight, his ability to grasp the kernel of a character or plot in a few words.

There had never been men in my family as I grew up. I was one of four sisters. Both my grandfathers were dead before I was born. My uncles and cousins were absent, either because they lived on the other sides of the world or were estranged from my parents. The only man I had as a role model was my father, honourable, if quite distant. I trusted him completely. I was naïve in the extreme, and foisted a romantic image on Nick that was both unrealistic and unfair on him. I thought in Nick I had found my mate and life partner, someone who would take care of me. When we argued, the next day by 11am a bunch of flowers would be delivered to the door. A few minutes later, Nick would ring and all would be forgiven and forgotten. I loved hearing his voice on the phone. It was his metier. He was gentle, loving and a great listener.

I remember on my 27th birthday, when I was pregnant with Samantha, Nick told me to come outside. Parked in the street was a brand new shiny black Fiat Uno. I gasped with delight because it was tied up like a parcel with a white bow on top and I couldn't believe he'd found a way to get the ribbon under and over the car several times. In that moment I loved the man with all my heart - the car came a close second!

Once, playing golf in Portugal, on a fairway running alongside a lake, Nick stripped off and began ducking and diving under the water. I watched, amused, because I'd never seen him go to such lengths for a missing golf ball before. I started to worry when he failed to surface, but just then, out of the middle of the lake emerged a hand, not clutching Excalibur, but rather his seven iron. My knight in shining armour! Unknown to me the week before, out of character, he'd hit his club on the ground in frustration and in the next instant, it had shot out of his hand into the lake.

From the beginning of the marriage, holidays played a large part – Nick was in the travel business after all. School holidays were spent abroad in Austria and Portugal. Friends and relatives were always invited which was great fun. A big treat was one long-haul trip either to Mauritius or Canada Heli-skiing each year. Nick's additional surfing and golf weeks meant that the rare moments I spent alone with him felt very precious.

Nick was an atheist but I didn't worry about us not having a spiritual connection. I figured it was a private affair anyway, and he seemed to be a good man, caring of and generous with his friends and family. In contrast, I was a Catholic with a strong belief in the spirit world, especially angels. I believed in reincarnation[10] and felt deeply that no one faith is better than another. We are all looking at the same thing with different coloured spectacles as a nun once told me.

Marrying the mother

On hearing of our engagement, Vera, Nick's mother, flew from Dallas to live with us for twelve weeks. Every night, instead of the two of us making passionate love, the three of us would sit down to yet another awkward meal.

"If you marry the favourite son, you marry the mother."[11] One of the first things Vera said to me when we were alone was: "You know Nick and I have a connection like no other – we can read each other's minds." On hearing this, my heart sank, but by then I was far too in love to back out.

Vera got married soon after she left school. She had post-natal depression with her first-born. By contrast, the birth of her second child, Nick, was quick and effortless. Blonde and blue-eyed, he became the apple of his mother's eye. He could do no wrong.

To escape her Crawley council flat, Vera persuaded Nick's father, Dennis, to up sticks to Zambia, where he got a job as an architect in the Town Planning Department. They were now living in beautiful colonial surroundings with servants, a tennis club, the ex-pat's dream. Vera told me that all the staff adored Nick and couldn't do enough for him.

Nick, age six, and his brother, age eight, were sent to an English boarding school and Nick's parents divorced a year later. When Tom, our son, turned six, I remember Nick saying to me, "how could they have sent me away this young? Tom is still wetting the bed and sucking his thumb." The experience toughened Nick up and made him self-reliant, but I can only speculate that, from this time on, he learnt to keep his feelings to himself.

Vera is nothing if not resourceful. After her divorce, she asked herself where the greatest concentration of men to women on the planet was – she found out that Malta, with its army, air force and naval bases, had a 10:1 ratio of men to women. This inspired her to set up a fashionable boutique on the island. Nick told me that, as a seven-year-old boy, he would sit on the stairs, unable to sleep until he knew his mother was safely back from one of her nights out. *Eventually she married an airline pilot, Derek, and persuaded him to join East African Airways, thereby returning to her ex-pat lifestyle, this time in Kenya. Vera told me Derek was the love of her life. In the same breath she revealed he had once tried to run her over – "but I was young and too quick for him!" – I remember spilling my tea in response.*

Years later, when her marriage was beyond repair, Nick helped a desperate Vera leave her second husband and return to England – a kindness she never forgot. Nick and his mother went into partnership, founding a holiday company together. Vera manned the phones from her Twickenham house, placing adverts in the Observer, while Nick and Alex went out to the Swiss Alps to run their first two chalets.

Nick once said to me that he could never not be successful. Eventually Alex took Vera's place in the partnership and by the time they were 25 years old, these two lads had bought their first hotel. When I met him two years later, Nick already owned his own house in Fulham.

Meanwhile, Vera had left England and found administrative work in a hospital in Saudi Arabia. There she met her third husband, Keith, an American, twenty years her junior.[12] *Vera kept telling him to get his hair cut like Nick, or dress like Nick – an annoyance both for him and Nick.*

Nick, Vera and Keith began a one-hour photo business together, which lasted several years. After their marriage and business dissolved, I received manic letters from Keith, informing me that Nick and Vera were keeping money from him.

I felt Nick had never cut the umbilical cord. Four days before our wedding, we were driving to Hampshire, where Nick's medical records were, to have our jabs for the honeymoon. As we hit the Hammersmith flyover, I put this question to Nick; "if Vera and I were drowning, who would you rescue?" Despite two lanes and no hard shoulder, he slammed on the brakes and told me to get out. In my defence, Nick had no faith, had never been baptised and I desperately wanted to be sure he respected the vow, 'forsaking all others'. We drove the rest of the way in silence and after being inoculated, arrived at Nick's father and stepmother's house for dinner. I saw them exchange worried glances when they saw we weren't speaking.

My fears were grounded. From the beginning of our marriage, Vera was ever-present. She helped look after the children once a year, to give us a holiday on our own, but it came at a price. For fourteen years, she stayed every other weekend when we were in London and came on most winter and summer holidays. On arriving, it was her custom to go straight to my cupboard and rifle through my clothes to see what Nick had bought me and then declare that she had always wanted the same. I remember once giving in and seeing Nick's horrified face as Vera paraded her 'new' jumper before him. Nick had only given it to me the day before. She would come in without knocking when I was in the bath and then stay and chat, which made me squirm. Why didn't I just ask her to leave? I once complained to Nick that Vera rang me two or three times a day. He told me that she rang him seven times a day! She was passed round the office to give him a break.

Our arguments were almost always about her. When Nick was around, she wanted his undivided attention and was not interested in me or the children. As I didn't see Nick much myself, I resented her taking up so much of his spare time.

It was thirteen years into the marriage and Vera had been staying for a month. One day she pushed me too far. I remember saying on the phone in an uncharacteristically calm and cold voice: "It is not your house, it is my house." She refused to have anything to do with me for ten months after that. A blessing in disguise!

Children

Samantha *was born on Valentine's day, after a 13-hour labour*[14]. *Alert, demanding, she seemed to be awake night and day, determined to miss nothing. She was crawling at six months, walking at ten. Petite, she had this unruly, white-blond hair. In Portugal, a woman ran demented down the beach; in Sardinia, a bejewelled, gnarled hand reached out from the back of a chauffeur-driven Bentley, both women wanting to stroke this impossible mane.*

She was spotted for a film at two years old but got chicken pox the day before casting. Encouraged, I enrolled her in a Huggies advert. Two-year-olds were, somewhat ambitiously, expected to walk down a catwalk one at a time. One boy pushed past Samantha, who pushed him back in return. The boy howled, setting off other children. The parents were told to take him out and so attacked me for ruining their child's career. The day ended with Samantha dressed as a cave baby, fur nappy and club, sporting the look they wanted, seriously moody because she WASN'T wearing Huggies.

Samantha has always had an enquiring mind. She learnt to read very quickly and then devoured everything in sight. I have seen her walk into a pillar at Heathrow airport because she was so absorbed in her book. She almost got straight A*s in GCSE's, in a mood on the day of her results, because two of her grades were only A. She also got straight A's at A level. However, that feisty girl received two suspensions, one when her whole class dyed their hair pink one hour before prizegiving; the second when she and three friends poured concentrated washing-up liquid into the school fountain. It had been an object of interest for scientists in the holidays because of its 17th century eco-system, now destroyed along with a prehistoric newt, the only one of its kind on the planet, well WAS the only one of its kind.

Nick and I always called Samantha the 'shop steward'. As the oldest, she was always demanding her rights and the rights of her siblings. She was always putting on plays, suborning her siblings and cousins, and even us grown-ups, in her productions.

Samantha's competitiveness led her to become an all-around sportswoman – golf, tennis, skiing, you name it. It definitely helped sharing digs with six lads at Uni. But something else of her grandmother's spirit appeared. Throughout those three years, she mentored an 11-year-old girl considered 'at risk' by social services. This girl's only ambition was to get pregnant and thereby get a flat of her own. Partly through Samantha's encouragement, she became a hairdresser and is now a solid citizen.

Samantha was an impossible teenager herself but only until she reached the age of thirteen. I blame the Spice Girls. I can see her now in her pink and blue make-up, tottering on black and silver platforms, in a lurex mini dress to match, looking to my undying shame like an underage hooker. Her dress sense has since improved, thank God!

My second daughter **Emma**, is the wild child and free spirit of our family. Her birth was over from first twinge to first cry in under four hours, with no pain relief and only twenty minutes of excruciating pain. Later that day, as I crept down the corridor of Queen Charlotte's Hammersmith for a desperately needed shower, I heard this furious scream behind me, demanding immediate attention, and realised with horror it was coming from my own child's pair of lungs. Another feisty daughter.

Emma cannot be taught, anymore than a cat; she was born in the year of the cat after all. She teaches herself, and when she decides to do something, nothing will stop her. For her school 'private enterprise' aged eleven, she created a range of accessories from denim material. She dusted off our sewing machine, read the instruction manual from beginning to end, and having learnt to thread it, she was off. I watched her put a zip in a make-up bag and unpick it eight times until she was satisfied. I would have thrown *the infernal contraption across the room. She picked up a silver award, not a gold, but I reckon she was the only child to be given absolutely no help from her parents.*

Emma went to Hurtwood House for sixth form. Her art teacher told me that she spearheaded her year in her complete lack of fear and single-mindedness. She would think nothing of going outside, picking up a handful of dirt and rubbing it into her canvas. Her sketch pads looked like something out of the day of the Triffids, as she painted and glued textiles on textiles and scribbled upside-down if necessary.

Emma is an out and out creative, very sensitive, and easily flies off the handle. She went to City and Guilds Art School. For the first year, the tutors tried to get her to analyse her work and wondered why she ran out in floods of tears saying, "I don't know. I just do it." Accepting that her method was intuitive rather than analytical, they left her alone for her last two years. She preferred to work at home. For her final piece, she stitched 192 stuffed armless dolls from old white sheets, sewing into the night to complete the installation. She fought tooth and nail to get the staff to build her a space, seven feet by seven feet by seven feet. By lining this room with the dolls she created a padded cell conforming to Victorian measurements. She then hung a stuffed, life-sized woman from a naked lightbulb, with floor-length black hair, big red lips, red finger nails on hands, and feet dragging on the floor. Not quite what they were expecting! I watched one set of parents, having viewed the several rooms of paintings, peer into her doorway, only to step back in horror.

Emma has always been fearless. This led to several accidents in her terrible twos. Nick and I were in A & E every fortnight – I thought they would start to suspect me of Munchausen by proxy. She sniffed a red berry up her nose and had to be operated on immediately. She fell off a wall and broke her front tooth. The end of a paper napkin tucked into her collar, caught fire on a candle as she leant forward, and burnt her face. Luckily Jo, our quick-witted

New Zealand help, was looking after her then, and kept her face covered in a cold wet towel for an hour and a half. By the time she was seen in A & E, they said they would have done the same and well done. The scab fell off within ten days and within two years all discolouration had gone.

Emma is the most overtly spiritual of my children. I think this inner journey was kick-started at age nineteen when a number of close friends died. Her first boyfriend Gabriel was practising a Parkour stunt and fell off a four-storey building. Another friend looked down at the A to Z on his lap and swerved into an oncoming vehicle. One boy committed suicide, tying himself to his bedroom curtain rail. Another jumped in front of an oncoming train, and yet another died in India from contaminated cocaine. In her first year at Art School, she was given a small room, which she painted completely white. In one corner was a shoebox in which lay a little, stitched, stuffed white figure. On the wall hung a similar figure, with arms outstretched in the shape of a cross. On a small white table lay an open Bible. Otherwise the room was empty. It was a very moving experience to be in there.

***Tom** is my oldest boy. Born a Sagittarius, he is straight as a die, witty and quick, with a photographic memory. Until his A levels, I never saw him do more than ten minutes of revision at a time. Just by listening in class to his History teacher, he got 100%. I once tested him on two sides of Latin vocabulary when, after his usual ten minutes, he said he knew them. He got every one right. The next day, thinking it was a fluke, I tested him again and again, 100%.*

This enviable memory made Tom bone idle and he cruised his way through his school years, proudly declaring that he, "did the minimum to get by." He almost came unstuck at A levels when he blew his RS paper. He knew he would only achieve a C and Leeds wanted 3 B's. In the next two weeks, Tom worked, as he admitted, as hard as he ever had in his life, to get his Drama up to an A grade to balance the books. On the day of the results, finding out he had, as he expected, achieved an A, B & C, he managed by 9.30am to speak PERSONALLY with the registrar of the faculty for Broadcast Journalism at Leeds.

"Sorry Tom but we've had such a strong intake this year, your C has let you down."

"It's not a problem because I want a gap year so I am perfectly happy to retake any modules necessary. The real issue is that I am planning to teach in a school in Nepal when the exams come round next June."

"Oh Tom, you are just the type of student we are looking for! I will ring you in three days' time when I have cleared this year's intake and see what we can do."

True to her word, the registrar rang and told Tom that she had found a precedent and he would not have to retake IF he made a radio documentary of his time in Nepal and sent some work references to her at once. Again by luck, he had just been working for ITN and had two references to her in 48-hours.

That sums up Tom to a T. He manages to wing his way through life, but when he wants something, he has the charm and determination to get it. Perfect qualities for a journalist and presenter.

On his gap year, Tom visited the Favelas in Rio. A boy about his age, approached him in the street and asked him if he would like to have an alternative tour of the slums. His Headmaster at Wellington College had told the boys, in his end of year speech, to 'trust'. Tom looked into this boy's eyes and decided to trust him. A minute later he began to have doubts as the boy said he could bring his friends but must come on foot after dark.

Tom walked beside the boy, his two friends behind. Children, he noticed, were playing Cowboys and Indians with real guns. One teenager, very jumpy, was bouncing a Kalashnikov on his knee. Tom found out that it was this boy's first week manning the initial checkpoint to the head honcho and he was understandably very nervous. Tom was asked if he wanted to meet the chief. In for a penny, in for a pound! After several checkpoints he was surprised to be greeted, not by Marlon Brando or Al Pacino, but by a thin, 27-year-old post-graduate in specs. He told Tom that the only way out for the children was education. He told Tom he was far safer inside the slum. No one wished to give the police or government any excuse to close the place down. In fact, the only loose cannons they had were the crackheads. They were housed apart and guarded because of their unpredictable behaviour. Tom was asked if he wanted to take a look. No guesses at his answer. Tom told me it was truly sinister. They entered a house in darkness. An electric light bulb was switched on, illuminating a sea of white faces with zombie eyes. As they left, he turned to see the faces staring at him from the windows. 'Shaun of the Dead' or what!

At the end of the tour, after they had had a meal, Tom paid the sum agreed. Tom asked his guide what he would spend it on. "Books. I want to go to University like the chief."

Tom has always been a natural sportsman, in all the teams, and has never had to work at it to be a good amateur. Still, he used to hate losing, but particularly hated playing badly. I remember once when he was ten, I was marking a golf card for him. We were only on the sixth hole, when Tom began throwing his toys out of the pram. I said if he dared to step off the green, I would drive home without him. He did. I grabbed my bag and stormed across three fairways to the car. By the time I had reached the house fifteen minutes later, my anger had subsided and I wondered guiltily if he had any money on him for the train from Richmond to Barnes. Two hours later, Tom walked in, having been too embarrassed to borrow money from the office or my friends. He had trekked all the way back in his golf studs, with his bag on his back. It was a lesson for life, he now tells me, as he has never lost his cool playing sport since.

A similar incident happened to Tom in the Alps when he was 9 years old. After a big family lunch at a mountain restaurant he'd gone to the loo. No-one had realized and the two taxis left without him. Wearing ski boots and carrying his skis, he figured the only thing he could do was start walking until someone realised and came back for him. It turned dark, the mountain pass totally unlit. At one point he lost the snow-covered road and found himself following a cross-country track to the river. Realising his mistake, he cut through the deep snow back to the road. He told me afterwards that he kept repeating "I am not dead yet," over and over. Hours later, exhausted and tearstained, Tom came crawling into my bathroom. "Hi Tom!" I said, thinking he'd been in the other taxi. "What do you mean hi? I was left behind and nearly died!"

Tom is the darling of his grandmothers and has never talked down or up to anyone, whether nine or ninety. Teachers either loved or loathed him because he had absolutely no concept of 'them and us.'

***William** is my youngest. He's a dreamy boy with no grasp of time, often missing buses, trains and planes. He has a powerful imagination but I never realised just what a unique vision he had until he started getting behind a film camera.*

William was the easiest baby and, as a result, we never got a babysitter but took him with us everywhere. As a three-year-old, he came with us to evening performances of Michael Flatley's 'Lord of the Dance' and 'Jesus Christ Superstar'. At the former, he sat entranced until, at a less riveting bit, he looked up and exclaimed "Oh what a beautiful ceiling!" Lots of giggles from the stalls. At 'Jesus Christ Superstar', he sat with his feet up on the empty chair in front, completely enthralled.

William, when little, was continually making things and had complete faith in the creative side of his nature. Nuts, bolts, wires, plastic, tape, string all went into his installations. At primary school, he stayed behind to assist the Art teacher with extra classes for the younger boys. His drawings had mastered the three-dimensional to a degree well ahead of his age group. He hated lessons but loved sport and his peers.

At six years old he was assessed to see why he was getting behind academically. A psychologist came to our house. I was allowed to stay in the kitchen, but just to observe. William was wringing his hands with nervousness. The first question was, "Where does milk come from?" Silence. "William, where does milk come from?" Finally a small voice said, "a cat". Next question, "What is in the sky at night?" Silence. "William, what is in the sky at night?". Eventually he said, "the sun," I knew he was the rabbit caught in headlights and my heart sank to my boots.

The assessor decided to change tack and drew out a board with pegs on it. William's demeanour altered instantly. He became alert and curious. He was told to look carefully at the pattern made by the pegs and to rearrange them in the correct order. He paused for a moment and then his hands, like a skilled typist, flashed across the board moving various pegs. In ten seconds he stopped. The man asked him if he had finished and, confidently, he said yes. A few puzzles later and William's insecurity had vanished. He sailed through the test and when the man returned to the two original questions, "cows" and "moon" were his immediate responses. The assessor told me that William would always be a round peg in a square hole as far as school was concerned, but, "trust me" he said, "I've been doing this job for 25 years; William will be a success."

I've held these words to my heart during some horrendous parent/teacher meetings, through hours of homework, and watching his confidence ebb in a schooling system totally unsuited to him. He was diagnosed with border-line dyslexia and so given little extra help.

Despite this, William got three A levels and gained a place at film school. William has busied himself writing film scripts, working on material as cameraman and editor with his brother, and I see glimpses of the old William emerge. Amen to that.

However, like his grandmothers, William is great in a real crisis. When Samantha was helping produce a commercial in Kiev, ten extra bags of props were needed immediately. Dropping everything, William raced to Heathrow where he found waiting for him a motley assortment, most bags kilos overweight, all badly packed. The kindly female member of staff, seeing the bemused smile on his face, stepped in to help. She told him to go and buy two more bags while she fetched a lighter from those confiscated. He would have to burn through the plastic ties securing each bag and repack them himself. William set to, and the queue building up behind him, instead of getting irate, were cheering him on. One woman even fetched him a cup of water.

On arrival at Kiev, William was hauled aside by several scary-looking security staff. He had been briefed to say the bags were for his private use. At least he could answer with conviction when asked did he pack the bags himself. He was told to open one in front of them. It was full of old planks of wood. They all began laughing and waved him through.

Samantha and the crew were staying in a hotel similar to the 'Grand Budapest.' After a night with them he flew back home. No sooner had he got through the front door than his mobile rang. It was Samantha, to say that she'd just described his saga to the director. This man had been so impressed, he wanted him back on set as his assistant. In forty minutes, William was back at Heathrow.

Help

It is impossible to be a mother without stoicism. Endless sleepless nights, endless repetition of mindless tasks. Endless crying or whining. Endless feeding, winding, nappy changing, dressing and undressing. Of course there are many wonderful moments. A baby's cheeky smile looking up from your boob can't be beaten.

Later on, it's stoicism of a different nature. Five hours driving per day with four children at four different schools. Add homework, extras and the daily battle with the television[13] and finally reading a story to them feels like a huge victory. They're now looking and behaving like angels in order to extend bedtime for as long as possible. I remember reading them 'Holes' and, just as the Warden opens the vial of poisoned nail polish, announcing, "that's all for tonight": Pandemonium!

It's Wednesday. I am running on to poolside whilst double-parked, throwing the two girls to Lauren, their swimming instructor, then sprinting to the car. Sitting in the back, breastfeeding William, while listening to Tom do his spelling and numbers. Back to the pool to get the girls dressed. As we leave, I'm trying to slip past the vending machine without them seeing it. Back home. Letting Tom watch TV because he has done his homework, whilst trying to get the girls to do theirs.

I first needed help when Emma, my second daughter, was ten weeks old. We had just moved into our new house and the builders began work the next day. Nick was flying around on business as his company expanded and his schedule was never the same week on week. I couldn't rely on him for help and so began employing a series of au-pairs. Outstanding was a 17-year-old, Swiss-Italian called Sonia. I knew, if there was a fire, she would find a way of getting my children out. She achieved one of the three highest grades in the country for English spoken as a foreign language.

She did better answering 'Mastermind' questions than I did. By contrast, we had Carmen from Spain. One day, while reading a magazine with headphones on, she failed to notice Tom, age one and a half, jump into the pool without armbands. By a miracle I had just arrived and, seeing him go under, ran the length of the pool, leaped in fully clothed and fished him out.

This incident made me realize I needed someone full-time. Through 'The Lady' magazine, I employed a series of New Zealand and Australian girls who were all utterly reliable, and good companions to boot. The most outstanding of an excellent bunch, Jo, came to work for us when Tom was born and returned again for William's birth. She adored the children, particularly William, and became a dear friend. I reckon if you have the gumption at nineteen to get to the other side of the world to work there for two years, you already have what it takes to cope with four active children.

In 1994, I was very lucky to get Monika from the Czech Republic for two years. She was beautiful inside and out, quiet and confident with an amazing sense of when to stop and chat or give me space.

Monika's previous job had been working for a family in Kent. She hadn't been there long when she began to feel distinctly uncomfortable. She found the mother lying on her bed on one occasion and on another rifling through her underwear drawer. The husband walked out of her shower stark naked. After their 'dinner parties', she would clean up the used condoms. The final straw came as she was washing up. Someone cupped her breasts from behind and she realised with horror that it was the wife. A few hours later, she was on a plane to the Czech Republic. Amazingly, she had the guts to return to England and work for me.

Monika adored William **(14)**, *my youngest, and was in turn loved by all my children. She had a brilliantly dry sense of humour. Thank goodness, because Vera, my mother-in-law, was running a B&B in*

Whistler at that time and during the low seasons in spring and autumn, came to stay with us. She used to lie on the sofa in our conservatory ordering Monika about. One morning I came into the kitchen to find Monika and Sao, my cleaning lady, scowling.

"What's up?" I asked.

Monika explained that Vera was treating her like a servant. Sao retorted, "You're lucky, she treats me like a dog!"

A few days later, Nick and I had a blazing row when he told me that Vera was going to stay a few days longer.

"Monika, Sao and I can't bear another minute. You are never here. You don't know what it's like. They will walk out."

One evening, Vera was giving Karen (our nanny at the time) yet another lesson, this time on how to butter her bread, Sybil Fawlty in tone. Karen eventually got up and left the room, frustration finally getting the better of her. I found her silently screaming in the kitchen and joined in.

Looking back, I want to thank these wonderful young women for giving me so much support in the face of a very absent husband and a very present mother-in-law. I felt I knew the girls better than I knew Nick. I would not have got through all those years without them.

*

I

In 1990, when we'd been married for six years, Nick told me that the company was really struggling and I would have to tighten my belt. He told me not to buy anything but essentials. He said heli-skiing and trips to Mauritius were over. For seven years, I spent nothing on myself. Now, nothing new and expensive hung in my cupboard for Vera to covet. I worried about Nick and the perilous state of his business, which was on his mind the whole time. Discussing our relationship was simply not on the agenda. As long as I asked him on the phone about his business he was interested; as soon as I changed the subject, I could feel his boredom. "Is that all?" was his way of bringing any conversation to an end.

In the early years, on hearing Nick's car on the gravel drive, I would drop everything to run out and embrace him and he me. But I remember a significant shift when one evening he remained in the car on the phone. This he did more and more. On that occasion, I stood there for five minutes waiting for him to finish the call, and then he told me off for loitering! I never came out to the car again.

When I was 31, Samantha four and Emma two years old, we went to a self-catering chalet in Zermatt, taking with us an au-pair. One evening Nick said he was off for a drink and would be back for supper. By 10.30pm I had cleared everything away. By midnight I was really worried. By 4am I was murderous and decided to do the laundry. Nick walked in and, on seeing me, turned as white as a sheet, a phenomenon I would see several times down the years.

One afternoon, a few years later, Nick returned from golf, again white-faced. I thought maybe he'd had an accident. He told me that Chris, his really close friend, had asked him if he was having an affair. Chris had found out from his wife, who'd found out from my daughter Emma's godmother, who had found out from my twin-sister. I was shocked, but impressed that Nick had come straight to me. I rang my sister, who told me that she had heard it from another friend. I told Nick I was going to follow this lead. He said I would be stooping to their level if I did. He said that he and I could rise together above these rumours. I said I would think about it for three days. I was livid that all these women had gossiped behind my back rather than to my face, and for that reason, in the end, I decided not to pursue the matter. From that moment on though, I never fully trusted Nick or the friends around me again. I began to keep my own council, but this only increased my feeling of loneliness and isolation.

By 1997, Nick had steered his business into less perilous waters. I was over the moon when he said we could go Heli-skiing again. We had both loved boarding school and now we could afford to send Samantha and Emma to my old school. I decided I no longer needed an au-pair as Tom and William were at primary school. I hoped Nick would have more time to be around for evenings and weekends, but gradually the reverse occurred.

As the new century unfolded, Nick began to arrive back late from a 'work trip' every Christmas Eve. I would hear his key turning in the lock upstairs, then his feet brushing back and forth on the doormat, the keys dropping on the shelf by the door, and then the heavy tread as he came down the stairs to our semi-basement kitchen. I would be wrapping the last of the presents at our large pitch-pine table. He would kiss me on the top of my head, fill me in on his last few days abroad, and then back upstairs to bed.

In 2001 we had the chance to buy a chalet in St Anton, Austria, that we had rented for years. Due to an obscure clause, at the moment of signing **(15)***, we relinquished our right to it. Nick was then faced with a fierce legal battle for two years in a bid to retain it. As a result, he said that he needed to be with his lawyers in Vienna almost every other weekend in preparation for the court hearings. I wasn't convinced. I asked him on several occasions during those two years whether he was having an affair. He told me I was "paranoid" and "delusional", that he was simply overworked and that, one day, when he had sold the business, we would have time to be together. Tied to four children, with no help, I felt I had no choice but to believe him.*

Nick and I had never even considered having a joint account. From the beginning of the marriage, Nick had set me up with a monthly 'housekeeping' account. This was comfortable, but if I wanted any extra money I had to ask him for it. Now, seventeen years on, I was suspicious enough to think of hiring a private detective, but the bill to investigate Nick, who could sometimes travel to three countries in a week, stopped me in my tracks.

I had thrown myself into doing up the villa in Portugal and now I threw myself into doing up the Austrian Chalet. When we first married, we dreamed of having a villa and a chalet. Now the dream had become a reality. I so desperately wanted to believe everything was alright.

It was Christmas, 2001. I had come out early to St Anton to put the finishing touches on the chalet, and was busy hanging curtains, mirrors and pictures, arranging the furniture and dressing the beds. I remember Nick helping me to wrap presents that Christmas Eve. Eventually he went to bed. I decided to call it a day when at 2am, a mouse peered out from under the armchair!

When Nick's friends and relatives arrived on Boxing day, they were astonished at the transformation. I wanted the chalet to feel romantic. It must have worked, because the next morning I knew instinctively that every couple had made love, with the exception of Nick and myself. I asked the wives and they all said, "How did you know?". I was miserable all day and that night told Nick what I'd found out. Not for the first time, I begged for sex, longing for that afterglow of intimacy we had once had and that I sensed in everyone else. With an irritated expression, he pushed me onto the bed, not even bothering to remove his clothes. The joyless act was over in minutes.

Just as suddenly, I am jolted back to a time when I am 21, working as a ski-club party leader in Italy. "Go to bed, take the day off, you have flu," my colleagues tell me. It is 2.30pm. The hotel is silent. I'm lying in a darkened room, so ill I feel paralysed. I hear a key turning in the lock. I can't even raise my head from the pillow. I have no energy to resist, I feel a weight press down on me, I feel my legs being pushed apart and pain as something is thrust up and I am crying silent tears. I have no strength in me to call out, to struggle, but as the bed shakes and I clench my eyes shut, I pray as I've never prayed before, "God, get me out of this."

Suddenly there is the unmistakable sound of a fire alarm. The thrusting stops. The hotel owner rolls off me. Relief and sadness penetrate the fever: relief that God came to my rescue (thank you! thank you! thank you!), and sadness that I'm no longer a virgin. Was I saving myself for this?

And then I'm back on this other bed, and again the thought is, "Was I saving myself for this?" The despair is overwhelming.

CONNECTION

"The bond of all companionship, whether in marriage or in friendship, is conversation."

— Oscar Wilde, *De Profundis*

Correspondence

The getting of mail is important to any prisoner, but for the foreigners in Bang Kwang it was a lifeline, often the only contact that they might have with the world outside. Many of our gripes were about the inconsistency of mail deliveries. Men would loiter around the administration section waiting for the post, me included.

I received letters regularly from my mother and through her, Denise got back in touch. When Quinlan was old enough, he began to write postscripts at the bottom of his mother's and later, grandmother's cards – half a dozen or so missives a year. The banter was often about the merits or otherwise of Manchester United (Quinlan) or Chelsea (Me). Once he was old enough I would send him cards and letters on a regular basis.

Andy in the library of Block Six, Bang Kwang 2000

Some of my friends also kept in touch. John, an actor from New South Wales wrote to me often, and actually broke his journey to London on one occasion to visit me. I'd known him for years, being an even older friend of my wife. His letters detailed his work as a performer, and sometimes he would send me a dozen or so books from his bookshelves. He was undoubtedly the greatest single contributor to my reading matter, and therefore to the building's library. He spent a small fortune on postage and new books over the years, and I shall be eternally grateful to him for his support. His exhortations to have courage and optimism were always heartfelt and I read them and was cheered. He was a rock for me throughout my stretch.

I got a letter from New Zealand, the sender being an American actor called Cam. One photo he enclosed, was of him talking to Anthony Hopkins, another of him looking most saturnine on set, but the one that struck me most, was a copy of an X-ray of his body. I have NEVER seen so much metal inside a human being, not one who was still active at least. His back was pinned and bracketed to an alarming degree.

Cam took time off work to go on a comprehensive road trip of New Zealand. He sent me postcards from all over the country, ending with one from the southern-most tip of South Island. The scenery was spectacular; volcanoes, mountains, forests and lakes, glaciers even. I managed to keep and look at them for ages as a form of escapism. I told him I was a little surprised that Auckland was so close to a damn great volcano. Cam wrote back saying that the whole area, indeed the whole country, was a veritable seismic time-bomb, part of the 'Ring of Fire'.

The nearest I myself have come to a natural catastrophe, I was feeling the outermost edges of a small earthquake in Snowdonia, a hundred and fifty miles away from the trembling hillside on which I was standing at the time.

Visitors

Foreign, or white western prisoners, generally have no one in the country to visit them. So when I am called out, knowing that the consulate is not due, I am intrigued.

I pass through the gatehouse, then the wrought-iron gates which separate the main accommodation blocks from the forward areas of the prison. I glance up at the big central tower with its radio antennae, searchlights and klaxons and admire again the way it leans to one side. I go through more gates, getting perfunctorily patted down each time.

The long visit area stretches about fifty yards. The first bit is for embassy visits, a bench on our side, a wonky shelf for our elbows and both bars and fine mesh chicken wire between us and the Foreign Office wallahs. Further on, in the main section, there is a four-foot-wide dead zone beyond the bars and mesh to another identical barrier. Beyond that sit the visitors.

I wander down searching for a face. A young farang is there, also seemingly searching, so I ask him who he's waiting for. To my surprise, he says my name, so I sit down opposite him and ask how it is he's here. He replies that he saw my name on a noticeboard in the guesthouse he was in, on the Kho San Road, a well-known backpacker hang-out which produced an abundance of visitors as I was subsequently to find out.[16]

He's a student on a gap year – I will meet many such – Alec by name, from somewhere in Hertfordshire. He seems a little overawed by the actuality of this place, but as the conversation starts to flow, he loosens up and becomes more animated.

I try to remember what it was like to be nineteen, I was a student too, of sorts, but my recollection is hazy, vague. The remembrance of the long hot summers of '76, seems not to contain much in the way of specifics, only impressions; the grass in Chiswick Park burned to a patchy brown by the relentless sun, the days spent in the cool of the common room or the pub up the road, waiting for a train at Turnham Green, the first sighting of punks in the corridors of the college. It all seems so long ago. I feel old.

He leaves, promising to get me coffee and cigarettes from the visitors shop, and he's off the next day on his long flight home. His purchases arrive the following day. In all my years, dealings with that visitors' shop were kosher, though there might be delays.

A 21-year-old called Alison visited me three times. From the Northeast of England, she'd set out with a friend on their post-university round-the-world trip. She was refused entry into Australia, having on her record a couple of grams of ganja. She was sitting out the three weeks in Bangkok, then flying direct to New Zealand to re-join her companion.

The strangest, the most disconcerting visit I ever had was from an American, about forty, who arrived with a boy of eleven or twelve, his son. His stated intent was to scare the living shit out of this already frightened looking lad, so that he wouldn't be tempted to stray from the straight and narrow. I suppose I could have refused to play along, but the man's determination was plain to see. Better the lad got it from me, rather than from some evil bugger who delights in messing with young minds.

A woman called Jane visits. Slim and boyish with a shortish haircut and wearing long trousers and a man's shirt, she asks the usual questions and then pronounces herself mystified.

"You are obviously intelligent," she says.

"Knowledge and intelligence only get you so far," I reply. What was missing was the third leg of the tripod, some measure of wisdom. She would later write from East London, to say that she had re-invented herself as John. I can't say I am surprised and wish her, sorry him, all the best.

One day my visitor is not a stranger but a friend from my past life, Sarah. I am eager for news of mutual friends but other than to speak of Sian, a bubbly and lovable Welsh woman, she has little to impart. It is the first inkling I have of the dispersal of my old circle of friends.

Stu and Tracey from Manchester come to see me, and we stay in touch. Over the years many of their family will visit, and keep in touch with regular letters, cards and photos. I'll always have a lot of time for the Malones of Manchester, even if they do support Manchesterbloodyunited.

One day Leicester Steve gets a visit from Gale, who would once have lived just a few miles away from him back in Blighty. No tourist she, but an ex-pat who has lived in Thailand for years. The visit energises her and she sets about informing, cajoling and generally browbeating as many British women in Bangkok as she can, to become prison visitors. As a direct result of her efforts, some of the ladies become not just regular visitors but friends. We look forward to their visits, perhaps even more than they themselves realise. They become a big part of our lives.

Allison is a tall, lithe, fifty-something with curly hair and a glint in her eye. When she comes in with a heavily strapped leg, I ask if she's had a fall, perhaps tripped on one of Bangkok's notoriously uneven pavements. No, she got it during kickboxing class! Sue S. with short grey hair and a ready grin, is always cheerful. Sue K, a bubbly, dark-haired woman I take to be in her thirties but later discover is over 45, shows up with her 18-year-old daughter. She always calls me Zee Zee, after ZZ Top, whose front men I suppose I resemble, with my beard, dark glasses and cap. Another of the ladies, Kathleen, moved to Singapore, but still drops into Bangkok every now and then.

Gale is undoubtedly the motor driving the group and makes the most trips up river to us lags, trying to visit all those who need the company and, acting as co-ordinator and conduit for such funds as might be sent their way. Her efforts, along with those of the other ladies, is invaluable. Their company by itself is enough, but they all go beyond the call of duty, offering compassion and selfless kindness which none of us will forget.

Pat, (a blonde mother of four beefy sons), is one who attached herself to the ladies group without having been in any of the ex-pat associations. She lives on the 32nd floor of an upscale development in Bangkok and has a car and driver at her disposal. She has an easy, infectious laugh, is really great fun to talk to and loves risqué humour, so the kind of gag that a prisoner tends to hear is meat and drink to her. She's also able to gauge any clothes size at a glance: when she gifts me new T-shirts and shorts and much later some clobber to go home in, it fits, no bother. She's lived away from Stoke-on-Trent for thirty years and seems in no rush to go back.

Bill, a Massachusetts man, came to visit me and proved to be a great and true friend. He had been in the US Air Force for about 22 years, finishing the equivalent of a masters. Many people, Cons or Screws, thought that Bill and I were related, brothers perhaps. A police description of either of us would have been nearly identical. His hair, thinning out like mine, had grown long and was kept back in a ponytail. Glasses and

Inside visit, Andy and Bill 2011

beard, again like mine, though he kept his face hair a good deal shorter and tidier than I did, sat atop a frame that had expanded considerably since serving in the military. In fact he took to the role of Santa Claus with gusto, making appearances at orphanages, schools and so on, buying himself the full outfit to make the best impression. At one home for some seriously disadvantaged children, he made quite the stir by arriving in a helicopter.

I became extremely attached to Bill. He would come almost every Tuesday morning on a small motor scooter. It was Bill who told me how he could speak, using voice and image, to a friend in Massachusetts twelve time zones away, using Skype, for FREE. I am fond of 'snail mail', but this venerable institution may be on its last legs.

When I described to one consul the relative freedom with which we associated with each other, the lack of regulation, no work for foreigners, he said, "it's almost like a prisoner-of-war camp."

I shot back, "we <u>are</u> prisoners of war, aren't we?"

He raised his eyebrows. I said, "the powers-that-be first declared prohibition of various drugs; then they declared war on drugs. Ergo we are prisoners-of-war."

He actually said "yes, I suppose you are right."

*

I began as a child by writing 'Thank You' letters to relatives and godparents. Once married, I wrote Christmas cards, with letters enclosed, to family and friends that I didn't see from one year to the next. In them I painted a picture of the model happy family. I started at A in my address book and by the time I was writing to poor Sonia Zanardi, I sounded like a zombie. As a result, I avoided writing to anyone else for the rest of the year.

I made an exception with Nick and the children. I wrote Christmas and birthday cards to Nick to express my undying love and to apologize for being crabby. I cherished the cards from him. I believed all the beautiful things he said. He always declared how much he loved me and our life with the children and that he looked forward to our 50th wedding anniversary together.

2004

BBC

June

I am called out, along with Jody, a twenty-something young Brit with dual Zimbabwean citizenship. In our mandatory pale blue visit shirts we're led into a building with air-conditioning and tinted windows, used for VIP visitors and high-powered conferences. Inside waits one of the assistant directors of the prison. His name is Banham and he addresses us in reasonably fluent English. Michael Connell, a 20-year-old inmate from Manchester, is also present.

Banham smiles at us and says, "The BBC want to make a documentary about Bang Kwang and they want British prisoners to be in it. We want them to show how hard it is and how long people must stay in Thai prison if they do drug business in Thailand." he explains. I lean forward and smile at him. I can do genial as well as he can.

"What do you want me to say and what do you want me not to say?" He smiles again. We understand each other.

"You tell how hard, you show how you must live. You speak about sentence. You do not speak bad about guards, about Bang Kwang, about Correction Department".

I nod. "Ok, I'll do it," I say. If I fulfil my agreement with him, he'll owe me a favour; not a big one perhaps, but it's something. The other two follow suit.

I am not going to rubbish the screws, I'll be here years yet (that would be lunacy), but I AM going to take the opportunity to have a damned good dig at various UK ministries. They are responsible for extending our gaol time way beyond that which they assured us we were to serve.

Two days later we're sitting in the same chairs, only now there are four Farang guys across from us. Three screws position themselves fairly close to us.

The guy, who I presume is the producer, begins by saying how tricky it has been to arrange for this to happen, that it took almost two years to organise and how excited he is to be the first to be able to film inside the fabled *Bangkok Hilton*. I cannot resist puncturing this inflated ego.

"You've missed the boat", I say. "Australian TV did a documentary in here a while back". He looks truly disconcerted. I tell him it was a pretty limited affair, a bit of interviewing of a couple of Aussie prisoners.

He brightens up a bit at this, saying that they will have more wide-ranging access, filming inside the various buildings, including, to my surprise, Death Row. I suggest a good potential shot, from the top of the central guard tower at 6.30am. He'd get all the cell block doors opening and convicts boiling out like bees from a disturbed hive. I am being a bit mischievous here. I've piqued his interest, even though I know there isn't a cat-in-hell's chance they'll let him up that tower.

He starts the usual run of curious tourist questions about our day; how we live, what we do to keep ourselves amused. Jody starts yakking on about TV, how we have satellite, sport and movies. He's starting to tell them about the blue movies that are available when I kick him under the table and shoot him a meaningful look.

Everything he's been jabbering on about is against regulations. He'll land everybody in the cack at this rate. He's as eager to please as a puppy and has the self-preservation instincts of a concussed kitten.

Come Monday, I find out that Jody has dropped out; good luck for us, hard cheese for the Beeb. I trudge through the last knockings of a heavy squall to get to the first session, in Building Nine, a small block with three packed dormitories on the upper floor of a building on concrete pillars. Cons who work in the grounds and the kitchens live in there. With no special wall or even wire fence around it, Building Nine sits near the nick's main drag and I've not been inside it before.

The crew set up inside a dormitory and I look around. Each prisoner seems to have their own blue plastic-covered sleeping mat, at least three inches of foam. There are at least ten big fans in the ceiling too, so that no spot is left with dead air, and there are barred and netted windows at both the front and the back of the room, with an actual view outwards, which the windows in all the main blocks don't give.

This is the Bang Kwang equivalent of five star digs and I am impressed. The crew don't even spare a glance, so I point all this out to them. The paint on the walls and the lino floor covering appear to be brand spanking new as well. I am starting to get that Potemkin Village feeling. The crew are bustling, setting up lights, looking for the best camera position. I am given a clip-on mike and small battery, sat in a chair facing a window, and we begin.

It is almost unbearably tedious. There are two strands to the questions; those about the prison and those about my personal experience before, during and after my arrest and conviction. The first I can answer pretty much by rote, as I'd had lots of practise with the succession of curious backpackers and tourists who had visited me.

The second is more difficult to address, as I have to admit to having acted, not just stupidly, but in direct opposition to one of my few strongly held beliefs, to wit, heroin is bad and I'll have nothing to do with it. Such an admission leaves me feeling distinctly uncomfortable and irritated with myself and I ask for a break. As I puff on my roll-up, I lean on my walking-stick trying to regain my composure. I resolve to cheer up and give them what they want, which is someone who can string together a complete sentence and hold their viewers' interest.

That afternoon there is a new twist. For some reason, the prison has decided against allowing them to walk around filming amongst the general population. They claim safety issues. This is patently ludicrous. They would be a hundred times safer in there than on the streets of Bangkok, or Balham for that matter.

But that's how it is, and now they ask me to basically do their job for them. A screw is to film me as I do a tour of our cellblock and its compound, with me doing my piece to camera. It's left up to me to decide where to stop and explain what is in front of us. I do it with some aplomb, I think, and the business is wrapped up with the crew asking me if they could get me anything. I ponder a while and ask them to try and get me a 3-band radio, including short-wave, so I can listen to the BBC World Service. Mine has recently given up the ghost.

The programme goes out a month later, in early July 2004. People write to me as a result, offering sympathy, encouragement, help with books and magazines. One chap suggests that I recite "Om" all day, reckoning that several million "oms" later I will be released as a truly enlightened being. Carol from South Birmingham starts to write after seeing the BBC documentary. She would later send me some photos of herself in her days as a stripper, speciality a couple of large pythons. A clipping from her local newspaper shows a picture of her by her fireplace. One of her pythons has slipped up the chimney and the fire brigade has been called to come and get it out. The most welcome letter comes from my old friend Jill, with whom I'd lost touch many years before. She will continue to write to me at least once a week until I am released.

2005

Samantha returned from her gap year, a cornucopia of earrings and dreadlocks, but full of adventures from around the globe. Among tales of swimming in crocodile-infested waters in South America and having her valuables pinched on her first night in Sydney, was her story of visiting a British prisoner in Bang Kwang prison, the notorious 'Bangkok Hilton'.

*

Leicester Steve and I are called out to a visit, meeting Tony, a Brit from Building Four en-route. Three British gap year girls have navigated through the increased restrictions on visitors to see us on their last day in Thailand. The luck of the draw puts me in front of Sam, a gorgeous 19-year-old with curly blonde ringlets and penetrating blue eyes.

She is truly interested in our situation and I hope I answer her questions to her satisfaction: by then I'd been doing broadly the same for some years with any number of banana visitors, but she seems far more energised and sympathetic than most and promises to write, having got the prison's correct postal address from me.

*

When Andy's first letter arrived in reply to Samantha's, she allowed me to read it. We both admired the dying art of letter writing at its most considered and fluent, a little formal, as if written in some by-gone age.

*

I wrote back to Samantha, imparting advice which I was in no way competent to give. I felt like an expatriate uncle, the black sheep with a heart of gold. It was a pleasant sensation to be writing in this mode.

I did not know that my letters were being shown to Vicky, Sam's mother; this was to have life-changing consequences.

*

Samantha's second letter from Andy is sadly lost but one particular scene stands out in my memory... He describes standing in the prison compound, a monsoon rainstorm drenching him. He puts his hand in his pocket and inside is a packet of cigarettes, now sodden, which he squeezes. Suddenly I am in his coat and my hand is squeezing the cigarettes and I can feel the rain running in rivulets down my face. I realize that I had wasted 47-years writing to people, giving them a chronological précis when a picture in words of a vivid moment would have conveyed so much more.

2006

18 April

I respond to a visit room call-out. Once there, I spot a beautiful young girl. I am sure I haven't seen her before but she looks somehow familiar. I introduce myself and she tells me she is Emma, Sam's sister, the younger by a year or so. She is on her gap year round-the-world trip, just as Samantha was.

She looks a little dishevelled, as well she might. The annual three-day water festival, or 'Song Kran', the custom of dousing all and sundry with water and flour, most definitely extends to attractive Farang girls. I am inclined to be most cheerful when faced with such company, and we become engrossed in conversation quite quickly. She's the artistic type, and while I've little to contribute to any such discussion, I am a damn good listener. She asks the usual questions about life inside and I answer as best I can, starting with what 'Song Kran' is like in Bang Kwang

The festival spans three consecutive public holidays, 13, 14 and 15 of April. It began as the ancient New Year celebration of Buddhist Southeast Asia. What it is now, is a weeklong carnival of chaos. There is food and drink aplenty and whereas in times past a bucket or cook pot full of water might be hurled over passers-by regardless of age or rank, pump-action plastic water guns are now in the arsenals of many. The most dangerous practice is to throw water over moving motorcyclists, and the scariest, dumbest thing I have ever heard of is a fire-fighting crew turning their hose on passing traffic, including a biker who was blown right off his machine, to roars of laughter from the watching crowd.

In our building, these festivities are conducted on a smaller scale. The larger Nigerians and the guards are off limits, unless they begin hostilities. Since the wash troughs are always to hand, the supply of water is pretty well inexhaustible and I learn to wear my oldest, tattiest, clothes for the duration.

A particular target are the lady boys; they are effectively participants in a three-day wet T-shirt competition. The one known as Nong, being possessed of an impressive surgically enhanced chest, is the most popular target of all. She – all lady boys are referred to as she – takes such pride in her D-cups that she doesn't in fact wear any support garment. After about the twentieth or thirtieth bucketful, she removes her top and spreads her arms proudly, causing a brief cessation in the deluge, but after this pause for admiring glances, gets about half a dozen buckets full at once, causing her to run off squealing.

I warn Emma of the dangers of Thai traffic – vehicular rather than narcotic – and she is about to reply when the damned phone cuts off without warning, signalling an abrupt end to the visit. I try to mouth the words, "Say hi to Sam" but I don't know if she gets it, and she waves as she leaves. I am only seven years and change into a fifty-year stretch and I have no expectations of ever seeing her again.

Emma to Andy

May 2006

Andy,

Sorry for writing on scraps of paper. I am disorganised and I don't like neat, formal letter crap anyway. So I was glad to see small water droplets on your letter.

I just got back from Berlin, where I went to visit a friend, see lots of art galleries and actually do some drawing or painting (which I did not get round to doing, as usual!) [...] I am studying (if you can do that) at City and Guilds, an art college in London. I always thought at eighteen, I'd move out of home, but I just don't think that's going to happen. I am staying put, for now anyway.

Well, I am on my way to the doctor's 'cause I got infected mosquito bites and these huge blisters on my feet. It's freezing here but I have to go around in Burmese flipflops (which are actually the best and most comfortable) with drops of blood coming from my ankles. Seems pathetic I know; I'm sure I'm being a hypochondriac, but with the wet weather in Asia, nothing heals and then gets infected. Does that happen to you?

I can't believe that you say it must have been a disappointment to meet you. I could not have been happier. I particularly liked your rose-tinted old skool glasses. But I did get pissed off that you were so far away and that I had to look through a small space to see not even your WHOLE face, which by the way has much character. You should not hide it under your hat!!! (and glasses).

So after I got cut off from you, which was particularly sad, I took a boat down the river to the hotel, to get ready to go to Sri Lanka. The boat trip showed me all of Bangkok and let me think a lot about you and your situation. I felt that it was/is very unfair for one mistake to give someone so much pain. I have done many things already in my small life that probably should put me away for a lot longer than you!! I guess I believe in chance. It's what you make of it all, wherever you are and whatever you have. I don't know much because I'm only young and dumb, but that's what I felt. You could do more with your life, which I can see you have, in your time there more than some of the assholes out here. It's just chance that they happen to be let loose or have power and you do not.

I guess I'll tell you what I did next. I went to Sri Lanka to meet up with this charity called Swimlanka. They teach children who have been affected by the tsunami not to be scared of water and get them to swim. Most people on the island cannot swim and they are surrounded by water. It's madness! My first group that I attempted to teach, or swam with, were all orphans from the Tsunami. This (Dutch?) charity set up a portable shallow pool and place it by/on the beach and they go from village to village doing this. So I got involved for a couple of weeks.

I hope you don't think, after my charity account, that that's what you were. I felt as if I was going to see a friend when I came to see you. Sam had talked about you a lot. She hadn't got a letter from you when I spoke to her and was very jealous that I had got one and she had not. Sorry about my shit pronunciations and punctuations of everything. Anyway it was the greatest thing to see you. I felt that I was appreciated a great deal and it was pretty funny when the other guys who came to see you passed back the phone pretty quickly. I felt honoured.

I just drove with my mum to see some antique stuff and she was freaking out 'cause there are cameras for speeding everywhere. On one camera they have already made eight million pounds. So I have just been thinking that for one of my art projects I am going to do something about being watched all the time and under surveillance. They are trying to introduce these ID cards in England as they have in many places, where your info is stored on them. They (being I don't know who) can see what you buy, when etc. in a second. You probably know way more about this than me. I guess the prison feeling is everywhere in small ways.

Well, I hope you have started the books I gave you, 'cause *War and Peace* is one SERIOUS book which I really want to read and am leading myself up to it. *One Hundred Years of Solitude* is also one I read; I thought the imagination and description fascinating. The kids stories I just thought would be a laugh.

I have made so many lists recently and if I could make one for you I would be overjoyed. Please tell me anything I can send or do for you or anyone and I will try my best.

Lots and lots of best wishes

to you,

Emma

xxx

PS. My mum would love a letter if you want to write to her.

Had I not responded to the above request, I doubt very much that I would be in the process of writing a book, and what I would be doing, and where, is essentially un-guessable.

Lady-Boys

Dutch Hans, the whoremonger, pulled a sly one, getting the lady-boy he was currently shagging, transferred to our cell. The extreme overcrowding at the time meant that once done, not even bribery could get it undone.

Manop, or Nop, was only vaguely effeminate, unless you saw her dressed in full tranny regalia, tottering along on the highest heels she could manage. Then there was a transformation. All of the lady-boys had at least one set of such clothes and would wear them only very occasionally. Most often, this would be on those public holidays, during which the resident band gave a concert, of ear-piercingly loud renditions of Western and Thai pop music. These were not just street outfits, they were streetwalkers' clobber. But in the normal prison attire of T-shirt and shorts, Nop, and indeed most of the lady-boys in Bang Kwang, tended to blend into the crowd, being unaltered by surgery. Unlike the one known as Nong.

Nong came into the penal system almost immediately after the surgeons had given her a quite impressive pair of boobs. I was talking to Jules, a Caledonian from Building Three, when I saw him do a classic double take.

"Wow, I can see a guy with breasts!"

"Not something you see every day then?"

"Not exactly, no," says he, obviously impressed.

Nong was one of half a dozen lady-boys who had come into our block, along with a hundred or so prisoners from Building Five, emptied of inmates so that a major re-fit could be undertaken. One, thin as a rake, bore an uncanny resemblance to Olive Oyl of Popeye fame. Another, more unfortunately, strongly resembled Bluto from the same cartoon. Bluto had a sort of nervous tic where she was constantly adjusting the straps of the bra that she wore. It always amused me that those with little or nothing to fill the garment, insisted on wearing one, while someone like Nong preferred to let her expensively acquired air bags jiggle and bounce around unrestrained. Just showing off, most likely.

Dat was another one of the new intake. Tall for a Thai, about 5' 10", with a moon face and full lips, she was not surgically altered, yet somehow contrived to be more feminine than any of the other 'katoeys', as they are known in Thai. A cheerful happy-go-lucky sort, she was an exception to the general run of lady-boys, who seemed to affect a moody, sullen disposition, becoming strident fishwives when disagreements broke out. For all the wild screaming and gesticulating, I never saw a scene descend into actual violence, at least not between the lady-boys.

I had managed to move in the first year into the 'Farang's' cell, no. 25, facing the top of the stairs. The cell was smaller than standard and when I got there contained nine men and three TVs mounted on units against the far wall. I remained in that cell for nearly 14 years. We were in a privileged position. I had no compunction in taking advantage of it

Nop stayed in our cell for quite a while. I was a little uncomfortable at first as Hans had contrived to place Nop between me and him. But nothing untoward occurred that I was aware of, and Nop spent most of his, sorry her, waking hours, playing with a hand-held electronic games machine. Nop's English vocabulary was limited to a few chosen words and as there was usually English TV on in our cell, the Game-Boy was the only diversion available.

There was an unwritten rule that silence be maintained from 9pm. If a person wanted to continue watching the TV they could do so using headphones. One night I was awakened by a heated, yet whispered, argument between Nop and Hans. Nop was wearing his/her cool weather-gear, long sleeves, track-suit bottoms, socks, scarf and bobble hat and was still feeling the cold. She wanted to switch off the fan above him – there were three hanging from the 11-foot ceiling – but when she had done so Hans got up and turned it on again. As soon as he'd sat down, Nop got up and switched it off.

Two or three more repetitions of this led to an escalation. As Hans tried to physically stop Nop, voices were raised. By this time everyone in the cell was awake and watching. There was a pause where neither spoke, but looked daggers from a distance of less than two feet. Suddenly Nop let rip with a right hook. Totally surprised, Hans went down like a marionette with all its strings cut. He may have been four inches taller than the lady-boy, but was relying perhaps too much on the 'lady' part of this appellation. In fact Nop had done quite a bit of training at 'Muay Thai', or Thai kick boxing; a single blow was enough.

Hans was a quivering mess, with bloodied mouth and nose, and in no state to continue the dispute. It was over, and so was Nop's stay in our cell. When I heard the next day that Nop would be moving to a Thai cell, I told her/him "But you won. He should move!" Nop grinned but said that, on the whole, it would be best if she were the one to go: Apart from anything else, what Thai cell would have Hans move into it! I hadn't thought of that.

So Nop moved on and Hans found that no other lady-boy in the building would henceforth even consider ministering to his 'needs'. Even those who indulged in casual prostitution would have no part of him, though he tried to talk them round. The Dutch government having recently signed a prisoner transfer treaty, Hans duly went back to Amsterdam for a spell in a Dutch gaol. Word filtered back to us that he'd been diagnosed HIV positive. Speculation was rife that he had contracted the virus before coming to Thailand rather than in the prison system. It was certainly possible; he'd come there specifically to acquire a supply of ya-ba, or Thai speed, with which to keep happy the stable of Thai hookers that were working in his brother's brothel back in Holland, and given his whore-mongering proclivities, may well have picked it up there. I doubt we'll ever know.

25 April 2006

Up until the time of Emma's visit, the tone in my letters to all and sundry was upbeat. I had come to terms with my situation, and knew that worrying would not alter it. This changed radically after Emma came to see me.

The mail, that had been held up because of the 'Song Kran' Festival, was now trickling through. I got a large card-sized envelope with my mother's handwriting on it and put it aside to read later.

When I opened it, after my afternoon shower, I found an Easter card, homemade by my mother on her computer and tucked inside, a letter in Polish. Translated, the opening sentence read, "It is with a sad and heavy heart that I have to tell you..."; my eyes brimmed with tears as I read that Denise, my former partner and mother to our son, at only 42 years old, had died. She had been admitted to hospital three weeks before with pneumonia and caught a superbug there.

I tried to read on, suppressing the whimper that was threatening to become a full-blown fit of weeping and wailing. The funeral had been a week before, the day that young Emma Oak had been to see me. I wept as the enormity of her death struck at my very core.

I would never see her again, never hear her voice, her laughter. Never have the chance to tell her that I'd never stopped loving her. Never.

And our son, now age 10. What of him? Bad enough that he had no memory of me, had no father in his life. Cards and such from a prison the other side of the world hardly counted, now he had lost his mother forever. I just hoped that Denise's mother, Maureen, would keep him under her sole protection. The only alternative would be social services and that would be too much to bear.

I saw nothing of my surroundings that day, or for several days after. My grief was total; it was consuming me because it was completely internalised. There was nothing I could do, and no one to whom I could speak. Friends and family were all six thousand miles and at least a couple of weeks by post away. I was unable to do anything at all.

After a few days, I penned a letter to Denise's mother, my mother also, and various others back in England. I was doing it without thinking, stream of consciousness stuff, at least I assume so. I was not re-reading what I'd written, just penning it, putting it in the envelope and sending it. It may have taken the extreme edges of the pain away. I cannot tell. I only know that I was knocked flat, and from being a prisoner who could both smile, and raise a smile, I became a far more taciturn and morose individual. I was plunged into the deepest pit of despair. Depression hardly seems to be an adequate word to describe how I lived, the next weeks, months, even years.

Even writing these words brings down on me such a wave of sadness, of loss and of grief, that I can scarcely function. I am back to the day that I opened that letter, the whole thing sharp in my mind's eye, a fist once more clenching around my heart. I am bereft still, more than eight years later.

Andy to Vicky, 1st Letter

30 May 2006

Dear Mrs Oak

I am sorry to sound so formal, but though Sam did once write with your first name, I cannot lay my hands on that letter. I got one from Emma yesterday in which she said you would be happy to hear from me directly, so here is my response. She also said that Sam was 'jealous' that she, that is Emma, had received a letter and Sam hadn't. My reasons for tardiness make for depressing reading and I've no wish to bring them down on my account. I shall tell you however and let you decide.

A week after Emma's visit, I got a letter from my mother, held up in the backlog built up over Thai New Year. It was the most dreadful, heart-breaking thing I've ever had to read. My Denise, ex-partner and love of my life [...] had died three weeks before the letter arrived, on 4 April. Our son, Quinlan was five weeks from his tenth birthday. As far as I can tell, she'd been in hospital, treated for a lung infection, possibly pneumonia, for a fortnight. Her mother and our son had been to visit her the previous day. She was weak but smiling and making plans for when she returned home. But I am told she picked up one of those hospital superbugs and died the next day, suddenly, without warning. When I read the news, all of five weeks ago now, I was reduced to a mess immediately, unable to do anything at all, much less write a coherent letter to anyone.

I felt totally helpless and frustrated by this tragic turn of events, stuck in a S.E. Asian jail thousands of miles away, and still do. I dare say I would have felt just the same had I been in England, but that is no consolation. Whereas beforehand, I was pretty well resigned to servitude, now that my son has neither parent to turn to, my absolute priority is to get myself free of this system.

I have submitted a plea for royal clemency[17], which is my only realistic hope of release anytime soon. The consulate are now aware of what has happened and make soothing noises... but being very vague and making no kind of promises. They are pressuring me into transferring back to a UK jail but at this early stage in my sentence, there is no advantage to me in such a move, the reverse if anything. Despite the conditions, being a foreigner in the relatively relaxed atmosphere of a Thai prison (particularly this one) is far and away preferable to going back to the British penal system and effectively starting from scratch. The British system does not take into account time served here in Thailand. It's a mystery as to how many years I would have to serve back in the UK.

Oh dear, this has been a morbid and utterly depressing letter thus far, hasn't it? But I had to get it out and I hope you will reply, so that my next letter can demonstrate that I am not all doom and gloom. In fact I am normally considered unusually up-beat for one in my position.

I must compliment you on raising such a splendid pair of daughters. They have both impressed me no end, and I really appreciate their making the effort to visit me, in Sam's case quite spontaneously [...] I am touched that they think me worthy of their continued interest and take the time to write to me as well. I understand from both Sam and Emma that you yourself liked my letters, which does my bruised ego no harm either. I am aware that I have a reasonable command of the language, not bad when one considers that it is my second language, one I didn't start to learn until I was at least three years old, having been raised as the eldest of four boys, in a Polish household. I must confess though, that despite an 'O' level in Polish, my vocabulary was always rather limited and Polish can only be considered my first language chronologically. I have not been back to the old country for twenty-five years, but when last there, I did slip back into the rhythms and cadences of the tongue so completely, that I was soon dreaming in Polish [...] The French [...] I am better at reading than speaking. I am told that my accent is passable, though I do occasionally betray flashes of Walloon influences picked up in the Ardennes and in Brussels. Of the Swiss-German I picked up on several childhood trips to the Alps, not a trace remains however. My command of the German is on a par with Basil Fawlty's, if that. My mother is the linguist, Polish, German, Italian, English and Spanish in that order in which she acquired them.

I learned an odd thing about the differences between Thai (and other tonal languages) and those of the rest of the world. In an experiment, an Englishman and a Thai had electrodes fixed to their heads, and then had random sounds made by a human voice played to them. The Brit had half his brain 'light up' as the side of this brain associated with language, meaning and reason went into gear, trying to make sense of the nonsense being played to him. The Thai, on the other hand; had both sides of his brain light up, including the side which we normally associate with music, while his brain searched for meaning, not just in the content of the noise, but in the varying tone and pitch in which it was delivered. So it would appear that occidental brains are hard-wired very early to do this, while for Europeans it is much more difficult. Feeling better for knowing this, I have since continued in blissful ignorance; the babble of voices here is never ending, how much more irritating would it be if I could understand the conversations of all those people by whom I am constantly surrounded? The talk one hears in English in here is rarely edifying, usually scatological or just banal. As it is, the greater hubbub of the locals nattering away just washes over me like so much white noise.

It is a fact that by far the greater part of letters received by prisoners are written by women, and I would be very happy indeed to continue to receive them from the ladies of the Oak household. I will try to write to the girls as soon as I can. I leave it to you as to whether or not to tell them of my personal tragedy. It is probably best if you did so, as I might be a little pushed for an explanation of my lateness, my preoccupation, and a new imperative to freedom – one which I thought to have suppressed long since as a defence mechanism.

Yours from the gulag

Andy

I will now always associate Emma's visit with Denise's death; she actually came on the day of the funeral, two weeks after she died and one week before I got the awful news in a letter from my mother.

I began to invest a large part of my mental energy in the possibility of getting myself free because of the new position my son found himself in, without either parent.

I had submitted a plea for Royal Clemency the previous year and now asked the consulate to write an extra letter confirming my new family circumstances. The foreign office response was predictable. They saw no reason to support my application.

I have recently heard it said that it is not possible to experience anger and depression at the same time. Whether or not this is true, I can certainly attest that one can flit from one to the other, in my case due directly to grief. Throughout the rest of 2006, in a veritable flurry of letters between Vicky and myself, my tone veered between the rage and frustration I was actually feeling, and the attempts I made to distract her and myself, by imparting some measure of personal and family information. There is an almost complete absence of conscious humour in these letters, which speaks volumes.

*

I was pleased when my first letter from Andy arrived, but surprised and saddened by his news of Denise's death. I will never know why he opened himself up to me when he didn't even know me. I wondered how I should respond given my own beliefs in an afterlife. I had no idea how significant this man would become. As Nick and I communicated less and less, I would find myself opening up more and more to this penfriend on the other side of the globe.

Vicky to Andy, 1st Letter

June 2006

Dear Andy

What a surprise and a privilege to have a letter from you. The girls have always let me read your letters or given me your news, so the one thing it didn't feel was strange. I am just so sorry about the news of Denise and I can understand your frustration. We are all wondering how we can help. I don't know any foreign minister but I know an MEP, a retired British ambassador and a prison officer (actually one of the nicest men you could ever meet). I am going to pick their brains...

Emma was wondering if you'd like her to visit Quinlan. Would you let her know?

You've been in my thoughts a lot and particularly since I received your letter. Have the girls warned you that I am a practising Catholic? I actually don't think you've lost Denise at all. You just don't have her physical presence. She knows exactly how you feel about her, realises how good a person you are and I would say she is the one person you can talk to whenever you wish [...]. I have a friend whose daughter committed suicide. A spiritualist told her remaining daughter that she loves to sit in their garden at the far end, looking back at the house. I have another friend who keeps hearing the TV on in her house when she goes to bed, when she's already checked that everything is off. Apparently, it's her husband's best friend who died in a car crash when he was twenty-three, and who likes being a part of their household.

Quinlan must feel devastated [...] No doubt you write to him a lot. Perhaps you should tell him how you feel about Denise and tell him some stories of how you got together, the good times. I was thinking that maybe you should keep a diary by your bedside[18] *of your thoughts and feelings, as if you were writing to him and then on your release, give it to him as a present (is that allowed?) You are such a brilliant writer. You could make him feel how you feel. For example, your description of the rain pouring down in the compound and the cigarettes in your pocket feeling sodden is as good as any professional writer. You caught the moment; please don't underestimate your ability. You have a gift...*

7 June

This letter has been lying crumpled in my bag. My youngest son is doing an entrance exam for a school called Worth, so I am sitting in the car park till he comes out in two hours' time. He didn't quite make the grade for his brother's school, so we're scrabbling round for places, before these boarding schools close for the summer. He feels a failure because the other three have always achieved. Is Quinlan as bright and literate as you are? Does he have your facility for languages? As a family we are pretty hopeless, although Samantha and Tom aren't bad at Spanish and Nick has to speak French in his business. I totally understand you not learning Thai. One of my favourite things about going abroad is being in a language bubble. For example in church I don't/can't listen to the Portuguese priest but can use the time for private thought and prayer.

So you are Polish and write in your second language, like Joseph Conrad, one of our greatest writers. He had the choice of living in France, Russia or England and lucky for English literature, chose Britain. I'll send you some of his work if you want. I once saw a first edition of 'Heart of Darkness' with his words in ink on the flyleaf. It gave me goose bumps. My brother-in-law is Polish, Charlie Skarbek. Our Polish builder, Jacek, tells me that his ancestors were in all the history books.....

At the moment everyone is caught up in World Cup fever. We've all become experts. I was arguing the merits of Ashley Cole, my favourite English player, to someone at a golf club. Only afterwards, my husband told me that this particular old man had captained England seven times... and I was disagreeing with him!

You are now in my prayers with two other very special people. We have a 24-year-old lad who has cystic fibrosis living with us. Simon was only intending to stay four weeks and has now been here for nine months! [...] He is always positive and never wastes one minute, as they've given him till 30 years old to live. He's a diabetic and has to inject himself with antibiotics for one and a half hours each day. His veins on both arms have now all blown, so they've put in an artificial tube running from his shoulder, via his heart, to his rib cage and he now injects into a valve lying just under his skin. He has the mucus pummelled out of him every weekend at hospital. He is managing to hold down a job in sports PR, which he loves, and has already been promoted. I think he likes living with us, because it offers the bustling family life he doesn't have as an only child.

My other VIP is Lauren. She was the children's swimming teacher, a larger than life woman, with the loudest wolf whistle and personality to match. (After twelve years of medical mishaps, she is now half-paralysed) and her immune system is shot to bits, so she has always got secondary complications. I have never heard her complain. [...] She has a devoted husband and daughter, Frank and Yolande, and I am sure, but for their love, she would have given up the ghost long ago.

I feel privileged to know her, to know Si, and now to start to know you. I can only imagine how you've managed to get through the last seven years. All three of you share one thing in spades - patience – although I can sense that your changed circumstances have thrown this at the moment.

Keep praying, keep writing, and keep giving my daughters advice and one day I am sure we'll meet. Work on your health, for your son's sake,

I will write to you when I have more news,

Love Vicky (Oak)

3 days later *– William got into Worth School – what a relief!*

The letter arrived at a critical moment in my youngest son William's life. He didn't get into Wellington, his brother's school, and was devastated. Tom my eldest, is bright, gregarious and lazy, the perfect candidate for Milbourne Lodge, the prep school both the boys attended. Tom thrived in this eccentric establishment, with some sublime staff such as the unparalleled history teacher, Mr Walton. I never met a boy who wasn't passionate about Mr Walton's lessons. Mild mannered, he kept discipline by promising that if the class behaved, he would tell stories about Douglas Bader, Colditz or the White Company at the end. In their final year, he related ghost stories from the war that had allegedly happened and were terrifying. I once stood in a ploughed field on a country walk, as Tom excitedly pointed out that the terrain matched that of the battle of Hastings. He then proceeded to bring the battle to life, in the spirited manner of his teacher.

Sadly along with the sublime came the ridiculous or more accurately, the appalling. Mr Crawford, a sergeant-major of a man, in shorts all year round and who got 'results' in maths, was known for throwing desks out of the window, or objects at the boys to make his point. In every class he picked on someone. William was dreamy, artistic and never ever going to be a mathematician. Mr Crawford made William's life hell. On Prize Day, William's art teacher apologised that he hadn't been prepared for an art scholarship. Instead, in the lunch break he was doing maths catch-up with Crawford and not art with her. Why had nobody informed me? I found out later that William had been put outside on the stairs during most of the maths lessons. This man delighted in humiliation. I myself heard him shouting at a boy that he was the runt of his family. I witnessed him sending a boy off the games pitch for being too fat. When the boys queued for their Common Entrance exam, Crawford wished everyone luck and then added, "though why you Oak are taking it, is beyond me." How William managed to bite back the tears and then sit for a two-hour paper is a miracle. Ridiculed by this teacher daily in front of his peers, William's confidence nose-dived in those years. What a contrast to the 7-year-old who hardly ever watched TV because he was too busy painting, drawing, constructing weird installations or concocting mind-bogglingly disgusting recipes. Years later, a mother rang me and said I thought William would love to hear that another victim of this man had by chance bumped into him, punched him in the face and then stood over him and said, "I've waited ten years to do that." William's face lit up.

I am sitting in Worth school carpark re-reading and replying to Andy's letter as William does yet another two-hour entrance exam paper. Nick, William and I have been visiting schools in a frantic attempt against the clock to find him something before term ends.

He is depressed and moody and will only reply in monosyllables to the headmasters we meet.

Years before, I attended a governor's dinner at Woldingham, my old school and that of my girls. I was seated next to Father Christopher, Abbot and headmaster of Worth. He was brilliantly witty and we received a lot of black looks for breaking into peals of laughter. His parting words to me were 'think about Worth for your sons'.

Now, recalling this, I phone the school and the secretary listens patiently to William's life story. She's not offended that her school is a last-minute choice; if he can do the school exam, be assessed by a psychoanalyst and meet the present headmaster in the next few days, he will have a place. This all sounds straightforward, except that William had just done common entrance and never wants to see another exam paper in his life. He thinks visiting a child psychologist makes him a freak and I am worrying about his meeting with the headmaster.

We drive through the huge wrought-iron gates and are faced with a crenelated, mullioned and many chimneyed red brick building, gothic in feel, with fields stretching away to the right. William sits up and looks around. He reminds me of a stray dog who senses that he has finally found a home.

We meet the Australian headmaster in his study. The setting is forbidding; three large leather sofas positioned on three sides, Nick and I in one, Mr Armstrong opposite and William small and alone in between. I am feeling his anxiety, but in the next hour and a half, I watch a masterclass by this head teacher. He tells William that he must be devastated not getting into his brother's school, that he must feel a failure. He leads William by small gentle steps, as if he is dealing with post-traumatic stress disorder, until William starts to speak, his feelings pouring out in spite of himself. He asks William why he would want to come to Worth. 'I could only go to a school that was beautiful' is the reply. He asks William to describe his best friend. William doesn't describe how he looks or acts but how he feels. He says he is 'anxious.' As Lucas, on the surface, is an extrovert, I realize this is very observant.

Mr Armstrong must have thought so too because, shortly afterwards, he gets up, shakes William's hand and tells him that on the strength of that interview, he would be delighted to offer him a place.

I would love to relay all this to Andy but I have only just started writing to him and fear that the 'wealth and privilege' of this will shout at him louder than the pain of a 13-year-old boy. I would love to write to him about the monks and the chapel, that the school exudes peace like no other; that the boys, when homesick at night, let themselves into the imposing 1960's crypt to sit quietly; that the sign outside the school gates, 'STOP/LOOK' once encouraged a man driving past to take it literally and eventually join the order of monks. What do I write about to someone whose world is light years away from mine?

My Early Years

I was born, John Anderson, on 27 August 1957, somewhere in West London, to a nineteen-year-old Norwegian au pair. She took the decision, after much heart-searching, to put me up for adoption. Indeed she had made this choice before I was born, but after the birth she wavered, until finally, to the relief of my adoptive mother, she decided that she should give me up. I was not to know all of this for a long, long time.

My adoptive parents had not had any children of their own and my adoptive mother Danuta, as I will always think of her, was already 33-years old when she took me into her embrace. My adoptive father was already 41. To retain a link with my birth name, they christened me Andrew with their surname Hawke.

left to right, Edmund, Andy and
Danuta, Wembley 1959

As is often the case, the appearance of an infant in the house seemed to kick-start the reproductive system. In fairly short order I acquired three younger brothers, Martin ('59) Peter ('61) and Nicholas ('62). My mother could not cope alone with the four of us and the addition of an au pair or nanny to the household probably diluted rather than reinforced parental authority.

Most of my father's generation of Polish émigrés considered themselves exiles, refugees from communist oppression, and were mortally afraid of returning. My father, Edmund, wasn't having any of this nonsense. As soon as he had the protection of UK citizenship, he began to make trips back to the country where his mother still lived.

Left to right, Peter, Niki, Martin, Cousin Marek and Andy in Poland 1968

My very earliest memory was being on holiday in Italy[19], and thinking I was drowning when left to sink or swim by my dad (I sank). All of our other summer holidays seemed to be in Poland. We drove there, first in a VW Beetle and later in partnership with a Morris Oxford. The time we spent at the checkpoints in Germany is oddly vivid – first the west/east German border, down the only designated road to West Berlin, then into East Berlin, finally across the border into Poland.

Our winter holidays were spent in the Alps, first a couple of seasons in Austria, then in Switzerland. We spent four winters at the same chalet in Flims, near Chur, and it was here that I was first struck by a physical problem that would plague me for the rest of my life.

I had done the usual winter sports activity, tobogganing wildly down wooded slopes. I remember winning a kid's skiing race and skating in the open air. But it was on the curling rink next to it that my life, and my world, changed.

I was standing on the ice, watching adults playing this odd game, laughing as a sweeper (moving his legs and feet rapidly) frantically brushed the ice ahead of the sliding stone released by his playing partner. I can't remember how or why, but I fell over, hard, on my left hip. I screamed and screamed and screamed.

A vague reconstruction of what happened next read: taken back to London by my dad, while my mum stayed behind with the other three boys, examined by an orthopaedic specialist and diagnosed as having Perthe's disease. As far as I was concerned, Perthe could have it back and welcome to it.

I don't know what treatment is given to sufferers these days, but what they did with me, was fit me with a set of calipers, similar to those fitted for polio sufferers. The left leg was immobilized by two lengths of steel. A padded strap prevented my knee from bending. The right boot was raised to equalize my gait.

I knew no better and dragged myself around as best I could, but the world of team games, of climbing trees, of running was gone for good. Oh, I tried to run and keep up, and I could manage a surprising turn of speed, but the handicap was too great. As for trying to sneak up on someone, forget it. The clank of metal and creak of stiff leather gave me away every time. Stairs and sitting were a real pain, what with the left leg being immobilized in the straight position. I spent a lot of time on the sidelines.

The only contribution I could make was with words. Already inclined to reading, I began to immerse myself in books. A bookcase in the hallway contained a 24-volume 1955 edition *Encyclopaedia Britannica*, and I would sit on the floor by it, pulling out whichever volume took my fancy and opening the pages at random, soaking up whatever I came across. I couldn't comprehend the mathematical and technical stuff but historical and biographical items kept me occupied. I became something of a smart alec. I still am, and use mimicry and jokes to deflect unkind words and to win over my peers.

Sometime in early 1966, I went into the Royal Orthopaedic hospital at Stanmore for major surgery on my left femur. My mother came to visit me every day, my father more occasionally. He had recently had a heart attack, his second in fact, and this would cause another change in our circumstances. After what seemed like months but was probably weeks, I left Stanmore to join the family migration to Ireland. I am sure that part of the reason we moved across the Irish Sea was the overwhelming burden of taxation on so called 'un-earned income' imposed by Harold Wilson's labour government. Since my dad had been forced to retire at the age of only 48, due to ill health, this was the only income he had.

We moved to Dundalk, just short of the border with Northern Ireland into a big Victorian terrace house on the main square, opposite a sizeable church. Each of the rooms still had a working system of signal bells, which would ring in the basement kitchen. We would ring them constantly, until we drove the big people to distraction. My dad disconnected them eventually.

My introduction to the Irish education system came via the Christian Brothers, which are these days mired in a paedophile scandal. Back then we knew naught of this; we were far more concerned with the continuous use of corporal punishment, meted out with a strap. Somewhere was a factory dedicated to manufacturing these instruments of pain and misery and there wasn't a boy in the school who wouldn't have cheerfully torched the place.

A few months later we moved into a large, brand new bungalow on the outskirts of town. The house had fields on two sides, a new-laid expanse of lawn, which I discovered was going to be up to me to mow, a two-car garage and a rocky inlet of the Irish sea five minutes away by bicycle.

I had to go back in for more surgery, this time to remove the metal inserted during the previous procedure. Recovery was far faster than last time and I was now in possession of two large thick long scars down the outside of my left thigh.

I was by now thoroughly unused to sport and had recently been fitted with glasses to correct my vision. I remember being led out to the playing fields to join in a game of Gaelic football. I wasn't about to wear glasses on the field but hadn't realized the absurd length of a Gaelic football pitch. I just couldn't make out the damn goal. Following my abject display, I was quietly dropped from the team and managed to keep out of most games thereafter, in every school that I attended.

Life in the Republic did not suit my mother; the separation from all her mostly Polish friends back in London left her miserable. There seemed to be nothing around to engage her attention. She eventually had a breakdown and went into a clinic for weeks or maybe months, I was too young to know. Dad cut his losses and decided to move back to England, though not to London. At Easter, my brother Martin and I were dispatched to a huge mansion somewhere in Virginia Water, run by nuns of some kind. There were about a score of kids in their care, parked there for the school holidays while their parents were otherwise engaged. At the end of this sojourn, Martin and I were taken off to a boarding school.

Divine Mercy College, known as Fawley Court, just outside Henley-on-Thames, was a 17th century stately home. The school had been set up to cater for the sons of the Polish diaspora. The money to purchase the property had been raised by the Marian Fathers from that community and about half the boys were from families living in England, mainly London. The rest were from all parts of the globe, a lot from Germany but also from places like Trinidad, Zambia, Italy, and most exotic of all, Los Angeles. The total school population was about a hundred and twenty at full capacity.[20]

I was still very young, not yet ten years old, Martin a couple of years younger still. He had a much harder time of it than I did and was quietly withdrawn from the school after my dad bought a fair-sized house in Wargrave, a village on the Berkshire side of the Thames a few miles away. This was where I went home that summer, but frankly I couldn't wait to go back to school. The seemingly constant moving from place to place had left me with no friends other than those I now had.

In retrospect, being at boarding school made it easier to adjust to life in prison three decades later. Out of bounds was designated by a dab of blue and white paint, the school colours, rather than a high wall with razor wire. The regimentation of regular meal times, classes, prep, (organized homework periods) and daily mass was, if anything, more all-consuming than that which I experienced later in gaol. The insistence on submission to the authority of teachers and priest, sometimes combined in the same person, was definitely more prevalent at school than in the prison system.

The school was not particularly well run and the rector, Father Andrew, asked my dad to come out of retirement to become its financial director, which he did. The food immediately improved and the fees were raised to the princely sum of £130 per term, to at least cover the running costs. The school was host to a great annual Polish cultural bash every Whitsunday, and that held in 1969 set a record that was never broken. 30,000 Poles from all over Great Britain and beyond, descended on Fawley Court, a great gathering of the clans. The sports field below the main house had a huge marquee on it, in which beer and 'bigos' were served.[21]

One way or another, my dad put the school back into the black. During his tenure he had acquired the nickname 'Fritz'. This moniker rapidly transferred itself to me.

At the end of '69, something must have happened at school that changed my parents' attitude to the place. The upshot was that I was moved to an English state school, Wargrave Piggott secondary modern.

I had been a year ahead and now had to repeat the whole of what I had been doing at school in 1969. At the end of the first term, when places in individual subjects were announced, I came first or second in almost every subject without trying.

The school was coeducational. I did make one slip that I regretted, in that I unwisely admitted to having had the nickname Fritz in my previous school. Instantly I became Fritz to all there and it wasn't until much later, after yet another attack of moving house, that I finally managed to shake it off.

I acquired a regular, if limited, smoking habit, a pack of ten Players No.6 at a time, puffing away in the bike shed or out behind the irregular screens of trees and bushes that dotted the edges of the playing fields. This casual truancy, after having been registered as present at the beginning of the school day, was not uncommon and was often unnoticed, By '72, before I had reached my 15th birthday, a handful of us would slope off from our various lessons, in my case quadruple chemistry, on Friday morning, to gather at the Duke of Wellington in Twyford for a pint or two. The place kept country hours, 10am till 2pm for the lunchtime session, which suited us just fine.

In hindsight, Norman the landlord must have known we were under age, but I believe economic necessity forced him to turn Nelson's eye on us. Apart from a hard core of four or five regulars in his public bar, he seemed to have no other custom. On a Friday or Saturday night we would often return to join two dozen or more patrons, not one of whom was drinking legally, but since we were always well-behaved, it was a mutually beneficial arrangement.

Then in June 1972 came the hammer-blow. On Sunday the fourth of that month my father had his third heart attack. I was ambling from the TV room to the kitchen when I heard his faint call for help from the second floor. On discovering him, I went to get my mother and rang 999. The ambulance seemed to take forever and the crew had some trouble manoeuvring him on a stretcher down the steep and narrow stairs. They drove off with lights and sirens. I sat on the stairs alone, my brothers asleep, until my mother returned from the hospital at around 2 am. She told me my father had died. She had been at the hospital but not actually with him in his final moments. I wish she had been by his side holding his hand, rather than the priest who stepped in. She was in bits. It was a sad house.

The funeral was a sombre affair held in St Benedict's church, Ealing in West London. Shortly afterwards my mother took me aside in my father's study and blurted out that I was adopted. I looked at her face intently and quickly realised that she was speaking the truth. An age later (in reality a few moments) I managed to speak. I asked a few questions, principally who my actual parents were. The details were sparse and vague. My Birth Mother had been a 19-year-old Norwegian au-pair called Ossa, the father unknown but presumed to be a Londoner she had met on one of her days off. I assured her that I regarded her as my REAL mother, despite this revelation, and she said both she and my father had always regarded me as if I had been their first born, their little gift from God.

I was not angry with them for not telling me earlier, much to the surprise of many. When I reviewed the scanty information, I realised that all concerned had acted as they saw it, in my best interest, and I certainly had no reason to complain of the life that I had been given. In those days 'closed' adoptions were the norm and adopted children routinely went all the way to adulthood without being aware of their origins.

No, I was angry with myself. How could I not have seen the signs? I looked at family photos with a new eye. True, all my brothers were different from each other; Martin really skinny, hair mousy-grey, slightly pop-eyed; Peter taller, chunkier, brown-haired; Nick blond, myself blonder still. But they all resembled each other nonetheless – particularly their noses – how had I never seen it? I resolved to pay more attention to what was around me. And life went on.

That summer my mother took my brothers to Poland, along with my father's ashes which were interred beside his mother's grave in Silesia. For some reason, she decided I could do with a bit of practical help with my French and found a family of Polish descent in France for me to board with that summer. Since they all spoke Polish anyway, this plan didn't amount to much, though I did pass French O level the following year.

The family I was placed with had a son, Marc, who was my age. We would roam the countryside and nearby towns on mopeds. In those days there were no issues with helmet laws or licenses. I was exhilarated by the sense of freedom and to this day a motorcycle is my preferred ride.

Back home eventually to a new school year – the one with O-Levels at the end of it. Just before I began, I went to a birthday party and was fixed up with a blind date. This was Kathy, a Texan by birth, freshly arrived from Rome with her newly divorced mother and two younger sisters.

In my world she was an exotic creature. She had an oval face, high cheekbones and long straight brown hair, a great figure and an international American accent. Her father had worked for UNESCO and she had been bounced around the world. Hormones raging, I fell for her hook, line and sinker. It was my good fortune that she found me interesting enough to go out with again, and so, for the first time, I had myself a genuine, regular girlfriend.

It was about three weeks later that we first made love. It was a revelation, it was wonderful and it became my new best thing. She said she had never done it before and I said I had. On reflection I think we were both fibbing to spare our blushes, but thereafter we fell into it with gusto.

A few more weeks passed and Kathy had her sixteenth birthday. Mine was ten months away, and she said that now at least I wasn't breaking the law. "What law?" I asked, to be told that it was illegal while she was under 16 years old;

"statutory rape" as she put it. Intrigued, I pointed out that I was still only fifteen; did this mean that she was now guilty? "No silly, it only works one way." I checked this later and found out that, by God, she was right!

We carried on regardless, meeting wherever possible, spending hours on the telephone talking about nothing in particular, saying, "you hang up first," "no you hang up first", etc. One day, just before Easter, she dropped a bombshell. Her mother had grown rapidly tired of her life in a suburban house in the A4 commuter corridor and decided to up sticks and go back to Texas. The decision was made. We were still just kids and there was nothing to be done about it. I went with them to Heathrow and said my goodbyes with a lump in my throat and a heavy heart. I never saw her again. We wrote to each other a few times and she sent me a picture of herself in a bikini on a beach somewhere. I kept that photo for decades, though I can't seem to lay hands on it now, worse luck. She was my first love and you never forget that.

Soon enough along came a series of O level qualifications. I did reasonably well except in the biology and chemistry exams.

I had been going up to London every Saturday during term time for a morning of Polish school. The O Level exam itself was in the Royal Agricultural Halls in St James'. When I put down my pen, I found myself in a predicament that would plague me down the years. I could not stand up, my back would not unbend, and I was locked in position. I had to wave over the invigilator and ask him to put his knee in the small of my back, hands on my shoulders and give me a sudden wrench back into the upright position. It hurt like blazes and my back and hip have given me increasing discomfort or pain ever since. At the time I shrugged it off. It

Passport photo, July 1974

would be another fifteen years before I was driven to ask my GP for painkillers, and that only to be able to sleep when the pain was too great. It was then discovered I had a kink in my spine, the asymmetry probably the cause of so much discomfort. From the time of my arrival in Bang Kwang until now I have been in pain almost all the time. I can sit or stand for no more than fifteen minutes at a time without having to alter my position.

After the Saturday morning lessons, I would go up to the house my father had bought the year before he died. It had stood empty for some years and my mother now planned to uproot us yet again and move the family to this derelict late-Victorian pile.

We moved in, just before term started. Almost none of the rooms were yet habitable, and we started out living in one room on the top floor. A kitchen had been made operational, as had a bathroom. Gradually, room by room, the house was fitted out, until a large three-bedroom flat on the ground floor for the family and two other flats, finally took shape.

I was now to be an A Level student at Ealing grammar. I was unhappy at having been yanked out of my settled existence, away from the friends I had made in Berkshire, and I was, I think, a sullen teenager. I certainly loathed the school and its single sex ethos. The other boys seemed to be ludicrously immature and socially graceless and I thanked providence that I had not gone to Maidenhead grammar.

I started to skip lessons and eventually stopped showing up altogether. When this came to my mother's attention, she arranged for me to attend a cramming college in a big house in West Ealing to try and catch up.

The chap who owned and ran the place doubled as both maths and history tutor. He was a colourful character. He told us at one point that he was in this line of work because he had made and lost a fortune, not once but twice and was working his way to a hat-trick. Gambling had been his downfall, he said, as he joined in our lunch-time game of penny pontoon, Freddie Mercury's 'The Seven Seas of Rye' coming over the transistor radio.

Somehow I ended up doing my A level courses from scratch, enrolling in September at what was then Chiswick Polytechnic.

The English teacher was, again, inspiring and engaging. He was also completely indifferent to any notion of discipline, with smoking permitted in class. When big Jack arrived one afternoon, still holding a 'Screwdriver' that he had not finished when in the pub, lack of rules became complete. The common room was always buzzing, as was the Tabard pub next door. When the time finally came to take the A Level exams, I didn't even notice. I wasn't sufficiently motivated to do well academically and subsequently had no focus. Apart from a love of language and a belief in the strength and power of words, I can't say I got much from my formal education.[22] Anything that I have learned is as a result of what I have read or otherwise discovered in my own time which fits me to be in a pub quiz team and not much else.

On the Train

The train was crowded when I got on at Queenstown Road. I was doing up a flat nearby, who's passive-aggressive owner was making the job well-nigh impossible and I was now going back to what felt like an equally unwelcoming home. Already pissed off, I couldn't believe that the only empty seats in the carriage were opposite and next to a skinhead with a boxer's face and tattoos. "Sod it," I thought, and sat directly in front of him. He glared at me but couldn't say anything because he was on the phone to his mate. "Yer, well [Wormwood] Scrubbs and AA have asked me to give a talk on alcoholism, but I can't do it, I just can't do it." As soon as the conversation ended, the word came out of my mouth before I had a chance to stuff it back in, "Pity." There was an audible intake of breath from the rest of the carriage. You could have heard a pin drop.

"Yer, what?" he leant menacingly towards me.

"Pity, pity that you are not going to give that talk. How long have you been dry?"

"Eight years and proud of it."

"Can I shake your hand?" I said and did it before he could believe what was happening.

"You are only one of two people I know who have kept off booze that long. You have my absolute respect. I work with builders who have done time and a talk from you would have had a marked effect on them. If you move only one person to change their life, it will be worth it."

I have read that in hostage situations, you have to avoid eye contact until you've been singled out, and then talk like mad to turn yourself from a statistic into a fellow human being. The carriage was still as silent as the grave but this man's face was visibly relaxing and softening. He started to tell me a bit about himself but got up as Putney came into view. "This is my stop. May I shake your hand because it's been an honour talking to you," and with that, he was gone. The honour was mutual. I realized later that my friendship with Andy had given me the passport to connect with this man.

Jobs

A careers officer had once asked me what I wanted to be. "Retired" I said, only half-joking.

Only twice did I take paid employment in a job which required me to wear a suit and tie. The first was with an oil company, Phillips Petroleum, at their offices in Victoria. The job was mind numbing and soul destroying. The view from the seventeenth floor out over Buckingham Palace's gardens didn't make up for that and I quit after a month and a half.

The second was closer to home, as a wages clerk to a company in Acton Vale. There were only two others in the office, an Irish woman and an elderly Sudeten German woman who was in charge. I now think that I'd been hired by her, partly because of my Germanic surname. When she discovered, from my chance remark, that I was in fact from a Polish background, her demeanour changed considerably. After a couple of months I was dismissed.

I did a lot of temp work at pretty much everything that didn't require particular skills or qualifications. Since this came through an agency, the pay was even worse, but there was constant change and no pressure to stay somewhere I didn't like. The light engineering and other firms on the A4 down in Brentford always needed bodies to make up the numbers, and often I ended up pushing a broom and being told to look busy if I saw a suit coming.

Being a kitchen porter during the summer was probably the sweatiest and dirtiest job, though the grub was good and we started and finished early, which suited me fine.

Eventually, with the acquisition of a cheap Honda C70, I had wheels, and my brother Martin had already been working for a courier company in the west end, so he asked that I be taken on. I duly started to bomb around central London ferrying small packages from one office to another. I actually liked this work and certainly got to know the streets of the city far better than I ever had.

I had recently taken up the game of snooker. The popularity of the game was then at its height. It was open from 11 am to 11 pm and I would occasionally play the whole twelve hours on the tables. When the barman quit, I offered to do the job and stayed on for about eight months. Then I heard that my old bosses in the courier company had opened an even bigger and better-appointed snooker hall in West Ealing. I joined the club and when they too needed another hand behind the counter, did long shifts there. I took advantage of the lull after midnight, when my shift ended, to play for free and improve my game.

Andy to Vicky, 2nd Letter

July 2006,

Dear Vicky,

I have just finished penning a very belated reply to Sam the wage-slave,[23] languishing off the coast of Turkey, when your letter arrived. Her last letter said 'Kos, Western Greece'. Honestly, what sort of people do they have teaching geography these days? [...]

How to properly begin; well, I suppose I had better start with the family, from which, after all, all else stems. I am the eldest (though apparently not the wisest) of four sons. Our parents lived in the SW corner of Poland.

They were married in early June '45 and fled the country, immediately before the commissars following the red army could get the machinery of control into place. They were almost sent back when they stopped in Austria, where the Americans were rounding up all the obvious DP's[24]. My parents reacted quickly; they went into a café-restaurant in their best clothes and sat drinking coffee and eating cake, replying in fluent German to inquiries as to their nationality.

When they arrived in London, my father's Polish university degree counted for nought, so he started again and became a chartered accountant. My father's brother had an 'interesting' war. My father had served in the Polish army and was left alone, but his brother was forcibly conscripted into the Wehrmacht, captured in Italy and then Shanghaied into a Polish brigade, thus serving on both sides.

We too are of the Catholic faith, though I would have to admit being a 'lapsed' Catholic, or on my worst days a 'collapsed' Catholic. I remember grousing that I was the only boy I knew that had to go to school every single day of the week – five days English school, Saturdays Polish school and Sundays, well Sunday school!

At age six I became ill with a childhood degenerative bone condition, 'Perthe's disease,' at about this time. The 'treatment' in the sixties, was to wear ungainly callipers for three years, followed by some rather invasive surgery...

It also left me with a lifelong habit; that of reading anything I could lay my hands on. I am still constantly amazed by how little most people bother to read, a situation which is only getting worse in the population as a whole and amongst the younger generation in particular. Since I must rely upon the state to educate my son, this seeming aversion to the written (or printed) word is worrisome to me. From what I understand, he has an aptitude for maths, unlike his father who knows enough arithmetic to count money but scarcely more, and a liking for sport, particularly football and Manchester United. That last is particularly galling since I've followed Chelsea ever since I can remember.

My three brothers and I have been educated, or interned or both, in a variety of establishments. Peter went to Cambridge. Niki, for reasons known only to himself, went to UEA and there got a degree in Philosophy. He spent the next dozen years or so working for a while, then taking off to foreign parts. He now lives near Valencia in a house which appears to swallow money, along with Liz his Bosnian-Serb wife.

Peter married a Polish girl and lives in Warsaw (my least favourite place in the entire country) along with their two, Zofia and Stanislaw, known as Stas' (pronounced Stash). Martin my youngest brother and his wife and two girls live two houses up from my mother in Ealing.

Enough of this reminiscing, me thinks, and on to other things. Though I might add here that my mother, Danuta, 81 years old but still with all her mental faculties, is also a practising Catholic and has an interest (the priests might think perhaps too keen an interest) in the phenomena associated with the departed, with spirits and so forth. We had a spiritualist faith healer stay in one of the flats in our old house in Ealing many years ago, which spurred the interest, no doubt. Myself, I am determinedly agnostic about such things. I feel there is enough going on in the world that we can see, not to be distracted by such considerations [...]

[...] Regarding my son's whereabouts, Denise and her mother sold their London homes in 2005, and went to live together with the children in North Norfolk to get away from London and it's problems. Quinlan has a half-sister, Ariana, as I may have already told you. She'll be eight in September, poor mite. But the young are resilient, so they say. In retrospect the death of my father when I was just shy of fifteen affected me far more and for far longer than it did Niki, my brother, who had only just turned ten years old. In fact it's Denise's mother I feel most for. To lose a parent is bad enough, to lose the only parent immediately to hand is worse, but to lose a child goes against the natural order of things. Children should mourn their parents, not the other way around.

Because of the physical separation from London, I'll have to thank Emma for the offer (to visit Quinlan) but decline; he wouldn't know what to make of it I am sure. [...]

[...] It remains for me to thank you for your kind words about my writing and your kindness towards a stranger. 'I have always relied on the kindness of strangers.' [...] No I don't think Blanche Dubois is me somehow! I believe I am writing just as you leave on holiday, but this will await your return. Many thanks for your interest in an old fool's predicament, my compliments also on your excellent daughters (and sons, no doubt) and my thanks to them also. Regards to one and all. Please tell Emma I'll write if she does (I am not sure who's turn it is!)

Yours from the gulag

Andy Hawke

*

In my second letter there was little or no attempt to make light of my situation, as had been my wont in previous years. Also notable by its absence was any mention of day-to-day life within the prison walls. I often found it difficult and sometimes impossible to commit to the mail any significant details of what went on inside. Our mail was not sealed, and was always in danger of being read and censored.

It would have been difficult to convey a totally accurate picture of the way life was experienced without reference to the casual graft and corruption and instances of more general criminal behaviour endemic to the system. It was best to avoid touching on such subjects.

In 2003 particularly, and also in 2004, there was a huge drive to be <u>seen</u> to be doing something about Thailand's 'new' drug problem, which was perceived as a massive expansion in the local supply and use of methamphetamine. This came in tablet form and had previously been known as a 'ya-ma' or 'horse medicine'. A press campaign succeeded in re-naming it 'ya-ba' or 'crazy medicine'.

The policy of giving huge sentences for even relatively low amounts of drugs meant that the number of ya-ba users in the prison system sky-rocketed, and stayed high thereafter. The consequences for us, the 'old' type of drug offender in the system, were dire.

Firstly, the amount of police activity and media interest generated by this 'war on drugs' was immense. The press and TV showed an almost constant stream of images of drug busts. Sullen-faced, newly arrested men – very few women – were paraded for the media, sitting behind trestle tables piled high with hundreds of thousands of tablets of Ya-ba (at £1.50 to £2 per tablet).

The second thing which shifted the media focus directly onto us inside the prison, tied in with mobile phones. An arrest of multiple suspects in Bangkok led to a simple question: who is the boss?" Thai suspects in Police investigations rarely hold back information, the police taking a decidedly physical approach to non-compliance. The answer was given, a name, and his location: Bang Kwang prison! "How is that possible?" the cops demanded, "Easy, we communicate by mobile phone." It was this that caused the midden to hit the windmill.

All of this took some time, the first phase of the 'war on drugs' kicking into gear in 2003. It was the brainchild of the Government of Thaksin Shinawattra, who had been a Lieutenant-Colonel in the Thai police in a previous incarnation.

The arrest rate doubled, and by the time Samantha came to visit me, the resultant convictions had swelled the Bang Kwang population to about 7,000 prisoners, with the crowding in the cells reaching ridiculous levels. We were not happy bunnies, but I did not even attempt to convey this in my letters.

Sam to Andy

18 September 2006,

(First page lost)

[…] I am currently spending everyday panic reading before I get back to uni. I have chosen to do a module on Rudyard Kipling and have three of his books to read. (I've only got through two so far – his autobiography and Kim.) If you know anything about him, I am always interested in your intelligent insights. […]. As regards the play I asked you to write, don't worry in the slightest. I completely understand and so long as I have first rights on anything you write in the future Andy, I am happy.

[…] I enclose in the letter a picture of my mother, my sister and I quite some years ago. I came across it today and thought you might like it, hopefully it won't get confiscated. I am the moody, blonde one on the left – of course! Thank you for correcting my geography and yes, I am now a lot more knowledgeable on the whereabouts of Greece and Turkey. […].

As always, I am praying for you, all my love, Sam.

PS Send my love to Steve and the others.

left to right, Samantha, Vicky and Emma, Portugal 1989

Andy to Sam

27 September 2006

Dear Sam

Thank you for the combination card/letter/photo that I received yesterday. It was post marked 18th, the day after the local military deposed the 'caretaker' prime minister (Thaksin Shinawat) [...]. He was out of the country, in this case in New York at the UN and as a result the coup was 'bloodless' [...]

[...] There hasn't been a military takeover in fifteen years, and it took the arrogance of the previous incumbent to provoke this one. [...]

[...] Meanwhile, when the Thai mega-corporation Shincorp,[25] was sold to a Singaporean concern, it was found to be a subsidiary of a company registered for tax purposes in the British Virgin Islands. The sole proprietor it turned out was T. Shinawat.

Big demos and a brouhaha by the opposition. [...] Enter the army; exit Thaksin, gone to spend more time with his money-over £1,100,000,000 of it, by the most conservative estimates. All paperwork slowed down and submissions for King's pardons have not moved an inch [...]

[...] As for Kipling, I read him when I was far too young to have any appreciation of his literary talents. He was hugely popular in his lifetime, the golden sunset of the empire, the Indian Raj in particular. His 'If' hangs on walls throughout the land; my mother has it somewhere [...]

If you've read his autobiography you'll know what he thought and felt; best you read a life of him by someone else to get a more rounded view though, both of the man and the time he lived through – you need context to fully understand some of the unspoken but assumed attributes and ideas [...]

Yours affectionately

Andy

*

Thaksin, quite deliberately, gave the cops carte blanche to go hog-wild in his first 'war on drugs,' resulting in the murders of over two and a half thousand people in two and a half months, by the cops mostly, or with their connivance. The king himself asked plaintively why not one of these murders had been solved.

I now realise that the coup-makers read their man correctly. They wanted this dangerous demagogue permanently out of the picture and found the most pleasing and efficient way of doing it that didn't involve shooting him.

'Riot'

I am drinking coffee and smoking a roll-up when I hear it. My head snaps up, as does that of Stoker Steve. We look at each other. We both recognise the sound of small-arms fire. We look back at the near wall, just as chips of concrete dislodged by a fusillade of shotgun and rifle-fire come flying up and over into our cell block's compound.

It transpires that the prison population next door, unable to access TV or radio reports on the bloodless coup, became vociferous. Their screws panicked and called on armed intervention goons. The result, mayhem. Two prisoners were shot dead, eight more seriously injured. The next day the screw showed photos of himself posing with a foot on the backs of his victims to sycophantic blue-shirts (trusties) and all and sundry in our block. His braggadocio and the fawning attentions of his audience made me sick to my stomach. Bloodless coup?

The immediate result was the influx of a few dozen men who had been involved. They were all young, the oldest probably only in his mid-to-late twenties. All were street gang members and amphetamine users. They were surly, violent and had no respect for anyone, including themselves. In short, they were bad news, as was amply demonstrated some months later.

One guy was suspected, rightly or wrongly, of being a grass. A young 'un whacked him on the noggin from behind with a glass bottle. Screws questioned the victim in the block's main office as his bonce was being patched up.

Unfortunately for him he had now been seen talking to the screws and the young boss, having lost face, marched his band through both office doors, intent on punishing the supposed informer. In the ensuing frenzy, they actually slashed and stabbed each other while the three screws leapt out of their way, one even climbing up on a desk. Us older lags could see all this going on through the windows and scarpered pronto.

The alarm sounded. All of us were ordered back to our cells. A squad of riot control screws dragged out about three dozen, laid them face down on the basketball court with plastic ties holding their wrists behind their backs and started beating the crap out of them with hardwood clubs. All were moved out forthwith, some to solitary, others to different blocks. They picked up additional sentences tacked on to the relatively short ones they'd started with in the prison next door.

*

Andy's letter is lying on the doormat when we return from our family holiday in Portugal. A few days later, I pick up a pen to write a second letter to him. I feel awkward telling Andy about our holiday. Will he think six weeks indulgent?

From the beginning of the marriage, Nick and I dreamt of having a villa when we could afford it. In 1999, an opportunity to convert a tired three-bedroom villa into an 'old' Portuguese farmhouse, presented itself. For two years I put all my energy into creating this romantic idyll, giving particular attention to our bedroom, featuring a seventeenth century Romeo and Juliet balcony, huge Indian four-poster marriage bed and private terrace. I imagined us sunbathing nude or having breakfast there after lovemaking. Our architect Stewart said, "this house was built with love". My frustration was, that after I had spent a year and a half transforming a nondescript house, there was still no sign of passion from Nick.

In the following twelve years, we were together on that terrace only once. We used the house for family holidays but never as a romantic bolthole as I had imagined. He always claimed he was too busy and stressed, keeping his business afloat and as a result his libido was down. He kept promising that one day he would make it up to me. We would make love once during the summer holidays, at the precise moment he could see I was going to burst, and bizarrely, I would feel grateful. On the rare occasions we went out to dinner on our own, I foolishly tried to discuss where we were going wrong only to be met with a wall of silence. I eventually realised that to have a 'nice' meal out, I needed to stick to his 'go to' subject, his business. Once I began working for him and went to the different hotels and got to know the staff, I also enjoyed talking shop. Funnily enough we were closer in those moments than at any other time in those later years of our marriage.

If I told Andy all this, would he empathise with my misery at feeling invisible and treated like a housekeeper, or would he think 'first world problems?' He must think I have a charmed and privileged life. I know I am very fortunate not to have financial worries; I've never been to the supermarket and had the credit card bounce on me as it has with some of my friends and family.

The nightmares of my childhood had come back to haunt me. I had a recurring dream; a throned figure, stone-cold and expressionless, staring straight at me, the face alternating between my mother's and Nick's.

I was born in the Chinese year of the dog. I am faithful and loving, but to keep my tail wagging and my coat shiny, I need to be stroked and patted and given lots of affection. Lack of physical closeness was having the opposite effect on my health. I had been diagnosed with chronic arthritis in my left knee, pre-cancerous cells had been found on my face and in my colon. I had developed asthma but was loth to take medication, instead being treated with homeopathy which didn't seem to be working. I couldn't go on a run without continually stopping for breath. Sometimes at night I didn't think I would wake up alive; I would be on all fours for hours, trying desperately to take in air. One night, I was forced to go to Kingston A&E because of a pheasant bone that had got stuck in my throat. When the receptionist saw I was struggling to breathe, I was seen straight away. No one took any notice of the bone. Apparently I had so little oxygen in me that by law they were not allowed to let me leave. I was rigged up with an oxygen mask and was eventually discharged at 2.30am. The next morning I coughed up that pesky two-inch pheasant bone!

I fold my wealth and unhappiness away and write to Andy about the children and my family history instead, secretly wondering how long I can keep going. I was suffocating in the marriage but who could I share these feelings with?

Vicky to Andy, 2nd Letter

29 September 2006,

Dear Andy,

It was a relief to hear your more upbeat tone in your second letter, rather than the despair of your first. I have been talking to a young female lawyer who worked for the Home Office on prison transfers from abroad. She totally understands your frustration with the consulate and the system. She's come up against it all the time. Her advice however, is to get transferred at all costs and once here in England, to get the lawyers to fight your case [...]

[...] If you get transferred but not immediately released, could you not begin an Open University degree course in English? You have such a fine mind and I am sure would relish the challenge. I can see you doing a creative writing course. You are not boring whatever you write about. For example I can 'see' your mother and father with their best clothes, coffee and cake in that restaurant, saving their skins, (at the end of the war), with their fluent German.

By the way, I think I would get on with your mother. Like her, I believe in a life after death. My sister's friend has seen spirits since she was little. One of her children also sees them. She says that as Britain becomes more and more secular, with less and less attention to someone's funeral or 'sending off', spirits do not move on, but hover on earth. She says it is driving her mad and the family go to Thailand for their holidays, so that she and her daughter can have a break. She says there are no spirits to speak of there, because the whole country is religious and the funerals are taken seriously by everybody. They are thinking of immigrating to Australia, which is less spirit populated. I can see you not taking any of this seriously, like my husband Nick, who is also agnostic.

Talking of Nick, my husband; he is a Chelsea fan like you, but I am 100% behind your son Quinlan. The boys and I are Man U supporters through and through...

... You are a year older than I am and the eldest of four boys; I am the eldest of four girls. For good or bad I've always been the responsible one, buried in books while my parents rowed every day; or more accurately, my mother ranted and raved and my father was silent. He had three scholarships to Cambridge and she had never passed an exam in her life. Mind you if you want something done, you ask my mother. I think she's a depressive and was deeply unhappy when married. They stuck it out for 24-years and when they split up, we three older girls were in our twenties and quite relieved. However my youngest sister, Itsy, was thirteen and went on a 10-year rebellion – sex, drugs and rock n' roll (she did get to no. 19 in the charts in the early nineties). She had a police record at age 10 for shoplifting (in a gang).[26] *She was visiting a boyfriend in Leicester prison at eighteen years old. She then went out with Jarvis, who ran acid-house parties [...] I had just married Nick when my sister came to him wanting to borrow £600 (20 years ago!). I told my husband to employ her in the sales dept. (he owns a travel company) so she could put some money aside each week out of her wages and the*

day she'd paid him back, she could walk out. Well, she ended up staying for two years; she cleaned up her act and won sales person of the year. Why I bought all this up, is that puberty is the worst time for anything traumatic to happen to a person; as you rightly said, you were more affected by your father's death than your younger brother.

Are there any books/plays/poetry I could send you? Vitamin pills? A cigarette and coffee are not the best breakfast in the world! Goodness, I sound interfering – once a mother always a mother.

Emma's just seen a note by this letter, "Emma – boyfriends last six weeks!" I told her to write to you and argue her case against that statement. The male model has disappeared and a guitarist, Luis, has taken his place. He has a wise face and seems quite calm (possibly pot). Looks like he needs a good meal and some fresh air. He's very likeable though. She's just started Art College [...] Her fees are twice as much as Samantha's, but she seems to be getting ten times the amount of tuition. I am not sure Samantha's degree course is all it's cracked up to be. It seems she will come out in three years, being able to write about the theatre but not actually work in it [...] Oh well, she's enjoying the English department and is looking forward to sharing a house with six boys and Polly, a great friend [...] She's already driven to Bristol with the first carload of stuff, sorted out the phone, electrics, a list of what needs to be done for the landlord, etc. She's the one child who could take over Nick's business.

Oh, Emma's just come in. Loved her second day. She drew a nude with a ruler and pencil – no curves allowed! Got both praise and criticism – just what she wants.

I told you about Lauren in my last letter – my friend who is half paralysed. I looked after her for two weeks after the boys went back to school, because her daughter and husband haven't had a holiday for four years. To be fair there

*were three of us, all unqualified. My shift was 7.30am –
8.30pm [...] Talk about being thrown in the deep end! [...]
pills and morphine every four hours, [...] the hydro pool,
washing her, changing clothes and sheets constantly, doing
the chores and cooking when she slept. Her daughter and
husband must be saints. However we had a lot of laughs
between her bouts of pain. I am probably on a dangerous
carers list. I wheeled Lauren to Richmond Park and decided
to take her on an 'off-road' expedition along the deer tracks
where I run. Needless to say, I almost tipped her out, hitting
a rut and buckling the wheel. Up to then we'd been singing
"Oh what a beautiful morning!" at the top of our lungs. I had
to abandon her and run to a gamekeeper's cottage in the
distance. [...] In the end they came with an ancient Land
Rover and another wheelchair – and the police! We've since
been back to John, the gamekeeper, who turns out to be a
healer. He hasn't been able to alleviate the pain, but has
taken a huge weight off Lauren's mind. In the last few
months she had been seeing the spirit of her mother-in-law
at the end of her bed and it was freaking her out. Lauren
was sure she was going to die imminently. John told her not
to worry, that her mother-in-law was there to help her, not to
take her to the next life [...] So now I don't feel so bad about
buckling the wheel; it was meant to be. You are probably
thinking, like my husband, here she goes again!* [27]

*Simon, the 24-year-old with cystic fibrosis, has now been
with us for thirteen months! [...] I think by Christmas he'll
have moved out. We'll miss him. He's like one of the family.
[...] One morning, while staying with us in Portugal, he went
into a coma. In front of all my panicking relatives, my boys
(age 13 and 16) took over. They knew exactly what to
squeeze into his mouth, to get the sugar levels up and
exactly how to take a blood sample and get a reading and
bring him round quickly and without panic. I shouldn't brag,
but at that moment I was a proud mother.*

Well that's it and you are probably thinking thank goodness – she's arrogant, talks too much and why do I need to know about Lauren and Simon anyway?! Well, they are the most remarkable people I've ever had the privilege to come across. Despite the fact that they probably won't live very long, they both have a wicked sense of humour (grammatical minefield just negotiated).

And next time I write, I'll let you know about William and his new school, which is too new at the moment to give an accurate picture of (grammar at an all-time low).

Please write with a shopping list and any more on the transfer,

Lots of Love

Vicky

Appeals and Heavy Penalties

In Thailand amnesties (reductions of sentence for good behaviour) were meted out on special occasions, particularly Royal birthdays, by the King.

By the time of the Queen's birthday on 12 August 2004, I had served 68 months and had been 'excellent class' throughout that period. I was thus eligible for the full measure of any amnesty. However I was given a very rude shock when the powers that be came up with a new rule. For drug offences only, the prisoner's case had to be closed, not just before the amnesty being granted, but before the date of the PREVIOUS amnesty. Therefore he could end up serving AT LEAST ten years longer than a murderer given the same sentence at the same time.

This discrimination for drug cases, already commanding the highest sentences internationally, made the penal code of the Kingdom of Thailand one of the harshest in the world. The Thais also had the death penalty, and were notoriously more likely to use it in sentencing drug cases than sentencing murderers, though only a smallish proportion of those so sentenced were actually executed.

Even those with what would be considered small cases incurred large sentences. The most ludicrous example was a Thai we called Bingo. This poor sod had been collared with a gram of heroin in a tiny glass vial. As well as the possession charge, he was given a 'manufacture' charge. He had changed the container in which the dope had been sold, which was usually a drinking straw. He got life for a gram, which constituted a mind-bogglingly disproportionate response to his offence.

The highest numbered sentence for an individual offence was 50 years, but as far as we could see it was only ever given to drug cases.[28] The frequency and scale of amnesties over the years, were reduced. Drug offenders, even minor ones, were incarcerated for longer and longer periods. And yet for all this, the number of drug convictions has gone steadily upwards.

Drug offenders, are considered by the guards to have higher levels of disposable income than run-of-the-mill murderers, rapists and thieves. So even though it costs the state extra to keep these people inside and the ballooning prison population is having to be packed in like sardines, from the screws' point of view this is all gravy. More drug offenders equals more money. And that's it folks.

*

There were now two other Brits in my block, indeed in my cell. Their presence, along with that of a Dutch-Canadian and a pair of Aussies, gave the "farang" body of prisoners an Anglophile cast and the addition of a 30-ish Polish lad, gradually drew me into a more interactive, gregarious life. As a result, my letter-writing slackened off and never really recovered.

All in all, my days were more filled than previously. My nights on the other hand, were bleak and empty, because that is when the weight of grief over Denise's death came to land on my heart and mind with overpowering force. I would wake each morning, exhausted and bleary-eyed, morose and generally numb. It took me ages to come alive for the day.

Andy to Vicky, 3rd Letter

11 October 2006

Dear Vicky

I just received your letter and decided I had best begin my reply immediately [...]

This does not mean I will be likely to actually finish this effort in one fell swoop. Even though it is only half-past noon and there remain three hours before we are chivvied back into our cells, the smart money is against it. For one thing, it is becoming ominously dark, and while a good thunderstorm is welcome for its cooling qualities, 'bad light' would inevitably retard play.

For another, I just came back from my second 'shower' of the day, and on rounding the corner of the longer water-trough, slipped on some green, slimy stuff and went Madras over Elba! The elbow was in fact bruised, but fortunately not on the writing arm. It could have been worse; people have been known to crack their craniums and expire forthwith in such incidents. I do not exaggerate [...].

[...] Sam wrote of her interest in an English 'module' on Rudyard Kipling. [...] It is very difficult to read a man like Kipling, always an outsider, in isolation. You have to appreciate the late Victorian/Edwardian milieu in which he lived and wrote, and how complete and all-enveloping the concept of the Empire was, in particular for his readership.

A crack of thunder has just punctuated my train of thought. I shall continue until the coming storm derails it entirely [...].

[...] Kipling was vilified as a racist and apologist for the perceived excesses of 'Empire' before that Empire had fully unravelled and the literati sneered at him for decades. But in truth, within the limitations imposed upon him by his circumstances, he was far more sympathetic to the indigenous population (of the old Raj), than almost any Anglo writer I can think of.

I confess I do not really know what Sam expects to get out of her time at university. If, as you say, she may come out being able to write about the theatre but not actually work in it... a theatre critic! She'd have to learn a nastiness, a sarcastic and snappy form of what passes for 'wit', which I don't believe lies in her personality. Also, she would have to learn to write in paragraphs; I love her letters but have to keep my finger on the page or I lose track!

Incidentally, the last side of Sam's last letter was entirely given over to a photocopied photo (tortuous language!) of you, Sam and Emma on a beach somewhere when they were young (er) and adorable. Some appreciative, if a tad lewd, comments were passed by an over-inquisitive lecher peering over my shoulder regarding the central figure, which was of course you! I said nothing of the kind, being the perfect gentleman.

And now to Emma: I confess I burst out laughing when I read that paragraph, particularly those first lines – the note: "Emma – boyfriends last six weeks!" And your proposal that she write arguing the case against the statement. Then the throwaway line about the 'replacement' as I'll call him, having 'a wise face' and seeming quite calm – possibly pot. I've known some muzos in my time and while it's true they are notoriously apt to indulge in various chemical excesses, the notion of him deliberately showing up to meet his gorgeous girlfriend's mother, while stoned on THC is a bit unlikely. If you are actually worried on the chemical score, try and check the pupils of his eyes; if normal, fine. If slightly or even greatly dilated, don't worry too much. But if they are right down to pinpricks, it's probably heroin (unless there's a bright light in his eyes) in which case, worry. He's highly unlikely to be taking cocaine because a) it is too expensive for struggling musicians and b) it turns a half-decent musician into a useless one, see ten disappeared and wasted years of David Bowie's life. As to these new-fangled drugs like Ecstasy and Ketamine (which I thought was a horse-tranquiliser), I am just the wrong generation. And that was far too long a paragraph!

Darkness looms and I must set aside this letter, as two hours have zipped by and I must prepare to be herded back into the block for another fifteen hours. I cannot write in the cell – there is no furniture as such, and though one might avail oneself of one of those little fold-out oriental writing tables, I am utterly incapable of assuming the lotus position required to make use of them.

12 October

Another day in this tropical paradise. Returning briefly to Sam's letter and my reply, she said you and indeed she, would like perhaps to contact my mother, so, I have dashed off a letter to my mother to give her some advance warning [...]

In the letter I just got from Danuta, my mother. She mentions (at some length) the spirit world and is apparently again in touch with some woman who is a medium or something [...] I cannot say with certainty that it is all nonsense, only that I have not experienced anything that has convinced me. The thing that strikes me most is the preponderance of women over men who appear to be able to pick up these psychic vibrations.

I would, however, take issue with your sister's friend regarding the Thais and religion. The funeral aspect, the proper sending off of the dead has, I agree, become not so much secularised as sanitised. People live so far from their roots in nature. [...] The process of dealing with death has become so clinical, that most people are only vaguely aware, on a subconscious basis, of someone's absence. The old practices of viewing the dead, the funeral mass, the burial with the clods of earth landing on the coffin, these things had a finality (what the moderns call 'closure', I suppose), that are missing in the conveyor belt cremations that have taken over the country.

Thais do still do the 'sending off' in the old fashion, it is true, but as for their religion, well, that's another matter entirely. The forms are followed. Almost every male will spend at least a few months in a monastery at some point in his life, and there are nuns as well as monks throughout the land. But do any of the masses even understand, let alone follow the precepts of Buddhism? This is far more doubtful. I caught a radio programme, in English, where a Thai opined that lip service and ritual were there but that understanding and belief probably, in most cases, were not.

This would almost mirror our own country, except that the Thais, in the countryside particularly, definitely believe in ghosts and demons. Intricate tattoos to ward off illness, knives and bullets or to ensure wealth, health or happiness, are done with slivers of bamboo by Buddhist monks. These 'temple tattoos' are ubiquitous and have, as far as I can see, nothing to do with Buddhist teaching whatsoever. They can even be done in oil instead of ink, so that the charm or bodily amulet is there but not visible – popular with the ladies that one.

There was a short break there, for a visit by the consular staff to us Brits, and I've just had a fairly hot curry for my lunch. I always go to these, though some don't. It's a chance to talk to people from other buildings that one would otherwise not see, to exchange gossip and news and, on occasion, much needed advice. Here we are in the fresh air all day, can read, listen to or watch whatever we want, cook our own chosen food, and most importantly of all, we are left alone.

Yet another Brit has arrived from Block Four. Almost no foreigners are in there but the two Brits who are, were driving him up the wall. One is a scarily loony guy. The other is an unrepentant paedophile and a thoroughly unpleasant character, though from a distance you'd think butter wouldn't melt in his mouth.

[...] I do thank you from the bottom of my heart for showing such an interest, and I will certainly keep you apprised of any developments. Fingers crossed, that may be sooner than I would expect. Half-an-hour or so until lock down and I am still nowhere near finished – looks like this won't be going into the mail until Monday. It's about 32°C and I am having trouble concentrating, so I will continue this tomorrow.

14 October

In fact the day after tomorrow, as yesterday was Friday 13th so I did nothing whatsoever (I know, superstition, silly really) [...].

[...] When I was first taken from the police station to the drug remand prison, I was immediately and systematically stripped and separated from most of my belongings. They even took a pair of flip-flops, though I saw everyone else wearing footwear, presumably for re-sale. I had no shoes and was depressed and saddened until I saw a man with no feet – he was knuckling himself about on a jury-rigged little cart, more like a skateboard. He was not concerned with such trivialities as shoes. I saw more maimed men in six months than in the whole of my life until that point. Any other problems I might have, paled into seeming insignificance before what these men [...] had to endure until the end.

[...] None of us here knows, can possibly know, how long they will actually serve, until the time comes for their release. All we can do is hope that something good will happen. Which brings me to another old story, Arabic or Persian, I think.

A criminal is brought before the ruler of the state, tried and found guilty and condemned to death. When asked if he has anything to say, he replies, "Yes, your majesty, only give me one year, and I will teach your favourite horse to sing!" Intrigued, the monarch grants the request.

Next day at the stable, a curious head groom asks the man "What on earth were you thinking? There is no way you can teach that horse to sing in a year, or a hundred years!"

"Ah", says the reprieved one, "a year is a long time, many things can happen; the king might die, I might die, or who knows, perhaps the horse will learn to sing!" Such is the nature of hope.

I cannot think of anything I would like to be sent except books; would you believe I am missing the seventh and last Harry Potter! I know childish escapism, but still.

[...] Thank you for the offer of help and the parcel. [...] I would like a copy of Terry Pratchett's *The Last Continent*, Carpe Jagulum, *The Fifth Elephant*, The *Thief of Time* or *Monstrous Regiment*. [...] It's pure escapist fantasy and very humanly funny. Not too many funny books to be found here. Try finding a joke in *The Decline and Fall of the Roman Empire*!! [...]

I must finish now, it's late on Sunday and I do want to get this in tomorrow's post.

Regards to one and all

Lots of Love Andy

*

Despite the fact that we've never met and thousands of miles lie between us, I have already started to regard Andy as a friend. It is always a treat when I see the tell-tale airmail letter on the doormat. I try to make time to read it leisurely, to appreciate the quality of the writing, and this one is no exception. Andy writes about Kipling with such grace that Samantha wonders if she can plagiarise it for her pending essay. I say that I don't think the English department will trace her work back to a prisoner in a Thai jail, but that 'borrowing' is something to be frowned upon.

Andy's mention of a photo sent by Samantha, of Emma, herself and me on a beach when the children were little, disturbs me. Which one did she send? For one horrible moment, I think of a photo of myself with huge knockers because I am breastfeeding, but then get a grip because Tom is in that, so it can't be that one. I do know that I need to put him right on one thing – I am now middle-aged so he needs to think again, otherwise when we finally meet, he's going to be a tad disappointed.

*

In her 3rd letter, now missing, she mentions reading a book (the fourth Harry Potter) whilst at the wheel of a car. The thought terrified me and actually coloured my perception of the woman I was writing to. It wasn't just irresponsible, it was insane; it was past Barking, it was positively Dagenham it was so crazy.

Andy to Vicky, 4th Letter

21 November 2006

Dear Vicky

[...] Having read your description of how 'exciting' you found the fourth Harry Potter, I've made a mental note to say, "I'd rather take the bus, thank you," if you ever offer me a lift (just kidding!). Having been a despatch rider, I don't even like taking my eyes off the road ahead to look in the mirror, let alone look down at a map as some do. Read a book? [...] Yikes!

I too am rushing, as sending cards at Christmas is a tricky business – I never know when they'll get there. More to follow, including cards for Sam and Emma.

Best wishes, thanks again

Andy

PS Do contact my mother.

*

I had written to Andy telling him that the Tri-Wizard tournament in the fourth book of Harry Potter was so exciting, I had read it balanced on the steering-wheel whilst driving down Putney High Street. I WAS in a traffic jam.

*

On their visit, just before 25 December, the ladies came dressed up in Xmas clobber, strobing hats, reindeer antlers and so on. Gale put through some cheap and cheerful Santa hats for us to wear. Better still, she gifted us some bangers and bacon and tins of baked beans (otherwise unavailable) with which to make a slap-up feast, as well as Christmas cake and mince pies.

These were things we really appreciated, and which we could only have been given by regular visitors living in the country.

Andy to Sam

6 Dec 2006

Dear Sam

I'm sorry to have been such a rotten letter writer, by which I mean the infrequency of my efforts […].

[...] For some years now the Thais have been calling me 'Santa' because of my beard [...] a Frenchman has offered (for a consideration, naturally), to cook us beef fondue, meaning Bourgignon I think, so that is my Christmas dinner taken care of [...].

[...] I came across a quote the other day, from a lady in a different artistic discipline, made thirty years ago. "One thing I have learned over the years is the difference between taking your work seriously and taking yourself seriously. The first is essential, the second disastrous." That was Dame Margot Fonteyn, the ballerina of her day. I knew there was something I liked about that woman. It wasn't ballet, that's for sure.

The 'Band', playing in the music room, is learning a new tune. Having played 'Hotel California' and J.J. Cale's 'Cocaine' so many times, hundreds, that I can no longer bear to listen to them, even on the radio, they've now started on 'Zombie' by the Cranberries; a great shame as I like that record and in three months it will grate on my nerves like chalk on a blackboard (deep sigh).

[...] Also, yesterday marked exactly eight years since my arrest and incarceration, not a particularly happy anniversary, and I spent the day trying not to think about it, failing miserably as usual [...].

Say hi to Emma and your mother for me.

Yours from the gulag,

Andy

The Africa House

In a vast open-sided shed with a corrugated roof, were the 'houses', or areas of lockers, commandeered by different groups of prisoners. Compared to the concrete 'house' where we farangs kept our possessions, Africa House, more often known as Nigeria House, was a rather more dilapidated and ramshackle affair of wooden lockers. The thirty-odd who lived here were a pretty noisy bunch. A conversation could be heard several yards away, an argument clearly audible in all parts of the compound. When they were not, ah, then there was some skulduggery afoot. At this time, in this place, the principal purveyors of retail pharmaceuticals were the Nigerians. Over time the original cartel split into three competing cartels. This caused friction.

When the hubbub and bad blood from this internecine warfare was at its height, Abu Bakar, a respected individual amongst their number, called for a cease-fire. Eventually, it was agreed that each group would operate every third day and that the other two would sit back and wait their turn. The immediate effect was suspension of hostilities. All parties pronounced themselves satisfied with the agreement and straight away took steps to get round it!

The Nigerians are a-buzz with news that Abu Bakar is due to come back from a three-month stint in solitary. This is highly unusual, as it is standard practice following a spell in Building 10, to be moved on to some other building. As usual Abu Bakar has managed to bribe his way back to where he wants to be.

He arrives like a comet, trailing a tail of convicts that have latched on to him as soon as he comes through the gate. He is an imposing figure, contriving to look somehow far taller than the 5'10" or so he actually is, looking sleek and well fed, wearing what appears to be a brand-new ensemble of sports shirt and shorts, socks and immaculate training shoes. A couple of prisoners are carrying his stuff. He opens up some lockers; they were his, and no-one, con or screw, went near them while he was away.

That afternoon is entirely taken up with conversations, pleas and counter pleas from the milling throng of Ibos who welcome him back. It's like watching the 'capo di tutti capi', the Don of Dons, dispensing justice, settling disputes, stroking and calming the troops. Other than a perfunctory introduction and greeting, he has no time for us then. Tomorrow will do. We are not short on time.

Abu Bakar is a Muslim. On Fridays Muslims may attend prayers in a hall between the major cell blocks, where they mingle with their co-religionists from the other buildings. The opportunities for the exchange of gossip, information and contraband, and for making future arrangements, are obvious.

Abu has been here ten years. He started on death row where he stayed with his leg-irons soldered together for over four years. Another heroin case, with a seizure amounting to 45 kilos, (fifty times what I was pinched with), he is clearly in the 'businessman' category of prisoner and wouldn't dream of dabbling in his own product.

Abu speaks French as fluently as he does English, and has travelled extensively throughout Western and Central Africa, as well as Europe and Asia. He appears to have access to substantial sums of cash, as his return from solitary confirms, and is treated with some respect by everyone, screws included.

Big George is another unique case: he has a strange medical condition. Under his left breast there is a six-inch long, inch-deep notch in his flesh, like that made by a lumberjack with an axe. The flesh on the two inner faces of this notch is an unhealthy-looking greyish-pink and uneven, like bubbles solidified. I ask what made this horrendous wound, but he says it just happened, something just began to eat away at his flesh. It has now dried and stabilised. An elderly be-spectacled senior Thai medic, Doctor John, took an interest in him. A letter from this jovial worthy, recommending a measure of Royal Clemency on medical grounds, was solid gold for George. A few years later this act of kindness would bear fruit. He had already had his original life sentence cut to 40 years and now it was reduced to 15 years. He had already served twelve and when he arrived back in Abuja, Nigeria's capital, he was pardoned and freed.

Chris is in his late thirties, about 6 feet tall and, unusually for the general run of African prisoners, holds himself aloof from his fellow countrymen. He is a keen chess player and a voracious reader, which marks him out still further, and since both are pastimes that interest me, we spend quite some time together.

The Jamaican, Lloyd, had lived in London for years. He was entitled to a UK passport but hadn't bothered to acquire one. Now the Brits won't touch him and the nearest Jamaican Embassy is in Tokyo. He has a partner and daughter in North London and I resolve to help him because he is becoming depressed and really needs a hand.

I tell him about the UK Charity, 'Prisoners Abroad', and then, since he isn't much of a hand with writing, I pen a letter to them, urging them to take him on their books. To my mild surprise and to Lloyd's eternal gratitude, they reply fairly promptly and in the affirmative. To the end of his stay in prison, Lloyd will rely almost exclusively on this slender lifeline, amounting to £90 a quarter. It is probably the single most constructive and helpful thing I do in my entire stretch and I'm inordinately proud of it.

One day, I get a visit from a big, bubbly 30-something Nigerian woman called Olive. When my mother visited me in Bambat she fell into conversation with Olive, who had been visiting a chap called Emmanuel, yet another Ibo. Apparently, Mum had asked Olive to drop in on me occasionally, perhaps get me some necessities from the visitors shop, and act as a conduit for news and for funds if necessary. And so, I am speaking to this pretty, lively and above all strong woman of the type of no-nonsense female who dominate the markets of West Africa.

She has arrived, wearing a black Lycra top and shorts with laces down the sides, leaving a wide vertical expanse of skin exposed. Her arms are rattling with bracelets and bangles, a large necklace is around her throat and outsized and elaborate earrings dangle from her lobes. Her hair is intricately braided and she's wearing bright red lipstick, which I can only just see because I am dazzled by the 24-carat smile from her perfect teeth. She looks glorious.

As she speaks, I become aware that we have gathered an audience. Almost every Ibo in the visit room stops to wave or to say hello, including Nigerian visitors on her side of the divide, as the authorities have not yet glassed in the two sides of the four-foot gap between convict and visitor. It is clear that almost every African knows her.

I am certain that she has no connection with the 'business.' She owns a women's clothes store in Bangkok and is a hard-working, prudent and cheerful Christian. She has a nine-year-old son, Joshua, to look after and while she looks to make proper use of every penny, she is open-handedly generous. There are few Nigerian women in the West African diaspora in Asia, so I suppose it is natural that all the men value her company. She is their reminder of home.

Alexandro, Alex, from Equatorial Guinea is a rarity. He had been a minor functionary at his nation's embassy in Paris. He was persuaded to go to Thailand and fetch drugs on behalf of his ambassador, being assured that he would have diplomatic immunity. It turned out that his country Guinea had no embassy in Thailand, and so, with no protection, he was busted.

Playing four-a-side football on concrete is all the rage in the cell blocks. The same space is used for basketball but football is far more popular. There are three tournaments every year, one between teams within the block, another between the blocks themselves, also played on our pitch in Building Six, and a third played on the full-sized grass pitch over near the front wall of the prison. The playing of ball games on the unforgiving cement in our yard has its inevitable injury toll. Knees and elbows are regularly scraped, sprained and broken.

In the early days, the guards permitted, for a small financial consideration, small groups of 'fans' to go to the tournaments on the grass pitch in Building 14, to support their teams. In one ad hoc competition, between four teams of Thai, Chinese (mixed nation), Africans and 'Farangs' or white Westerners, the farangs could not muster eleven players so a couple of Nigerians were drafted in as allowed replacements. When, during the course of an African versus farang match, little Nigerian Andy, co-opted for the farangs, shouted in Ibo to an opponent for the ball and received it, we howled with laughter. When he went on to score, the place went bananas, the affronted Africans complaining of foul play and little Andy turning five somersaults to celebrate.

Holidays

*left to Right, Emma, Tom, Samantha, William and
Vicky Mauritius, Dec 1993*

*To my undying shame, I once overheard a conversation my children
were having in their bedroom when they were around 10 years old.
One of them said they thought skiing was boring. They all agreed
and then another said, "not as boring as Portugal." They all agreed
again. Then one of them said the best holiday in the world was
Mauritius and again they all agreed. Spoilt or what, they were right
about one thing, the Saint Geran in Mauritius was tailor-made for
our family. This five-star hotel sits on a white sand peninsula
surrounded by turquoise waters, with every luxury provided. While
it is a honeymooners paradise, most of the guests at that time,
tended to be older, so the sports facilities were generally at our
disposal, whether it was the nine-hole golf course, tennis courts,
wind surfing or most importantly, water-skiing.*

*I loved this magical hotel but at night, when I had time to
myself, I felt a great sadness. The flower petals scattered on our*

double bed and the candlelit restaurants surrounded by moonlit water only served to highlight how invisible I had become to Nick. He had stipulated early on in the marriage that there would be no lovemaking at night because he was too tired. I had hoped the relaxed holiday mornings would provide us with a rare opportunity for being intimate. However, he firmly closed that door by booking a water-ski for 6am. I would wake each day to the sound of the boat's engine.

Neither of us had ever liked touching and kissing in public but now there was little affection in private and it was tearing me apart. My pleading and whining only drove him further away. I was so far removed from the proud, feisty girl he had fallen in love with. His wall of silence was insurmountable.

However Nick and I did share a love of heli-skiing. Every other year we flew to Canada with two of his friends. The first three days we spent in the ski resort of Whistler getting over jetlag. Nick would be wide awake at two in the morning with nothing to do so we would have sex. it was not passionate but at least it kept some semblance of a relationship going.

Once we were heli-skiing though, I wasn't bothered. For a week, Nick was my skiing buddy. I was almost always the only female in the group. I became one of the lads and I loved the banter, being pushed to the limit and skiing awesome terrain. In the eighties and early nineties, we would ski in Aspen or Alta and having got over the jetlag, take a Lear jet from the US to Calgary or Edmonton. It was in one of those early years that we arrived at the CMH lodge in the Caribous to find our American friends had dropped out at the last minute (it turned out they had just split up). John Kennedy Junior and his cousin had taken their place.

I was 29 at the time and John 27, so in our group of eleven skiers, I was the nearest to him in age. I remember the first night he was quite distant. The next day, after our safety briefing round the helicopter, I announced that if anyone took my share of the backpack, I would wash their laundry all week in return. Two hands went up with alacrity. So this is my claim to fame. I did John Kennedy junior's rather grey and holey laundry.

John was not the most co-ordinated skier I had ever seen. He lacked rhythm or training. He was an intellectual dreamer, forgetting his poles one minute, his gloves the next. We once searched for an hour before Art, the old boy of the group, found his ski. John couldn't work out from which direction he was coming when he fell, making the area of our search much larger. I remember growing hot and exasperated with digging and told him and his cousin that they needed nannies.

However, we broke all records for the amount of vertical feet a group together ever skied. My name is on a plaque in the Caribous with that of John Kennedy Jnr (when I last looked 14 years ago!)

On our last night, John seated himself next to me at dinner. He told me in depth of 'a cousin' who had a possessive mother who made it difficult for him to find and keep girlfriends. He asked me for my advice. Did my words change the course of history?

In that week we experienced the most stable conditions for sixteen years. We were able to ski on the glacier and one run stands out. Ernst, the head guide, led us down a slope so steep and deep and yet with snow so light, it felt like skiing in space. On reaching the bottom, we looked back but there were no tracks at all. The snow had closed back in on itself; an unearthly experience which sadly we never repeated.

Another amazing run I remember, was called 'Free Fall'. Cushions of the lightest, fluffiest snow had collected in crevices and by jumping from one to the other, we dropped down an almost vertical rock face. This was canyon territory and almost impossible to scale without ropes in summer. We had descended in winter with just two planks of laminated wood attached to our feet. I loved being in the moment, living on the edge, and felt a far cry from the housewife in Putney with clipped wings.

I remember skiing to one side of a trail and getting the strongest animal scent. I asked the guide what it could be, and he told me that we were crossing a stream and I had smelt a bear hibernating under its bank. Nick and I once paused in a wood for breath and saw a paw print about 1.5 ft. long. It was fresh and, unnervingly, there was only one.

I'm my happiest skiing in trees. It's like doing a giant slalom course with the excitement of not knowing what's round each corner. I always feel at home in pine forests, summer or winter. I've been told by a medium that I lived as a native American on the American/Canadian border, and belonged to the Lakota tribe. So at 39-years old, I was ecstatic to go with Nick, his business partner Alex and friend Adie, to the Monashees, to experience its famous 'deep and steep' pine-clad terrain. On the first morning I was surprised to see two other women in the group. So, it appeared, was the French Canadian ski guide Jean Francois. He told us with disdain that this lodge was for expert skiers only, that he had a cold and would give only one instruction: "SFD – Straight Fucking

Down". If we lost him, it was our own fault. Any questions? One of the American women, a brilliant skier it transpired, asked if we could enjoy ourselves.

Adie, Alex, and I lost John Francois after six turns on the third run. We traversed back in his direction, only to find the helicopter was making a high pickup and had stopped above us. One hour later we managed to sidestep in cup crystal snow to the others.

"You should have followed my tracks," Jean Francois said. The whole group thereafter became headless and paranoid. I decided to stick behind a two million foot veteran Monashee skier if I lost sight of the guide. That afternoon four others had done the same thing and we were, we learnt from radio contact, a quarter mile from everyone else.

We hiked along a logger's trail and eventually came across the group. "You should have followed my tracks," said Jean Francois again.

"Which of the eleven fucking tracks is that?" I shouted at him before I could stop myself. Let's just say that was only the start of it. My group tried to calm me down, the guide did a runner and in fifteen minutes was replaced by a young Austrian.

We never had Jean Francois again. I told Tom, the guy in the boot room, the saga. The next morning I saw that, "The Evil Victoria" had been written in indelible pen on my skis.

It didn't end there. When Adie went to get a drink at the bar that night, some bruiser from the top all-male group turned to him and said, "Did you hear of the fucking stupid group who lost Jean Francois?

"I was in that fucking stupid group!" replied Adie. A few days later, group one skied with Jean Francois and also got lost. That

night Adie went up to the same man. "Did you hear of the fucking stupid group who lost Jean Francois today?" Childish but satisfying.

Violence

Movies contrive to give the impression that violence in prisons is endemic. In England statistics are often advanced to show increases in attacks on screws and other convicts but the reality is less fraught. One thing most cons in Bang Kwang had in common was an enormous stretch yet to come. The best way, not only to survive but retain 'excellent status' for a reduction in sentence, was <u>not</u> to engage in unnecessary conflict (while always being ready to stand up if attacked, naturally) and since the average age in this maximum security facility was considerably higher than is common in the usual run of gaols, the testosterone fuelled mayhem portrayed on screen was exceptional rather than the norm.

On the other hand an inconsequential thing, the non-return of a spoon or a cup say, might trigger a bloody fight, or even a brawl if Thais from two different groups became involved, but such things were a 'nine-day wonder', as William Kemp would put it. Mostly the causes of any violence were financial disputes or previously existing friction such as Hong Kongers versus Singaporeans, or simply a build-up of bad blood between two erstwhile pals. Some Nigerians nursed impressive grudges and spent considerable mental and physical energy on keeping them going. I suppose it was something to do.

2007

Samantha and I made a New Year's resolution to visit Andy's mother, Danuta. We were expecting the door to be opened by a woman bowed down with grief. Instead a slim, smiling Meryl Streep greeted us.

Her first question to Samantha was, "Does Andy have a beard?"

When Samantha confirmed this, she breathed a sigh of relief. Afterwards, I asked my daughter what all that was about? She told me that to be allowed to keep the beard was a sign of Andy's exemplary behaviour. It was also the mark of respect shown by the screws to an older person.

Danuta, upright and elegant, invited us in for tea. While she prepared a tray in the kitchen, we were left to look around the living room at all the framed photos displayed everywhere. I couldn't help noticing that the blond, blue eyed smiling boy became, in the later photos, a moody, taciturn teenager. There was one photo in particular that caught my eye. His brothers, dark and slim, were standing and smiling at the camera. Andy was slouched on the ground, a forbidding Nordic presence refusing to show any animation. There were also one or two photos of a bearded adult alone. [29]

On that first visit, Danuta wouldn't be drawn into talking about Andy at all. Instead she talked about a book called 'Possession' which she ended up giving me. It was absolutely gripping when I did read it and I realised that she and I were on a similar spiritual path.

The next time we visited Danuta, the only thing she wanted to talk about was Andy. I think on that first occasion she was embarrassed. She had never met us before, did not know if we knew *anything about Andy, barring pen-pal platitudes and did not want to say anything that she shouldn't and might later regret.*

I wrote my fourth letter to Andy, letting him know of our visit. I didn't know it then but other than a Christmas card, I wouldn't write to Andy again for fifteen months.

*

Andy, Block Six, Bang Kwang, 2007

Andy to Vicky, 5th Letter

25 July 2007

Dear Vicky

Firstly, my sincere and profound apologies for not writing to you sooner. Actually I had begun a letter to you as far back as the end of April and then, after writing several pages, I put it to one side and was laid low by a succession of illnesses, none of which were major in themselves but which in combination, contrived to leave me in an altogether exhausted state.

Even after I had somewhat recovered from the effects, which were exacerbated by the oppressive heat and humidity lasting from April to the end of June, I was still not mentally ready to put pen to paper [...]

[...] Now to your question; yes, I did receive the books, including the signed one by Johnnie Mortimer – I beg his illustrious pardon, Sir John – and I'd like to thank you for going to the trouble of getting him to inscribe it personally; also to thank him for doing so. I've always liked Rumpole, both in print and in the excellent television series. I've also admired John Mortimer for a long time. He has been a champion of free speech and true justice for a number of decades [...].

26 July

I had to stop yesterday when the power to the fans went off and the temperature rose sharply to very uncomfortable levels. When the current returned, a storm blew up and darkened the sky, the wind blowing rain in over everything. Even with power, there is no artificial light available during our daylight hours outside the block. On the other hand, the lights during the fifteen hours we are locked up within the cells cannot be switched off. [...]

[...] I am glad that you and Sam went to see my mother, who then sent me some photos to show that you were there. Her expertise with a computer meant that these photos were printed on ordinary paper, which hardly seems like the real thing to me, but then I am old-fashioned in that regard. I've never owned, nor wanted to own, a computer of any kind. I've always said that I'll ignore computers until such time as they evolve to the *Star Trek* standard. Perhaps I am just a Luddite at heart.

Fri 27 July

Today I have just said goodbye to an old Thai man who is being released. He has been a prisoner since September 1980, twenty-six years and ten months. [...] Back in May, another Thai chap, a few cells up from mine was not so fortunate. He died of a heart attack about 8pm or so. A medical orderly was summoned, who, without entering the cell said, "Yep, he's dead alright" and left. The body remained in situ amongst its former cellmates... until the morning. Only then did a cop with fingerprint gear come and the family was informed. Indeed, they arrived at the gaol to claim the body for cremation. [...]

[...] It's becoming the norm in Europe, I believe, to dispose of the dead by burning. I can't say that I like the idea myself; the notion of 'a decent Christian burial' is perhaps too deeply rooted in my mind to approve of such heathen practices. I am sure the Bible has something to say on the matter. [...]

[...] The oddest method of disposing of the bodies of the dead must be that of the Farsi or Zoroastrians, still practised in India. They leave the corpses out in the open, usually in a high exposed place. In the cities this generally means the top of a high building. The idea is that the vultures should 'recycle' the flesh, all very 'green' no doubt, but the citizenry tend to make loud noises of outraged complaint when gobbets of flesh and bits of bone rain down on them, vultures not being renowned for their finicky eating habits.

The power has been cut again, the third time today – I have absolutely no idea what they are playing at, it is only our section at the back that is without power. I shall have to continue some other time, else the page will be spotted with drops of sweat from my fevered brow (bad eyesight and fading light requires me to bend forward to within inches of the page) [30] [...].

[...] Here it has rained at least once and often three or four times a day for weeks now. A big thunder and lightning storm will last for an hour, cooling the air wonderfully. The sun will then break through, blue sky and white cloud will be around for a while and in the space of two or three minutes we are back in stormy weather. [...] The rush to 'develop' the place led to most of the canals being filled in, with predictable results, i.e., the streets awash every rainy season. The inadequate (I am being polite here) sewerage system regularly fails to contain its raison d'etre and the rainy season is also the 'season of sickness'.

Changing the subject, how did you fare on your mission to transform the newly acquired hotel? You said the architecture looked East German. [...] I assume you mean the style we used to call 'Soviet Brutalist'. [...] My aunt Dorothy used to be the manager of a 'Novotel' down in southern Poland, which being relatively new actually used to function reasonably efficiently [...] but it never ceased to amaze me that you could go into a hotel restaurant [...] at lunchtime for a meal and find a sign up saying 'closed for staff lunch'. I am not making this up! [...]

My regards and best wishes go to all of you.

Yours once more from the gulag

Andy

Corsica, 2007

Once all our children were at boarding school, I was desperate to get back to work. Nick offered me a trial job of doing up his Austrian pizzeria on a shoestring budget. I went with my twin sister Sarah, as we'd worked together on decorative finishes before having children. Donning overalls and head torches we painted the whole place red and green and white. I'd had curtains made and my daughter Emma painted a series of abstract paint-spattered pictures. I brought Peter out from England, a wonderful Polish builder, to do electric and plumbing work and line the bar with green and red mirror.

Nick's takings doubled so I was then sent to do up a nightclub in France. This time I hired my sister Sarah, my brother-in-law Ben, a friend of his who was a graffiti artist, four sixth formers which included Tom, two cousins, and my friend Suzanne's daughter. I drove the lorry with Jacek, our Polish builder, through the night, rattling with paint, paintings and sheets of coloured glass. With my theatre design background kicking in, we went to town, mixing Baroque and Street. By the time the nightclub was ready to open, we had reupholstered the leather seating and hung striped taffeta curtains in reds, greens, purples and blacks. On the black walls I painted giant gold roses cascading down and hung rococo mirrors.

Canvases were mounted of black and white photos depicting skiers with red skateboards or purple skis. Graffiti in the same palette was everywhere. The three bars were distinguished by being mirrored in either red, green or purple.

From that job I earned my stripes to tackle the hotels in the company portfolio that were on 10-year leases and needed some life injected into them. A beach hotel in Corsica was one such. It had originally been built as a casino by the Corsican mafia. This was the first time since the seventies that a sizeable amount of money was to be spent on it. I had been told that the owner and his sons were tricky. I found them to be the opposite. The owner, a plumber by trade, was not impressed when foreigners in suits turned up to tell him what to do. He warmed to me though when I volunteered to paint the stairwells on the rickety scaffolding he'd rigged up. None of the decorators on site would touch them because they weren't insured. I didn't think I was, but someone needed to do the job. On my first day, I was so nervous, I left a sweaty handprint on the wall. Two weeks in and I was balancing on one foot and leaning out over the void to cut in.

The first task I gave the team was to get rid of every glass door and all the obsolete air-conditioning ducts. Together, the architect and I designed 10-foot high hotel entrance doors in ebonized wood, chrome and glass, which when open, gave the guests a view through the reception areas to the sea. I got the thumbs up from Nick for the whole hotel to be painted terracotta, with cream canvas awnings everywhere.

My next battle was to get the pools painted yellow so that, when filled, the water would look pale sea green. My specialist painting team found the extra hours to do the two larger pools before their contract ended. I was left to paint the baby pool myself. All would have been fine, but I was suddenly told by Andre, the hotel manager, that the deadline for filling the pool was 24-hours. By 4pm on a Sunday, my last roller had disintegrated from the *chemicals in the paint. No problem, I thought; I had some mini rollers to hand but by 7pm they had also disintegrated. By 9pm, in the pitch-black, I was down to my last 1" brush and praying it would finish the job. Francois, the good-looking French handyman, wandered over to say that the kitchen had plated up some supper for me. "Vicky", he says in the sexiest Parisian voice imaginable, "have you heard of a company called 'Club Mediterraneé?' I am sure you could find a job with them for better pay and better hours."*

I was conscious, as the main hotel became transformed, that the grounds were now looking shabby. With three days left until the guests arrived, I was trying to persuade Jean-Marc, the hotel owner's son and groundsman, that all the plants, barring seven evergreen trees and bushes around the front entrance, would have to go and to put white pebbles in their place. I was trying for a clean Zen look. I told him to imagine the entrance as a theatre. Seven black figures standing silent was a powerful look. Lots of colourful fairies dancing round, while pretty, would weaken the effect. I persuaded him to create a single rose bed on the other side of the driveway for the 'fairies'.

While I was working a 12-hour day, I was sleeping in staff accommodation away from the hotel, in a room that, for some inexplicable reason, flooded every morning under and around my bed. The ceiling's polystyrene squares used to fall into my hands as I got out of the shower.

Eventually the hot water was turned on in the hotel itself, so after dark, I ventured up for a bath. Without thinking, I stripped off and only then realized the bathroom I had wandered into had no plug. Starkers, I slipped into the bathroom next door. No plug there either. Two floors and twenty baths later I found a plug, but foolishly hadn't registered the number of my original bathroom, the one with my clothes in it – luckily, I never ran into the night porter.

My painting team were gone but the wives of Francois and Jacek agreed to step in as decorators to help paint the hotel signage with me. At 9pm, with 48-hours to go until the guests arrived, we persuaded the tallest man on site to climb up our scaffolding and on tiptoe, in flipflops, paint the last few inches of the entrance sign. At 9pm, with 24-hours to go, we got the stuccoed entrance wall painted, by handing passing staff a roller and tray and asking each person to give ten minutes of their time.

On my last night André hosted a dinner for me with the managers. Raising a glass of champagne he said, "Here's to Vicky, whose stubborn pig-headedness got this hotel open on time." In truth, it opened on time because everyone rallied together as a team and worked beyond the call of duty, but still, thanks André for the compliment.

*

Vicky to Andy, 4th Letter (Unfinished, Unsent)

December 2007

Dear Andy

I am <u>so</u> sorry I haven't managed to write to you before now but I've been working around the clock since September to get three hotels refurbished for Nick my husband's company. I only got your letter when I returned from Portugal in September and I was delighted after not hearing from you for so long.

So much has happened in the year since I last wrote to you. On the good front, I spent from March to July refurbishing the incredibly tired hotel in Corsica that I told you about. Nick had to look after the children for ten weekends. I took a team with me, of specialist painters – well; impoverished but highly talented art graduates, my sister and a friend who can do everything from wallpapering and painting to upholstering a bar in leather. Ours was one of three teams; the other two were a larger Polish crew and a smaller group of English builders. The hotel looked like something out of the Eastern Bloc, but positioned in the most beautiful location, two hundred metres from the sea, with a mountain range as backdrop.

The highest peak seemed to beckon me, so on the two days I had off, I climbed it – first, with a 21-year-old waterfront assistant manager – we took nine hours from start to finish which included being chased by wild boars. He ended up telling me his life story which was that he had been sexually abused by the headmaster of his choir school. Six boys agreed to testify, but five of the victims backed out at the last minute. This 12-year-old had to stand trial alone. He lost and because of the ensuing press and publicity, the family had to leave their home and he had to change his name. Then he proceeds to tell me he got a girl pregnant who he doesn't love and who is having the baby in October (now gone). I tried to give him the best advice I could, given his quest to travel the world. I never saw him again because the next day he got transferred to another hotel. [...] [31]

My second climb was with the head Polish builder Jacek, where I was lucky to come out alive.

He and I decided to follow the river from estuary to source. We followed a babbling brook to two waterfalls [...] Fixed ropes led to a rock pool. Behind that was a 30-metre rock-face with no ropes. Jacek managed to find a way up but I got stuck. He broke off, tested and then held out a branch, bracing himself to take my weight. Just as I started to freeze with fear, because one false move and I would fall to my death, I could see, as if magnified, the places to put my feet and so abseiled up to safety. Thank God the stick held.

Three hours later we reached the source but there was no way I was going back down the same route, A dense fog *had closed round us so the only thing for it was to stay in the woods and work our way down to the mountain road. We were in the 'maquis'.[32] Brambles dripped in barbed-wire festoons from the trees. We parted them with our hands, trying not to cut ourselves. Our hair tangled up in the thorns while our back legs, catching on the lower tendrils, sent us sprawling in the mud and boar tics.*

Three hours later we reached the road as the light was going. I looked as if someone had lacerated me with a razor blade in a crosshatched pattern all over my limbs. Now, half a year later, you can still see some of the scars. My left ankle was dripping blood.

Looking back and seeing the waterfalls side-on, my knees started knocking. It was almost vertical for 1,000 feet.

The whole climb took 11 hours round trip. Now you can see why I am going on about it.

*

I was in the process of writing this to Andy in December 2007. However, I never completed or sent this letter because I was in a state of shock. 'On the good front' I could communicate. 'On the bad front' I simply couldn't face telling him.

The First Discovery

Meribel

November 2007

"Freddie was found drunk and has been suspended."

I was stirring a white sauce in the hotel kitchen, with the phone tucked into my shoulder, so I could only just hear my sister Boozy's anxious voice passing on the news of my nephew's latest school escapade. As I rang off, I made a comment about Freddie's father's drinking to a few of the painting team who were also preparing supper. Sarah, Freddie's mother and my twin-sister, came in at that moment, overheard me and justifiably went ballistic. When I had steered us both out of earshot, she blurted out...

"Get your own stable in order!" Silence.

"Explain what you mean by that," I said, "or get off this building-site."

In the split second before Sarah spoke, every sinew in my body screamed, a piercing sound rang in my ears, the hairs on my arms stood on end. She began to shake uncontrollably and then blurted out that Nick had been having affairs for the last ten years.

I felt as if the ground was giving way under me. Pandora's box had been opened, I knew nothing would be the same again. I had wasted my love and loyalty on a man who didn't care a damn about me. My life with him had been an illusion. The image I had of myself was well and truly shattered. All my fears had been well-founded but this realisation provided no comfort. I knew deep down it was the beginning of the end of the marriage.

It took all my willpower not to grab the black paint we had on site and graffiti abuse all over the hotel's walls. Instead, Sarah helped me ring round everyone I trusted during our breaks. All, barring two people, knew about Nick's affairs. One friend simply said, "ask your children".

Feeling sick to my stomach, I rang Samantha during our morning coffee break. She burst into tears and told me she had found out, aged thirteen, after accidentally reading a text on Nick's phone. I felt terrible having to ring off and go back to work, so during the tea break six hours later, I tried her again and she was still crying.

She had kept this secret to herself until five years later; in 2004, Emma, Tom and William also found out after seeing a text on Nick's phone. We were in Portugal and I had gone on a run. Tom, age fifteen, accosted Nick, who confessed. Tom told him to give up 'the woman' and to come clean with me. Nick told them he would, if they promised not to tell me themselves. Had it really taken me ten years to find this out? What a secret for my children to have borne alone for so long.

I had been warned by one friend I rang that, when I confronted him, Nick's first words on admitting to infidelity would be "only once". She said it was a standard response. When I got back to England and accosted him, Nick's first words to me were "only once." He refused to say anything more, so that night the whole family gathered in the kitchen. Nick looked pale and drawn. Samantha did most of the talking, telling Nick that he owed it to me to tell the truth. She said that if we were to divorce, there would be no question who we would live with. "Mum has brought us up." Nick didn't say a word.

A few days later, when Nick came into the kitchen, I asked him to sit down.

"I'm just off to do the food shop. Your father is arriving to stay for Christmas in four hours. If you don't tell me the truth, I am going to take myself off for a few days and you will have to explain what has happened to the children and Dennis and organise four days of meals on your own. I can only sit here for fifteen minutes. Any later and I won't have enough time to get round the supermarket."

We were sitting at opposite ends of the kitchen table. I looked down at my phone. Five minutes passed. Silence. Ten minutes passed. Silence. Just as I started to get up and go, Nick's whole body began to shake involuntarily. One word emerged,

"Ten."

"Ten what?"

"Ten years."

He told me that he had spent ten years seeing call girls and prostitutes and would meet them in Vienna or Paris.

I asked Nick whether he had fallen in love with any of these women. He said, "yes", but that the affair was now over. I said, "didn't he ever worry about transmitting sexual diseases to me?" Silence. "Were there any children out of these liaisons?" Silence, and then, "not that I know of." I knew he was telling me the minimum, but other than "ten", I wasn't convinced I'd heard the truth. This had been the pattern of our conversations for years; me bombarding him with questions, he returning my gaze in silence or giving me evasive answers. I could sense I wasn't going to get any more out of him. At least I hadn't resorted to my usual pleading or whining.

I don't know how I got through the festivities without giving the game away. The children and I found the faking of Christmas cheer to friends and relatives almost impossible. Coincidentally, for New Year, we had booked the hotel in Meribel where only a few weeks before I had found out about Nick's infidelity. On New Year's Eve we went to Nick's business partner's chalet. I felt so miserable that, as William had a temperature, I used him as an excuse to get back to the hotel well before midnight. There didn't seem to be any reason to celebrate the future, which I saw stretching interminably ahead of me. I held back the tears until William was in bed and then cried into my pillow.

From this point on, the breathlessness and arthritic pain in my left knee worsened. At night, the sense of loneliness was overwhelming. By day I was rushed off my feet which kept the black dog at bay.

2008

Vicky to Andy, 5th Letter

10th June 2008

Dear Andy

Five months plus since I last wrote to you. I know that's unforgivable but trust me they've been psychologically among the worst in my life. I suspect the response from you to that remark is, you Vicky aren't even off first base in the hell stakes. Maybe, but I never had a proper boyfriend before Nick because I was never prepared to go out/live with someone who wasn't <u>the</u> *one – couldn't see the point. As a result I invested everything in the marriage, literally for better or worse etc. [...] till death us do part. Ten years ago, possibly by a gradual process of immersion in children, home, etc, versus his business abroad, he relegated me to loyal housekeeper and found sex elsewhere. So I haven't fared much better than you in that department!*

Having found out from my sister in November that, "everybody knows Nick's been unfaithful," I also found out that Samantha, age thirteen, picked up an email, guessed and without going off the rails, kept it to herself. Five years ago, my other children intercepted a message from a woman. They accosted him and made him promise to drop her [...] In return they wouldn't tell me. [...]

Well the truth is out now, although he won't give me more than an outline and so my head goes round and round with the possible permutations of the last decade (was it longer?). Sometimes I think I might go mad. Certainly I don't sleep much [...] I am more irritable, and find I can't relish life like I used to.

The children have been fantastic, jollying me along, giving me more hugs than usual. It didn't quite extend to Tom working really hard for his A levels though. That was definitely asking too much! He's been offered a place at Leeds reading Broadcast Journalism. He refused to apply for anything else, "Not interested." The jammy bugger got offered 3 Bs (one of 35 out of 500 applicants) [...] It looks like it might be A/B/C in which case he's going to have to use all his powers of persuasion, so that he doesn't have to blow his gap year with retakes. Well, we all wait until 14 August for results and go from there.

Back to the bigger problem. Sorry Andy, but it's going to be a letter full of self-pity, which is just about all you need. I told Nick that when he had a crisis in his business, he got the best experts to advise him. I said our marriage was in crisis and we needed to see the best marriage expert [...]. Three months later we had our first session with Keith. This councillor gave me hell, but in the second session on my own, he apologised and said it had been a strategy to even the playing field, to give Nick a reason to come back. We went to two more sessions separately. On the third session Keith gave me a questionnaire to fill in. On a scale of 1-6 do you change your mind, all the time ... sometimes ... never? Are you concerned about what people think of you ... all the time ... sometimes ... never? Are you influenced by your close friends ... all the time ... sometimes ... never? And so on.

Apparently, I have an ability to adapt (not hugely), am a borderline loner, and am not totally self-confident,[33] *[...] He said that Nick portrayed a personality that had absolutely no inclination to adapt or change. [...] He said that, in thirty years, he had never come across such an inflexible personality.*

He concluded by saying that we could patch up our marriage, but that in time Nick would get bored and stray again. He said I would be, "deeply unhappy." Our profiles really didn't fit.

Since then, and it's been two weeks, Nick has been making a real effort with me. On his birthday he took us all (children and me) to a restaurant I adore in Barnes. He's played golf with me twice. [...]

[...] Keith says that in my quest for truth and justice, I mustn't, "over egg" my point now but just to let things go; I think he means don't nag. Maybe now the stuffing has been knocked out of me, I will be easier to live with. Keith said to me that people in history who fought for truth and justice rarely got want they wanted. I said, then how did he explain Nelson Mandela? I got him there! Silence in response.

8.25am 27 June Friday

I've been given three tired hotels in Val d'Isere to refurbish. [...] This whole episode has made me determined to stand on my own two feet, to have a website, become computer literate [...]. My sister, Sarah, comes once a week to give me a lesson. Watch this space Andy. I might be down but I am not out!

Samantha has finished her degree and got a 2.1. She's standing here in the kitchen emptying the dishwasher with 'official programmes' printed on her black shirt because she's about to go to Wimbledon to sell programmes. She never stops. She's trying to break into the film/TV production world, so is looking for a runner/secretarial position, to get her foot in the door.

Emma has moved out with Luis, her guitarist boyfriend, to a flat in Camden. She's got one more year at Art College [...] has a job on the side designing shoes for the supplier of Top Shop.

William, my youngest, has just broken his collarbone, so five weeks minimum no sport. He'll go mad, as he's not what you'd call a bookworm. He was skateboarding down a steep grass hill and came a cropper.

I've got my 50th this year. I've asked Simon and Lauren to make a 5-minute speech each and I was wondering whether you could write something that Samantha could read out [...] While we haven't met, you know more about my inner life than 99% of the people I know. Anyway no pressure. You don't have to but it would mean a lot to me as you are in my thoughts in one way or another almost every day.

[...] Hopefully Tom gets to Thailand on his travels and comes to see you next year. He's not as pretty as the other two but he's got a good wit and a good heart. A favourite with the grandmothers.

Andy, do write. I love receiving your letters. I am just about to go into the dentist, so I'll sign off now.

Love and best wishes

Vicky

*

This letter is remarkably clear and upbeat given my mental state at the time. I remember being so glad to get the bloody events of Nick's confession out there to at least one person who might understand the pain if nothing else. I was having suicidal thoughts at that time, but knowing Andy and his depressive state following Denise's death, I was underplaying my own emotional fragility. There were days when I didn't want to get out of bed, many nights when I couldn't be bothered to undress. That November, I was doing up five hotels in the French Alps and was given one of the hotel vans to ferry myself, my crew and materials between Val d'Isere and Tignes. I worked on my own and drove fairly recklessly, once in the early hours spinning the vehicle a full 360 degrees. It narrowly missed the parked cars and ploughed into a snow bank. I had a death wish, so wasn't too bothered. There must have been some sense of self-preservation though, because I still said my prayers on my knees by the bed and brushed my teeth. When I closed my eyes to pray, all I could see was Nick humping women of all shapes and sizes. When I wasn't formally praying, I was literally begging God to get me through another day. At church I was overwhelmed by murderous thoughts but as I walked out, prayer came easily. I used to teach my children to say sorry, thank and ask God when they prayed. 'Sorry' and 'thank you' had gone out of the window. All I asked for, now, was truth and justice to clarify the situation and the ability – each second, minute and hour – not to lose the plot completely and find my children taken from me.

*

Screws

The salaries paid to prison guards are not high, though higher than that of the average agricultural worker, or low-level factory hand. However they do enjoy a level of job security and benefits unknown to the majority of the working population. A little help given a prisoner for a small contribution, something for the rice bowl, or 'tea money', leads to larger and more organised scamming, often of the machine that is employing them. The odd carton of imported cigarettes becomes a couple of ounces of heroin, a few magazines evolves into the wholesale and retail disposition of TVs, videos and computer games.

The interaction between screws and cons, to the financial gain of one and the satisfactory material benefit of the other, requires trust and respect. Sadists, martinets and jobsworths do not fit this bill. It is the jovial, the happy-go-lucky, the helpful, and the non-judgmental type of prison officer who thrives. They work nights and days, sometimes 80-hour weeks. Less than half of the 250 or so screws on the payroll are assigned to duty within the individual blocks and their compounds. This duty is considered highly desirable for its access to the steady trickle of un-official cash that keeps the machine going.

The screws spend more time with the prisoners than with their wives and families or with their 'mia noi' or minor wives. They can only afford the minor wife, the new pick-up truck and the well-appointed house because of the extra money they make in their dealings with the cons. In some cases this can be a matter of several times their official salaries. They don't have to fake being happy and friendly: they really are.

As far as I know, all of Thailand's prisons are laid out as separate cell blocks, each sitting in a walled compound of a much larger area. Originally the prisoners were expected to grow a quantity of their own food. Each block is run as a semi-autonomous fiefdom by its building chief.

The graft starts there, with a working building that specialises in, say, furniture-making, taking and filling orders from buyers outside, that never show up in any paperwork. The convict labour might be paid a pittance. The best of them will get better wages and be provided with small necessities or luxuries, be relatively pampered, in order to keep them sweet.

The six big blocks are different. Here there is some extremely badly paid work, usually for outside contractors, but only a fraction, less than half, of the convicts would be engaged in it. Avoidance of this tedious and unrewarding labour can be secured by payment of two or three hundred baht a month. Multiply by the four, five or six hundred who happily fork out that sum and already the nucleus of the screws retirement fund is in place. Call it a hundred thousand baht a month, 1.2 million baht (£25,000) per year, per block.

The screws' ranks seem to be mostly attained through the passage of time, reflecting their education and perceived social status. The chiefs were in the best position of all. They would keep something like office hours, 7.30 or 8am in the block, off by 4pm or even earlier. They would not work weekends. Some repeatedly refused promotion in order to maintain their income stream and the easy nature of their day. Most screws didn't do very much but the chief did bugger all. Once I saw a long-serving chief sitting back, relaxing in his comfortably padded chair in his air-conditioned office. He was being ministered to by no fewer than six Thai convicts, two massaging his legs, two more his arms and the final two using tweezers to pluck his ear hairs! He was like some dissolute sultan being pampered by eunuchs. Come to think of it, a couple were lady-boys, though that isn't quite the same thing at all!

When I arrived, almost every cell had at least one television. In the forty-eight cells in our block, which housed over a thousand men, there were probably 150 TVs, if one includes the dozen or so in each of the two corridors.

They had been brought in by a screw and the Nick-up per set had to reflect, not only the time and effort put in by that screw, but the backhander to the screws on the various gates he passed on his way in. CD and DVD players were smuggled in from the notorious floating market at Nonthaburi, just a short way downstream from Bang Kwang. The tapes and discs might be bought as a job lot by a prisoner, who then either sold them or rented them out piecemeal. The screw would either get the cash up front or had a slightly different arrangement.

Cash was forbidden but of course it was there, in the millions of baht, greasing the machine. The only realistic way for it to come into the prison was in a guard's pocket. Occasionally it would be passed to him by an outsider as cash, along with his commission, ten per cent on small amounts and five per cent on larger ones. Most often it was easier to simply pay the money directly into an account. The card would then be given to a favoured screw.

A constant fresh supply of cash from without was essential to the continued smooth running of the money river, and the screws were eager to facilitate this current.

The purchase of food, packaged and fresh, was allowed by prisoners. Officially we could spend up to 200 baht per day (later 300) with no deferrals from one day to another. The stock ordered was supposed to correspond with the orders by individual prisoners but this system was comprehensively ignored. Prisoners were happy to pay slightly more (between 10% and 50% in fact) for immediate access rather than wait two days for delivery, which might not even happen. The screws used part of the cash to buy the supplies and kept the rest. They were silent partners in the food supply chain, with a literally captive market.

The block shops sold soap, toothpaste, and toothbrushes, washing powder, shampoo, shaving cream, mirrors, buckets, charcoal burning ovens and the charcoal to make them work. They sold bread, eggs, milk, coffee, coffee-mate, tea, sugar, cooking oil, margarine, Coca-Cola, Pepsi, energy drinks, lemonade, Lipton Iced Tea and sometimes three different kinds of ice-cream. There was a profusion of different cakes and biscuits and potato crisps, peanuts and cashews, four sorts of jam, marmalade and peanut butter. I couldn't get Marmite though and I went through withdrawal for a few years.

A separate shop sold fresh meat, fruit and vegetables, and was also open seven days a week, every day of the year, regardless of holidays. It was all marked up by about 30% but it was there if and when you needed it. If your credit was good, well, you weren't going anywhere and many did in fact buy on credit, paying at the end of the month.

The actual running of the shops, including all the bookkeeping, was done by convicts, who made just enough from this work to cover their own food bills with perhaps a little left over. Many, with no support from outside, also did work for other prisoners, cooking, laundry, electrical and TV repairs. A few ran tiny restaurants, and many with an entrepreneurial streak, ran tiny stalls in what was in effect a market area, located in the dining hall next to the Africa House.

Since clothing, sheets, blankets and pillows were not provided, a thriving retail sector arose to fill the gap. A parcel or a donated sackful from a visit might be the start of a career as a market trader. The screws made no money out of this line, but allowed it to continue in the interests of the common good.

My allowance of £90 a quarter from the UK charity, 'Prisoners Abroad,' was sufficient for my needs, but was in no way representative of the cash stream throughout Bang Kwang. It was a mere tributary to the real golden goose, or perhaps geese.

A drily academic book by a couple of Thai university professors was entitled *Guns, Girls, Gambling and Ganja*, these being the four pillars of organised crime in the country.

Although the first two pillars were definitely out, the other two were major enterprises in Bang Kwang, one building chief in Building Two became briefly famous for his ability to provide beer by the pallet-load and Johnny Walker Red, Black or Blue Label at extremely high prices (up to £50 per bottle).

Block Two was notorious as a junkies building (even in a prison with scores of junkies in EVERY block) and the revenue stream from this was immense. Where the other enterprises were so commonplace, so overt that concealment was barely considered necessary, here it was essential.

The ease with which heroin was available demonstrates the flow rate of narcotics into the prison. The prices charged approached those on the street in Europe or America. Even though the stuff was heavily cut, the daily consumption must have been in the order of 40 or 50 grams of pure heroin in my block alone. It was being used on death row and in solitary. Sometimes a prisoner would check himself into the hospital (Building Twelve) to try and stop himself using the stuff, but they'd usually fall right back into it when returned to their building. Every single screw knew that drug use was widespread, but if some nitwit was caught with drugs on his person, no attempt was made to ascertain where he had obtained it, since the answer might implicate a fellow officer, and that way lay a can of worms.

Once the drugs were in the block, the business end was in the hands of the convicts. A large consignment might first go to a single prisoner. He would then determine the price per ounce. The retailers, usually Nigerian or Thai-Chinese would then put out the tiny wraps, using runners to deliver to the end users.

An example of the cash generated by the trade can be demonstrated by the bankroll seized in the crackdown of 2012. This was forced on the screws from above, and the amount discovered in a locker (which the Nigerians claimed had belonged to a deceased Nigerian named Obi) was pretty big – roughly 900,000 baht (£20,000). A similar figure was found in assorted currencies, mainly Euros, Sterling and US dollars. The second part of this represented 'going home' money. The Thai money was their operating capital and covered their day-to-day expenses.

Since a kilo of uncut heroin was about £8,000 in Bangkok, these lads had substantially increased their investment, even after allowing for the grease to the hand of the screw who brought it in. To the screw, it might be three years official salary.

Although there were instances where convicts died or went blind from drinking inexpertly made prison hooch, I never heard of anyone overdosing on heroin in any Thai prison. On the other hand, the sharing of needles, in the 1980's particularly, resulted in an explosion in the figures for HIV infection, and my early years there saw hundreds of fatalities, until the prison medical authorities (to their credit) instituted up-to-date HIV/AIDs treatment. Theirs was the first and the best such initiative in SE Asia and it's one of the things for which they can be justly praised.

The other pillar of organised crime was gambling. Building Six was known for being the most well-heeled, and the need to fill the hours of wakefulness resulted in a large-scale, wide open, high-rolling gambling culture. Many prisoners liked to lie in the cells during the daytime, as the high ceilings, spinning fans and relative emptiness made them the coolest places to be. So an enterprising convict employed in the administration section hit on the idea of 'charging' convicts to stay in their cells during the day. This was an instant success.

A few, like me, were happy to pay a couple of hundred baht a month to be able to go up in the heat of the afternoon, to nap in a cool cell, or watch a satellite TV. A larger number paid more for all-day access. A screw came up about once an hour, to collect the 'rent' from the guy running the games. The atmosphere was so relaxed that the prisoners felt able to add extra cash to the rent, so that the screw could send a 'boy' up with more Pepsi, water, ice and maybe some nibbles. Before long, a small shop selling all of this, along with a kettle to make coffee, was established in the corridor between the cells. It was a casino, it was Vegas, and it was a huge river of money, far larger even than the drug business, and it was run exclusively by Thais, though anyone could play.

An early warning system, starting at the building's gates, or possibly with a friendly call from one of the outside officers, would warn us of any search by screws from outside the block, or worse, from outside the prison by Department of Correction goons in black commando uniforms and jump boots. When this happened, it was all hands to the pump; screws, trusties and cons alike frantically hiding evidence. Even the TVs and videos were stashed down the un-used back stairwell, the bottom of which was boarded up to prevent detection and the upper gates carefully locked with a rusty padlock, ostensibly untouched for years. This worked for over a decade.

At night, after lock-up and headcount, the games continued. Prisoners notionally assigned to one cell might pay 50 baht or so to be in another for the night's game. Most often they would stand outside the locked door of their cell for the head count then when the screws had gone, wander down the corridor to play mahjong, dominoes, cards or dice for the rest of the night. I generally did quite well at blackjack, but seemed to be practically golden at baccarat. When I left Bambat, I considered myself retired from gambling.

These multi-layered systems of corruption helped create an atmosphere of bustling and vigorous business; there was always something interesting happening somewhere. The screws were so integrated, they would routinely shed uniform (shirt and regulation boots), to wander around – when they could be bothered to leave their air-con guard shacks – in T-shirts and flip-flops, not even carrying a baton or club for protection. If a convict went ape-shit and attacked them, a dozen other convicts would instantly come to their rescue. A population of murderers, rapists, bank robbers, kidnappers, drug dealers and an assortment of corrupt prison guards, somehow contrived security and material satisfaction along with minimum risk. That this actually worked is nothing short of miraculous.

I heard one delightful story to illustrate this. The cops in Bangkok were for years puzzled by the apparent existence of an organisation of car thieves, but couldn't pin-point their premises for re-spraying and re-plating stolen vehicles. After many years, an informant was finally found who could be cracked under pressure. It transpired that an automobile mechanics training school at Klong Prem Prison in Bangkok was receiving stolen vehicles within an hour or two of being plucked from the streets, then subsequently being driven out with a different coloured paint job, new plates and forged papers. Mercedes were a favourite. They got away with it for years.

As I said to my friend once on a visit, "Well, what do you expect, the place is full of criminals and the prisoners are nearly as bad". The guards were, almost to a man, as ready to commit a range of felonies as the convicts they were meant to be in charge of, and indeed occasionally ended up on the wrong side of the equation. This was usually due to a combination of arrogance and ignorance, greed allied with a sense of entitlement, coming with the uniform they wore.

Almost every aspect of day-to-day life in Thailand was ruled by bribery and graft so ingrained in the body politic that it wasn't even worthy of comment. In Thai TV news broadcasts, the English word 'corruption' is used because there is no Thai word with the same negative criminal connotations, a foreign concept indeed.

*

I was avoiding all my old friends, feeling detached or miserable by turns but foolishly one dinner party invitation I did accept. The conversation was tedious in the extreme until one of the guests remarked that his son was going to do a 'Gap year' and that one of his destinations was Thailand.

"It'd be fantastic if your son could visit a friend of mine in Bang Kwang prison. He gets very few visitors."

"Why is he there? Drug trafficking?" (said with suspicion)

"Yes"

"Well, I'm not putting my son in such a dangerous situation. I mean this man might give him something to deliver."

"I don't think so, with a sheet of toughened perspex and a grille dividing them. They would be talking on a phone."

He wriggled out of the conversation at breakneck speed and ignored me for the rest of the evening. I vowed that either I never accepted such an invitation again or spent the rest of my life knocking down prejudice, whether middle class or otherwise.

Book Club

Since discovering that Nick had been cheating on me, I was not sleeping and felt like I was in a permanent twilight zone. Sudoku book after Sudoku book was filled in feverishly.

I had been persuaded to join a book club and at night I dutifully read what seemed like a monthly dose of adultery. Our literary group had been put together to help Julia get over HER cheating husband and they had no idea about mine. Ironically it was Julia who saved me from going mad. She would arrive every month by kicking off her shoes and planting her feet on a coffee table or sofa. She would then proceed to dis any book she hadn't chosen. Her arguments allowed no room for dissent and were nearly always polar opposites to mine. I rarely came up with the quick repartee. However, the next day on my run, instead of looking at every tree for its gallows potential, I would try and come up with some arguments of merit. She even sparked anger in me, rather than the indifference I felt for everyone else. In hindsight, I loved our book club, but at the time it was literally all I could do to engage.

Now I look back with fondness at the six of us, so much less boring than the characters in 'Jane Austen's book club'. Helen was the chairman and instigator of the whole affair. She nearly always spoke first and set the viewpoint for everyone else. For a time we had Sandy who was completely deaf, so we had to sit opposite her in order for her to lip read. Her preferred method of discussion was to lecture us for five minutes and then fall silent. We had Jenny in the group, who announced at the first meeting that she was dyslexic and loathed reading. She would download summaries of all the books and if necessary get her children to read them. When it was her turn to choose a book, she would take the advice of her husband or the local bookshop owner which meant that she never put herself in the firing line. I, on the other hand, picked my absolute favourites. On one occasion, I decided to choose the short biography as my topic and picked 'Dibs'. 'The Butterfly and the Diving Bell' and 'The Last Lecture', knowing that Jenny could read one at least and therefore contribute. We had invited my friend Antonia to see if she wanted to join. Everyone gave me the thumbs up for 'Dibs' and 'The Diving Bell'. However Julia waved her copy of 'The Last Lecture' in my face and told me with disdain that she resented paying good money for it! I found myself unable to speak for fear of hurling bad language at her or the plate of smoked salmon sandwiches I had left on the table. Luckily, the dishwasher came to my rescue and I loaded it as loudly as I could, which the others correctly guessed was the signal for everyone to leave. Antonia remained for a post mortem. I said I was so sorry that this was to be not only her first book club but her last, "Oh no!" she said "I've never had so much fun. To watch you and Julia sparring is entertainment I'd pay good money for."

Andy to Vicky, 6th Letter

16 July 2008

Dear Vicky

I just received your letter. [...] I did write several sides to try and convey what I felt for you at the time, but discarded both efforts as 'not fit for purpose'. [...]

[...] I was deeply saddened and distressed by your news. Meeting your daughters, your subsequent letters to me, all of this put in my mind a picture of a happy, healthy, physically and spiritually wholesome family, an ideal to admire and to emulate. Knowing how badly I felt about the disillusionment following your revelation, I almost wept for thinking how it must have affected you. I am truly sorry that this has happened to you Vicky. You are a good-hearted soul and you certainly didn't deserve such treatment. [...]

The only person I talked to of your situation was a sixtyish English lady who was visiting me in late December and January. She herself divorced, advised that you see a lawyer. I replied that you had not arrived at such a pass yet and were a practising Catholic besides. She said simply that you should "think of it as a financial transaction."

[...] On no account allow yourself to be bamboozled with the notion that it takes two to cause a breakdown (break-up?). It only takes one. Your actions and the actions of your children in trying to spare you and to shame him into changing his behaviour are clear evidence that this is so. Regardless of his supposed 'alpha male' status, this puts you, not him, in the drivers' seat from now on. You have already lost that which you cherished and treasured, while he still faces the threat of doing so. This gives you a degree of leverage, not to 'nag' as you put it, but to insist on your due. He was almost certainly counting on your religious belief to avoid any disintegration of his domestic arrangements, not to mention the financial consequences. Being married with a family may well be an important constituent of his self-image, to which the philandering is simply a supplement. [...]

The only advice I can offer you is not to allow yourself to be taken advantage of. [...] I should point out that my own experiences in this area are certainly no model to follow, and that my advice and opinions are therefore suspect, though I hope that my motives can be taken to be sincere. [...] I can add no more on the subject, at least for now, so I'll change abruptly to another.

20 July

The rainy season is upon us – a grey, damp day following a stormy night. Good; it made it cool enough to sleep comfortably. We Brits are in something of a quandary right now [...]. A Royal Princess, no less, well-travelled and educated, is a prime sponsor of the reform and implementation of parole regulations. Parole for foreigners was almost never granted. The meat of the proposal is possible parole after serving one third of a sentence or 10 years of a life sentence

[...] The purpose of parole is, after all, to give the prisoner a chance at freedom based on his promise (parole) not to re-offend. [...] We can only hope that the measure is signed into law for foreigners as well as Thais. [...]

28 July

I am very glad to report that we appear to have dodged the bullet with the new restrictions (regarding mail) [...] The only remaining vestige of them is the unfortunate necessity of a photo ID of the sender being affixed to any parcel, as well as a full list of the contents being within said package. There is an odd restriction of 'no more than two of any one sort of item' but I can hardly believe that this applies to books.

I confess I have no idea as to what to do regarding your query re: something for Sam to read out from me for your birthday party: the thought of it freezes me into immobility! Odd, I didn't think such a simple request would have that effect on me, but it has.

2 August

Changes in U.K. Law [...] have instigated a disaster of epic proportions. [...] In a nutshell, the new Automatic Release at half-way point of sentence will not apply to us. [...] Instead we are told that we must serve half of the portion of our sentence which remains after transfer! This means that time served abroad counts for nothing and that I will have to spend a minimum of five extra years in an English prison even if I transferred tomorrow. My friend and I are now writing furious letters of complaint to various Ministries, MPs, newspapers etc. I must break off here to concentrate on trying to get the powers-that-be to undo this monstrous injustice [...]

Yours in haste

Andy

PS HAPPY BIRTHDAY!!

*

2008 was a year to make me both sad (for Vicky) and incandescent with rage (for myself and my fellow Brits in foreign prisons).

I could relate to Vicky's despair. I felt it myself when my own relationship with Denise fell apart, and I lost her and my son.

Going into prison compounded this feeling of emptiness, of hopelessness, and just when I'd begun to reform my broken psyche, albeit on an extremely modest scale, she died. That shattered all the newly glued-together bits of me, of my hopes, for good and all. The man I used to be was gone, as was all he had ever been or dreamed of being. I was entirely unsure of what might replace him, and it is partly this uncertainty which I deemed made me unfit to presume to write some kind of piece to Vicky for her 50th. I did not trust my judgement anything like enough to do that.

I was entirely consumed by the UK's new release regulations, and my letters to Vicky, indeed my letters to all and sundry, reflected the new priorities in my thinking. I think that my focus on this took away the overpowering, suffocating blanket of despair that I was otherwise subject to. I wrote to lawyers, to *Inside Time*[34] and wrote small bits for the web.

In a sense it represented displacement activity. It consumed me, it energised me, and it gave me purpose.

Angels

I'd already had two close brushes with death. At eighteen years old I had a near-fatal accident that profoundly changed my perception of life and death. I was on a student skiing trip to Courmayeur in the Italian Alps. To get to and from the slopes, everyone took a cable car. One day a boy persuaded me to walk back down the mountain instead. It was a beautiful, balmy spring evening, with not a breath of wind. He said he'd done mountaineering and would show me how to 'bunnyhop' with feet together, to quicken our descent.

What this lad had not factored in, was that I was a complete novice and wearing ski boots with no grip. Suddenly I lost my balance and before either of us knew what was happening, I was sliding head first on my back, accelerated by my shiny anorak, towards a precipice two hundred metres ahead.

Suddenly I had an out of body experience and was looking down at myself flailing helplessly. I heard a voice near me say, "You are going to die." I was filled with a sublime sense of peace, which seemed to last an eternity but was probably only a few seconds. Next thing I knew, I was standing a few metres from the cliff edge, looking up at my friend as if nothing had happened. He, on the other hand, was as white as this sheet of paper. He had been convinced I would die. What he told me he then saw, was me rising into the air, doing an Olympic backward somersault and landing perfectly, feet together, arms out at the side, with my back to the drop.

This happened twenty-seven years ago, but it feels as if it happened yesterday. I have gone over and over the event, but can find no scientific explanation that holds water. There were no thermal winds to hold me up. The ground was steep and thick with snow. Even if I had hit a hidden rock or tree trunk, yes, it could have *stopped me, but I would have ended in a heap, as I have in many precarious off-piste situations since.*

How did I not die? How, when I am hopeless at gym, did I do this perfectly balanced somersault? I believe, though I'm sure most won't, that there was a guardian angel either side of me, flipping me over and landing me firmly on my feet. When I was eighteen, this idea of angels being present was something I instinctively knew I couldn't discuss with anyone. I'd probably be locked up. Even our parish priest would have been sceptical. Angels are mentioned throughout Christian services, but with no thought to their immediate reality than the stone cherubs above the altar.

It was not my time to die on that mountain. I don't have a fear of dying anymore.

One of the lowest points in my life was being told by Keith, the marriage guidance councillor, that I was ten years too late to save the relationship.

In that final session, my illusions about our marriage were well and truly shattered. People have asked me why I didn't leave Nick at this point. I had never considered it an option. I had made a vow for better or worse. I plummeted from that moment into the abyss. I left Keith's practice feeling there was no point in going on now that all hope of love between us was gone. I stared at the tube lines, wondering how I could throw myself across them and end all the misery. For a year, I looked at branches above me and wondered about hanging myself. I wanted to return to the peace I had felt during my near-death experience.

I couldn't go through with it. I wish I could say I was saved by a concern for my children, but I was in much too dark and self-centred a place to notice anyone around me. I became a film director looking through the camera at this middle-aged woman asking the rush-hour crowds to let her pass. "Excuse me! Excuse me!". Having got to the edge of the platform, she can't decide whether to lower herself carefully onto the tracks, stumble, or take a running jump just as the tube emerges from the tunnel. Well, by the time I had thought of all this, the train had stopped, the doors opening.

While running or walking in Richmond Park, I would see overhanging branches and discarded blue plastic rope everywhere. I'm so bad at throwing, how would I get the rope up and over? Would I need to bring a chair? I never concentrated on knots at Brownies so what if the noose didn't hold and I found myself sprawled on the ground with a sprained ankle? For a year, I only saw dead trees and plants and only in black and white; the colour had drained from my life.

One day I walked into Waterstone's and could not go a step further. I closed my eyes and begged God to choose a book that would get me through, even the next hour. When I opened them, there in front of me, wall-to-wall, was a book display, not of the latest Dan Brown or Stephen King, but 'The Miracles of Archangel Michael' by Doreen Virtue. It even drew from me a wry smile because it was so in your face and I wondered what assistant could have had the chutzpah and permission to put out at least eighty copies of the same book side by side. I found out months later that it was an American girl and I asked her why. She said she had a sudden compulsion and went with it. She saved my life.

The book was a revelation. It got me through my depression and led me to develop an awareness of an angelic presence that had been lying dormant for over thirty years. I began to associate the blue plastic rope I saw lying around with Archangel Michael. I'd see it just out of reach when I stopped to stretch on a run and then find myself smiling. When I found a small, discarded piece on the ground, I'd keep it in my pocket as a talisman. I already knew about the Angel calling cards of white feathers, double numbers and coins. A few days after Nick's disclosure, he asked me for a game of golf. It was a beautiful evening and St George's Hill was looking particularly stunning. However, I felt so miserable and murderous, I could hardly hit a ball. As I walked off the fourth green, I prayed to Archangel Michael for help to park these destructive feelings, at least until I'd got back to the clubhouse. As I left the elevated fifth tee, I was astonished to see, laid out in front of me, a carpet of blue plastic rope remnants and white feathers placed carefully in a crosshatched pattern. I played the rest of the round peacefully and well.

I read all of Doreen Virtue's books and eventually went to one of her workshops in Salzburg. Dressed in a long blue and green gown, this angel guru was tall, blonde and blue-eyed. Her voice was deep and clear, and she spoke deliberately, rather like an interpreter. Four hundred people from Europe and beyond attended, and it was a pleasure to be with like-minded men and women.

One of the exercises, of the many we did that weekend, stands out in my mind. Doreen asked us to pair up with someone in the room we didn't know. That should have been easy, but everyone appeared to be speaking German. I had noticed one woman, in her thirties, speaking with an American accent, so I approached her. She reluctantly agreed and introduced herself as Marisol. We were told to turn our chairs to face each other, to hold hands with knees touching. Once we could picture the outline of our partner, we were to close our eyes and WAIT. We were not to force it. After fifteen minutes, just as I was resigned to seeing nothing, pink and purple flooded my inner vision. I saw a carved stone angel whispering in Marisol's left ear. Then I saw a colourful Renaissance angel in robes of blue, green and gold, whispering in her other ear. Those visions faded and then an older woman's face appeared, side on, again whispering in Marisol's ear. Her long hair was loosely tied back in a bun, with distinctive grey and white streaks. This, too, faded and a young man in army fatigues was standing within her outline.

At that point Doreen Virtue told us to stop and share our visions with each other. Marisol told me she had seen me surrounded by seven protective Archangels or seven of Archangel Michael, she wasn't sure which. She said they were thrusting a large scallop shell towards me, containing the word "TRUST" inside it. She had absolutely no idea that I had recently completed the Road to Santiago, whose symbol is the scallop, and that "TRUST" and "JOY" were my inspiration. I am so grateful to Marisol for this image, which I still hold close to me. She also saw a good-looking man leaning back in a relaxed pose, with straight, shoulder-length brown hair.

When I told Marisol what I had seen, she looked at me strangely and asked for my email address. The next day she contacted me, saying did I do readings professionally? She sent me a photo of her grandmother, exactly the woman I had seen. She said she adored her grandmother, who had died recently, and felt sure was advising her. Marisol then told me she had a fear of flying. She had gone to see a medium, who told her that, in a past life, she had been a pilot in the second world war and had died a horrible death when the plane caught fire.

We regularly email each other and pray for each other. Marisol is sure that the man she saw was my soulmate. She trolled through the internet until she found a photo of Vigo Mortenson. Well, there's no harm in daydreaming!

Andy calls himself a lapsed Atheist. I could never discuss Angels with him in my letters, whereas it's easy to open up with his mother, who prides herself on being spiritually open. He has probably written us both off as mad and maybe you have too dear reader.

2009

Vicky to Andy, 6th Letter

10 January

Dear Andy

There is no adequate excuse for not writing to you for four months, particularly after the very disturbing ending to your last letter [...]

How are you now? You sounded so positive before, particularly on the subject of parole. Has that all come to nothing?

Thank you for your sympathy regarding my marriage. Yes, a year on from 'knowing', I do have good days, but a photo of some sex chick or a film, book etc. on infidelity (and you'd be amazed how many there are) can send me plummeting. I was in Orly airport on my way to Corsica (to revisit the hotel I did up two years ago). I saw a grey-haired man in his fifties, giggling with a girl twenty years younger. I suddenly wanted to smash up the whole airport. I locked myself in the toilets until I'd calmed down. This summer (working on one of the Greek hotels), all the anger I had suppressed since Nick's revelation, erupted. I saw red and hit one of my decorating team on the back (I've never done anything that unprofessional before, or since for that matter); but she was bossing and baiting me, until I couldn't take it anymore. It ruined the atmosphere and was a huge mistake. A week ago, out of nowhere, I also thumped Samantha because she wouldn't stop baiting me at the airport. We're still not talking... I feel a bit like a wounded lion, a dangerous animal to be around.

I haven't been back to the psychiatrist. He did save me in those early days but going by myself now just seems like an expensive ego trip. If Nick is prepared to go with me, that's different. To be fair to him, he is trying to build bridges. I know the family unit really does matter to him. Business for him is as knife-edged as it's ever been.

I was meant to do up three hotels this summer. It's very likely that with the economic crisis, none of these projects will now come to fruition. [...]

12 January

I've made up with Samantha. She came and said sorry to me, which was humbling and we had a hug and a cry.

I've thrown in a photo from my 50th birthday (taken by the wife of our friend who climbed Everest for NSPCC – did I mention him to you?) I decided to make a speech, rather like 'the last lecture' and actually tell people what I thought [...] People were laughing uncontrollably or looking uncomfortable. Death featured heavily. I decorated the candles with dark brown ribbon and the invitations were black. Still, while it silenced a lot of people, it flushed out some like-minded friends, with whom I have since had some very remarkable conversations. I handed out notepaper and pens to all my children, nephews, nieces and their friends and I told them to take notes, as one of them would outlive me and write my obituary. Don't worry, I got Simon (the 24-year-old with cystic fibrosis) to speak afterwards, and Tom read out Lauren's speech, (unfortunately she was back in hospital), which righted the evening.

Do write back in reply to my questions and be your usual straight self.

Lots of love

Vicky

(Lost, Andy to Vicky, 7th Letter)

Vicky to Andy, 7th Letter

30 Sept 2009

Dear Andy

Disaster, Disaster! (well, I guess everything's relative). I got back last night from Portugal (ironically celebrating 25-years of marriage at the house there) and realised today that I'd left your letter, birthday card (which I only got two weeks ago) and my half-written reply, on the plane. I've torn all my luggage apart but there can be no other explanation. I don't mind so much losing my letter to you. I wrote a lot of it when I was feeling low, so in that sense, no great loss to you, but I hate losing your letters [...]

I also treasure you as a friend (and yes, I do neglect my friends.) Your birthday card could not have been opened at a more appropriate moment. I have been dreading this date – our 25th year wedding anniversary – ever since I found out about Nick, nearly two years ago now. I feel a bit like I am on death row (again relatively speaking). The children will be included in his life until the day he dies. Depending on how he chooses to play it, I will or won't, and at a date to suit him. At the moment he is struggling with every fibre of his being to keep his business afloat. [...] so I seem to him like a fly buzzing around his head.

This was the spirit in which we both started the weekend. However, your line, "don't forget to smell the roses", stuck in my head. [...] In fact, on [...] our last night, I just said I'd rather not go to a smart restaurant (we'd already had two stilted evenings doing that). Instead we went for a swim in the sea as the sun was setting. As it falls red in the sea, it seems to drip gold onto the waves. We then sat on some beach beds with a blanket, a bottle of champagne, two glasses and some smoked salmon sandwiches I'd made and watched the sun as it died away, leaving silhouettes of a few lone fishermen casting on the shore. The fishing boats out at sea were now looking like a string of pearls in the darkness. We reminisced about the good moments in the marriage [...].

*

I had omitted to tell Andy that I'd asked Nick if I'd done anything right in all those years. After a long pause, he said I'd been a good mother. I asked what had attracted him to me in the first place? Another long pause; "You were beautiful and dangerous." As we left the beach, he said this didn't mean he would be changing his ways. I tried to laugh it off by saying I didn't expect him to, but my heart was breaking.

*

Vicky to Andy, 7th letter cont.

I've come back to gloomy England with the boiler broken. Actually, somebody is fixing it as we speak. Still, I am trying to appreciate every day as it comes. Ironically, my sense of smell is shot to pieces as I have allergies to house dust, wine and lactose. My nose is permanently blocked or running.

Because of the arthritis, asthma and eczema on my elbows, your mother thought I was possessed by a spirit. I think the only spirit I am possessed by is unhappiness which crept up with a failing marriage [...] A psychiatrist I play golf with, told me that arthritis indicates unresolved anger and yes, I am angry as well as sad, because I feel I can't control my situation. When you mentioned your hip in the letter, I thought, aha; a fellow sufferer. In my book of healing we have to surround the afflicted area in our minds with a white light and then breathe deeply and slowly and let the anger go. In my case it's my knees. In terms of diet, avoid beef, pork, tomatoes, processed food, tropical fruits, berries, dairy products, caffeine and alcohol. Good things are pears, bananas, peaches, melons, apples being the healing fruit of all fruits. Other greats are porridge, almonds and honey (the darker the better). All veg is perfectly alright. So far, you've indicated that your breakfast consists of cigarettes and coffee.

I've just read back what I wrote and I think I am coming across as a self-obsessed, neurotic hypochondriac. If you couple that with a penchant for matters spiritual, then you are probably wondering why you have anything to do with this mad woman.

The other night I couldn't sleep, (a regular affliction that means I manage to get all my book club reading done fast). I got in the car and drove in three minutes to the gates of Richmond Park at 1.40am [...] "London's best kept secret" my next-door neighbour says. At night it is absolutely still, bathed in a blue, luminous light from the moon and the deer wander like shadows across the paths they would never go near during the day. Around the perimeter of trees, is the red glow of the sky from the lights of London. There is an energy and background noise of a city never sleeping, so that inside the park I feel I am protected by its blanket of silence. I wander through the bracken to a wood – 'Two Storm Wood' – it's called, and lie under one of the oldest trees in the park. [...] When I look up into the branches, it's as if I am looking at lace. The tree, which by day is just a large, old, gnarled oak, by night has a presence, a pulse or energy, like something containing the wisdom of ages. I feel as though, if I stay there long enough, I might obtain enlightenment. I returned home in this tranquil mood, to find that one of the children had removed the door-key from my keyring. So I lay in my car until 4am, when Tom luckily arrived back from a party and let me in. He looked at me as though I had lost it.

Talking of Tom, he was really pleased to see you. He told me it was a close run thing what with the shorts, flip flops, etc.[35] *And yes, he did arrive back from his travels with a beard, though not by the sounds of it in your class. He was also sporting two earrings in one ear. Was that your influence as well?*

He is now in Leeds starting his broadcasting and journalism course. [...] Samantha is working as her boss's PA at Academy Films and is much happier. [...] Emma got a 2.1 degree for Art. [...] She's now filling three large sweet jars with clay figures (Etruscan in style) and various plastic toys. Actually these are not grotesque but mysterious, as the resin crackled in places so it's more like looking at objects stuck in amber than suspended in water. [...]

Three days ago in Richmond Park, the sky was a pure Cambridge blue, against which silver birch leaves were shimmering in pale gold. Today near William's school, it was raining, so I stretched under a large oak and found myself again staring at a slim, pale gold tree trunk [...] which stood out amongst all the grey/green wet pine trees. All would have been magical if a woman hadn't come running out of a field telling me I was trespassing!

[...] You made a point about being institutionalised. I think everybody to a degree is, in the sense that they get used to their environment and don't like change. If they are always ringing in the changes, then maybe they feel safer not committing to one thing. [...] Correct me if I am wrong, but Bang Kwang offers you a certain safety and stability and your day is free, to a degree, to structure as you want. You always seem to be stretching your mind, reading and playing chess for example. You seem to be respected by inmates and screws alike. [...] I suppose I think of Ted Hughes' 'Jaguar' – physically curtailed but with a mind free to roam.

My mind's in a better place now, so I won't leave it so long to write to you.

Lots of love

Vicky

P.S. With the chess, do you have a limit on how long each move takes? I play scrabble with my twin sister. She's unbearably slow but devastating when she finally puts down the letters.

Andy to Sam

17 October 2009

Dear Sam,

Thanks for your letter dated 6 October. That was actually a sad day for me. I was told by my American regular visitor Bill [...] that my friend Kay had passed away. She'd been taken to hospital in an ambulance on 11 September and died that day. [...]

[...] I will miss her terribly and I am truly saddened that she has gone. [...]

Yours in haste

Andy

Kay

Then there was Kay. I first met her when she wandered into the New Inn, the oldest pub in Ealing, my hang-out since the late seventies, when it still had sawdust on the floors and gas-lamps that you could light a cigarette from.

It was now the mid-eighties, and she had just come to the area, having spent the previous eight years in Australia, and she had picked up something of an accent.

Over the next few weeks, she became a part of our loosely affiliated circle, and had a habit of sharing her life history, which was, to say the least, colourful. She had been born out of wedlock back in '53, to a 19-year-old mother, who had promptly shunted her into her grandmother's care, up in Burton-upon-Trent. This was the beginning of a lifelong history of abandonment 'issues'. Her mother got married a few years later and had a legitimate daughter, upon whom it would appear she lavished a mother's care. Kay didn't get much of a look-in, and certainly wasn't welcome at the new family home. I believe she nursed a bitter resentment of her mother for the rest of her life, and her feelings towards her half-sister were no better. Having left school, she moved up to London and got a secretarial job.

Here she immediately found a boyfriend. Unfortunately, he regarded her as a convenience rather than a necessity. She was easily impressed by his sports car and his free-spending ways. But then she got it into her head to try and trace her father, a Scot, who had immigrated to Australia. She conveyed this plan to her beau, confidently expecting that he would try to talk her out of it. He never did, so off she went.

She got to Australia, found a job pretty well straight away and then did a bit of detection work to find her father. She traced him to a building site where he was working, walked up to him when she'd identified his Scots accent and introduced herself by her full name, date and place of birth and said, "and you are my father". The man wept real tears, crying, "Och, ma wee hen" and so on in a Glaswegian accent you could cut teak with.

He had acquired a new family and, once again, Kay was perforce shut out, at the insistence of the man's wife. Kay's opinion of men was never particularly high, her opinion of most women was much lower, verging on the abysmal. The fact that <u>she</u> was a woman herself seemed not to figure in this assessment.

Demonstrating her flair for picking the wrong horse, her first boyfriend turned out to be a stone junkie. Her propensity to do as a man asked, led her to first try, then wholly adopt that life. She would shoot up in the spot between her fingers so as to leave no visible track marks, as, contrary to the picture that most non-users have of junkies, she continued to hold down a steady job.

This went on for years but her boyfriend, who was also something of an operator, getting high-quality smack from Penang in Malaysia, became too unstable and eventually she left him. She had other friends from whom she continued to obtain her supplies, but the inevitable stresses of junkie existence started to take their toll.

Overdoses began to claim her friends, and the spectre of AIDS started a panic. Mental health problems plagued a particular friend, a Kiwi, whom she eventually became instrumental in saving, by informing his family back home that they had better pay for him to return or they'd be paying for his funeral.

Once he was gone, she took stock. She was shrewd enough to realise that she couldn't kick the habit if she stayed where she was, so she decided to close the book on her experience of Australia and come back to England. It was a couple of months after this return that she came into our lives.

She took up with a guy called C. and stayed as his girlfriend for some years. He refused to contemplate a formalisation of their relationship even as loose as living together. The rowing increased in frequency and intensity.

They broke up and, strangely enough, remained friends thereafter.

A succession of boyfriends followed and she moved from one flat to another with regularity. She had developed carpal tunnel syndrome through her typing – she'd been pretty fast – so she needed to find something to keep her occupied. She had kicked the habit cold turkey, but to stay clean she knew she had to stay busy. A couple of casual or part-time stints as a house cleaner led to her going into it full-time. When she needed a name for her little concern, she chose the one I suggested, 'Spotless', a name to both inspire confidence and to live up to. She worked the jobs herself, but got so many referrals that she took on help, having five or six other women to help out and taking a small slice of what she charged for the work.

After all those apartments, she got a yen to live on a houseboat and, true to her impulsive nature, bought the first one she saw. I went with her to view it. *La Giaconda* was like a huge two-storey Portacabin on the water, moored on the Grand Union Canal just south of the Paddington Cut. I was extremely unsure. It had the look of something cobbled together by a man unused to building for water, which was indeed the case. Pine had been used instead of hardwood, definitely not a long-lasting timber for a water craft.

Since one cannot get a mortgage for a houseboat, Kay had to get a loan. She was forced to ask her mother, now widowed and very comfortably off indeed, thank you very much. The woman eventually agreed, twenty grand at fifteen per cent over ten years. Kay never missed a payment, in fact, she paid off the loan ahead of time, so anxious was she to get away from this obligation to her mother.

All this time I had remained her friend. I watched as she worked her way through various boyfriends and it took me a while to work out what the recurring motif was. It would start with the chap being wonderful, interesting, attractive etc, at least in her account of her newest beau. Imperceptibly the carping would start – little niggles of nuisance. He'd do this, or fail to do that. Mostly, these were things that everyone else could see from the off – how was it that she had not?

It goes back to this abandonment thing. She'd developed a strategy which seemed self-defeating on the face of it but which worked in terms of her deep-seated fear of being left. She'd pre-empt the chance of this, by precipitating a situation whereby she would be the one to leave. Since I had become her principal shoulder to cry on, I got the full story – or at least Kay's full story – every time.

My wife Jean had never liked Kay very much. After we were married, this got quite antagonistic, particularly in the brief period when Kay lived in the flat above ours.

My wife became convinced that there was more to this than met the eye. There was not, but my saying so wasn't making any difference, nor was the fact that Kay was going out with someone else almost all of the time. When my wife said that I either had, was having, or would have, an affair with Kay, I knew it was over. It was shortly afterwards that we split up.

For most of the next two years, I was taken up with Denise, and my own son. Kay would come round occasionally and, while my relationship with Denise was going well, the two were friends. Kay started to go out with my mate, and best man at my wedding to Jean, another Pole called Ed. This pairing followed the familiar pattern and Kay was starting to run out of potential suitors. At the time I went AWOL to Thailand, I think Kay didn't have a current beau.

When she found out what had happened to me, she wrote straight away. Her output averaged a letter every fortnight or so. Her life seemed to be a succession of problems, and I began to see in her narratives, a gradual expansion of a tendency which had already begun to worry me.

As I have said, an ex-junkie always remains vulnerable to relapse, but there is also another associated pitfall which is the replacement of one bad habit with another. Having avoided the methadone treatment, which is even more addictive than the heroin for which it is a substitute, she fell gradually into the next most common replacement: alcohol.

The first time I met her, she was drinking lager by the pint, as were most of those in that pub. Her intake increased, though since she drove every day to and from work, not too much. But when she moved to the houseboat, with a Tesco superstore three or four minutes' walk away, she changed her habits. Her local was the Grand Junction Arms and she'd go in there a couple of nights a week, usually at the weekends. After a crash in her old Fiat Panda – she was hit as she exited her own car park sober – she didn't drive for over a year. During this time her intake rose much higher and cheap supermarket vodka began to be a mainstay. The extent of this only became clear to me after I went to Thailand.

She was buying half a bottle a day. Since she was only about 5' 1½" tall this was a big dose of booze for such a small frame. She began to be ill.

In 2007 she sold the houseboat, for £10 grand. The superstructure was rotting and the price reflected the value of the steel double-hull and, more importantly, the mooring space. She moved away from London, first to the Welsh coast and a year or so later, to Derbyshire. She used some of the proceeds from the sale to come and visit me in Bang Kwang.

She arrived in April 2007, with her friend Angie in tow, as a travelling companion. This arrangement went wrong almost immediately.

First mistake: Kay suggested they only take one suitcase between two of them. This notion is inexplicable, and will baffle me to my dying day. On arrival they went out on the town for a couple of days and got fairly tanked up. Given that Kay was supposed to be on the wagon, this was not a good start. Angie then took it into her head to go off on her own, which was poor form considering that she was there first and foremost, to come and see me – we had also been writing – and also because Kay had paid for her ticket.

Instead of getting herself another bag, Angie just grabbed the shared suitcase and disappeared. As well as her clothes, Kay had her ticket, passport and money in it, so she was suddenly left high and dry. She arrived for our pre-arranged contact visit, in a state of great anxiety. I listened, incredulous, as she related what had happened to her. She had almost no cash, no way of paying the tiny amount she owed for her cheap hotel room on the Kho-San Road. She'd come up to the prison on the river bus, for about 25p. I'd brought out a couple of packs of cigarettes and gave them both to her, along with a lighter of prison manufacture in a mother-of-pearl cover. She was bewailing and bemoaning her fate throughout the visit. She was still wearing the same clothes that she'd had on when Angie went walkabout. She was, in short, a mess, both inside and out.

She had come out for three weeks, and it took the whole of the first week before Angie showed up again. She had swanned off to Koh Samui and Koh Phangan, a couple of islands in the Gulf of Thailand. After some heavy partying, she had woken up one day to find herself in a room of absolute squalor, surrounded by junkies fixing up. She fled the island in horror and came back to Bangkok with her tail between her legs. Contrite though she was, Kay could not carry on as though nothing had happened, and Angie changed her ticket and tearfully returned to London, without even having made the trip out to Bang Kwang to see me.

Kay visited me twice a week until she herself had to fly back. Re-united with her funds, including her credit card, she went out and got herself a tattoo on her shoulder of an eclipsing sun. This would have been her ninth or tenth such and she was to get two or three more in the next couple of years. Naturally, since this was Kay, the damn thing started to fester rather than simply scab over, and she was wearing a dressing on it when she came for her last visit.

I really hated saying goodbye to her. A recurrent theme of our conversations had been how much she missed me, and that she wanted to be with me when I got out. Her move out of London had resulted in a sense of isolation and loneliness. Since she had left the city, the temptation to reach for a bottle was great and she did succumb to it in the end. It was with dismay that I learned she had been diagnosed with cirrhosis of the liver, said organ being greatly enlarged due to the abuse she had been giving it.

Blow me down, if four months after our goodbyes, she was back again in August, smack in the rainy season. This time she found somewhere to stay close to the prison. But she didn't stay there long, the town having nothing whatsoever to recommend it to a traveller. She moved back to the Kho-San Road and carried on taking the cheap river bus to and from the prison.

She had already moved twice since she'd migrated to Wales. She now had a really nice flat in Aberporth, freshly finished out for the bargain rent of £300 a month. She was well pleased with her luck in finding the place, with its splendid views of the sea and gave me photographs of it and of her posing inside it. The rest of the visits were taken up with post-mortems of mostly lamentable relationships with men, and of her failed friendships with women. One guy turned out to be a closet transvestite and another beat her black and blue, the photographic evidence of which sent him to gaol, albeit only for a couple of months.

She expressed surprise that I hadn't actually gotten around to getting an official divorce from Jean. I said that I hadn't even thought about it.

I think this stayed in her mind because five and a half months after she finally went back to the UK, I received from Kay a proposal of marriage inside a Valentine's card, it being a leap year.

I sighed when I read this. Much as I loved her – and I did love her – it would have been the height of folly to have had any intimate relationship with her, let alone marry her. Over the twenty-odd years we had known each other, I would be the one she turned to but always as a friend.

I wrote back saying that, apart from the salient fact that I was indeed still technically married. I didn't particularly want to get spliced again. Her reply was hurt, disbelieving, she couldn't understand it – didn't I love her?

Back I wrote saying yes, I did, but that I wasn't even sure I wanted to co-habit with her, the very stumbling block that came between her and C... her first boyfriend on returning from Australia. There was something of a hiatus before her next letter arrived, but this time I wasn't the reason.

She had got quite ill and this time the doctors diagnosed Hepatitis C which could have lain dormant for 25-years – like the 'silent killer' it was.

On being discharged from the hospital, she did two things. One, she took herself to the nearest church and there took lessons on how to be a Christian, with a view to Baptism. Second, she booked a flight to Thailand to see me again. As near as I could work out, she was now using the last of the ten grand she'd got from the sale of her houseboat, and I wondered in my next letter whether it was wise to blow the last of her nest egg. She said it wasn't a nest egg, it was mad money and she just felt like going mad with it. She arrived at the end of May, about as hot as it could be. She'd booked a contact visit, asking specifically to come in the morning. I waited and waited and began to wonder what had happened to her this time.

I was finally called out after 1.30pm. I looked around but could not see Kay at first. Then I saw her, sitting on a low wall, twisting and turning and generally looking distressed.

She'd shown up in the morning clutching her photocopied visit authorisation. Since it was in Thai, she had not been aware that it was for the afternoon, not the morning session. So she had been hanging around outside the prison for five hours or so. It was the hottest day of the year so far, 38° or 39°, and she was in the early stages of heatstroke.

I got hold of a couple of big bottles of ice-cool water and Kay sipped a little of this. She poured some over herself, soaked a shawl and draped it over her head and shoulders, and recounted her latest tribulations. She'd mislaid her bank card before she flew out. She had got a replacement card before she left, but not a new pin number and was unable to access her funds through any ATM.

She looked ill and angry, and I was genuinely worried. I did not think her sickly appearance was due solely to the climate. She complained of the heat and of the chill, alternating between the two every few minutes.

I gave Kay a couple of small presents – a mother-of-pearl decorated cigarette box with a leaping tiger on one side and a rearing cobra on the other – the first to signify my present habitation, 'the Big Tiger'; the second her Chinese birth sign. To this I added a lighter, also of mother-of-pearl and decorated with dragons.

At our next meeting, she asked me once again if I would re-consider her proposal of marriage; if not, would I at least come and live with her. I looked at her, at her eager and expectant eyes, and I had to smile. I relented and said that I would love to be with her when I got out of this place. It was her 56th birthday.

During the last few visits, Kay spoke of other things, mostly of death and the afterlife. She was sure that she would die before me. I begged her to look after her body, that I wanted her to be there when I got out, that too many people had already passed away during my time here. She smiled and said that she would.

Our final goodbye was tearful and I watched her square her shoulders as she left. I wrote to Kay only twice in the next two months and she wrote perhaps three times. In mid-September my friend Bill came to visit me and opened by saying, "I've got some bad news". He assured me that my mother was O.K. – I hadn't even considered that she might not be – but that Kay had died on 11 of September.

I hung my head and thought about her face, her voice, her laugh. I realised how much I would miss her, knowing that she was there, somewhere. Bill told me that she had collapsed suddenly, been taken to hospital after she herself had called the emergency services. Nobody else knew and it wasn't until over a week later that the door to her flat was forced and the forlorn dead body of her pet parakeet was found. The minister who had baptised her so recently was now called upon to conduct her funeral. That I was not able to be there, I felt keenly. It was yet another plank removed from the floorboards of my previous life. I was missing her already. A wave of sadness rolled over me and I feel it over and over again whenever I think of her, which is often.

India/Australia

'Only connect.' – E.M. Forster

In 2009, Nick employed me to begin phase two of the refurbishment of the hotel in Corsica, to furnish ten bedrooms as a prototype for the rest, to be done the following year. While Nick had nearly brought me to my knees, the work his company provided had prevented me going under. I had a contact in India, Janine, a South African girl who used to cook for us. Five months of the year she wore her other hat, that of interior designer, clothes designer and supplier. She knew of a factory in Jaipur with a Jewish owner, Indian manager and German designer,

Nick agreed and within days I found myself on a plane to India. It dawned on me while I was in the air, destination hotel Dhoti Mahal, Delhi, that I was halfway to Australia, where my youngest sister, husband and two young children had emigrated. I asked Nick if I could extend the trip and I would pay for half the flight. I gave my sister, Itsy[36] twelve years my junior, three days' notice that I was coming for eight days. She was astonished and delighted.

I arrived in Delhi and a tuk-tuk was waiting to take me to the hotel. It was being driven by a 19-year-old with friend in tow. A guard tried to extract the friend who was clearly getting a free ride, but I said I didn't mind and off we went. These two boys plied me with questions, particularly about my two beautiful unmarried daughters. They were astonished when I told them they had boyfriends who could spend the night in our house. We got onto the subject of cricket and The Ashes and they were in full flow. We were approaching Delhi during rush-hour (is there anything else?) Lanes here had gone by the board. A sea of lorries, cars, taxis, dhurries, tuk-tuks, motor cycles and bicycles all competed for space along with India's sacred cows. I screamed as we narrowly missed a bus on one side and two cars on the other. A big mistake! I handed my driver an invitation to give me a roller-coaster ride. He laughingly told me there were never any accidents. I yelled out that every vehicle seemed to have a dent in it. At one point he accelerated into an ever-decreasing space and a buffalo horn glanced past my spleen.

Janine was waiting at the entrance of the hotel and dismissed the boys. I sadly didn't have a chance to thank them or tip them and prayed that they would get paid properly.

Janine was living in the hotel in return for refurbishing it. She was doing a superb job and the owner was giving her full rein. The hotel was in the old colonial style, built on four floors around a courtyard. An ornate carved stone handrail ran all the way round on the inside, giving the impression of an inverted wedding cake. Simple four-posters were in all the rooms with silk and satin cushions and rugs in pink, purple, grey and aquamarine, Mogul influence everywhere. The main reception room was in the process of being decorated. The ceiling was pink with a silver gilt cornice. One wall was covered in black and white stripes. A large round table had been spray-painted in purple. A huge chandelier hung from the ceiling and I relished seeing the end result.

Along the corridors, Janine had mounted Bollywood posters in antique wooden frames, wittily hanging real jewellery on the necks, ears and hair of the film stars depicted.

Early the next day, we took a taxi to Jaipur, travelling the same road taken in 'Welcome to the Marigold Hotel'. The old pink city was a wondrous sight, the energy and bustle of Delhi with the addition of working elephants lumbering amongst the traffic, body-painted in ornate pink, orange, scarlet and purple patterns, embellished with gold and silver, jewels and tassels.

The factory was modern. Within a day and a half, Martin, the designer, and I, had teased out an elegant contemporary bedroom in beautiful dark hardwood.

Janine put us up in a hotel where the shower head was a tap coming out of the wall and flooding the entire room, including WC and paper. There had been absolutely no tanking but the room dried in minutes. Nothing matched anything but I realised I had all I needed, soap, towel, light to read by.

We wrapped everything up the next day and took a train back to Delhi. Janine had booked first class seats because she thought I would enjoy the space and service. Secretly I would have loved to go third-class, to be part of the bustle and energy.

Janine had kindly and expertly organised everything and I knew Nick would be delighted. She was always very pleasant and polite to me. The only difficulty I found with the trip was her treatment of the Indian staff. She barked at waiters and taxi drivers, the machinists at her cottage factory, and the hotel cleaners.

On the way to the airport, when she began berating my taxi driver, I couldn't bite my tongue any longer. I found myself telling her about Andre, the brilliant South African hotel manager from Corsica. His advice in giving criticism was the "shit sandwich"

- Compliment, Criticism, Compliment. I said all I could hear from her was criticism. Of course it didn't go down well. She said I wasn't a single woman trying to run a business in India, and how would I know the first thing about it?

It's true, I don't know the first thing about it. But I felt I had to stand up to her. None of those people were in a position to answer back.

As soon as we had dropped Janine off en-route, I apologised to the driver for her behaviour. He instantly changed beyond recognition. Having been moody and taciturn, he now spoke beautifully and eloquently. We nattered all the way to the airport, he doing everything in his power – including going down a lane the wrong way– to get me there on time.

I arrived in Brisbane eighteen hours later, just in time to have supper with Itsy, Ben and their children. I had expected a week of housekeeping and babysitting. Instead I was shown around a beautifully elegant and organised house. Itsy had my grandmother's flair for cooking and interior design. Her children, Francesca and Jack, then aged eight and three, were a delight to be with.

The next morning, I went to have a shower and found a Huntsman spider, the size of a side plate, planted between me and the tray. I've heard they are not poisonous so the two of us lived harmoniously together until my last day when Ben came to collect my suitcase and was appalled when he nearly stepped on it.

During the recent floods, an evacuated family moved in with Itsy and Ben. The wife suddenly had an urge to rescue her books (a woman after my own heart). She and Itsy canoed through the streets to her house. Only the top five feet of each lamp post could be seen, but because spiders had crawled up them in such large numbers, they looked like seething lollypops! These two women watched, terrified, as snakes swarmed round their boat. They canoed to the top of the friend's staircase and she jumped out, leaving Itsy screaming her head off.

Ben was working and Francesca had school, so each day Itsy, Jack and I went off sightseeing. We spent a particularly memorable day on Stradbroke Island. I went for a run round the cliff boardwalk. In disbelief and delight, I saw dolphins organise themselves into six groups of four and together catch a wave and surf it. They leapt into the air afterwards, like footballers celebrating a goal. Two stingrays were floating near to the cliffs. Suddenly, I caught sight of a turtle between the dolphins and rays, swimming as if its life depended on it, terrified of both its neighbours.

We swam in a tea tree oil lake, which was literally like swimming in a cup of tea, a mixed blessing because I kept imagining crocodiles underneath me. My father's partner Luce went to the island's public WC on their visit and on opening the door to leave, was confronted by a kangaroo as tall as she was, eyeballing her.

All week, Itsy had been complaining about the cheap wooden beams in her barn-shaped drawing room. By Friday I had done enough sightseeing and persuaded Ben to help me paint them a pale cream. Despite the perilous scaffolding and Jack's wish to join in, we completed the task, staining the hardwood lintels ebony. On Sunday evening, an hour after completing the job, I was back at the airport.

*

About six months after Kay's death, came another heart-blow. On the last Saturday in March, my mother had a stroke. This was gut-wrenching news. She was 85 years old and recovery was going to be a tricky proposition. As the news filtered through in the five-minute weekly phone calls, her parlous position became more and more clear.

[...] I was into my twelfth year of imprisonment. [...] I had two friends die within three weeks of each other, just before I finally and belatedly wrote to Vicky. I told her that I felt depressed, but it was more than that. The cumulative effect of all the bad news on me was not just one of emotional wear and tear. I was becoming stretched tight while at the same time feeling trapped in amber. If my sentence was a marathon, I was coming up against 'The Wall.'

2010

Andy to Vicky, 8th Letter

27 November

Dear Vicky

My apologies for not replying sooner, an apology which also goes for Sam and Will. I've been stuck in a rut since my girlfriend Kay died, last year on 11 September. [...]

Then on the last Saturday of March, my mother had a stroke, leaving her without the use of her left leg and left arm. She was in three different hospitals before going home a few months later, only to be re-admitted almost immediately with a heart problem (caused by the medication she was on). Since Christmas I've barely written a line, so I guess that the stress, and indeed the distress, of all this, has finally caught up with me.

My mother, the last time I phoned, seemed much stronger. She has a therapist/nurse four times a day to help her and my youngest brother Nick is there in the evenings after work. She said to me, somewhat ruefully, that she was now a prisoner as well, and had to have help with everything. It breaks my heart to hear, but at least she can still speak and her mind is as sound as ever.

Does Will still want to do his gap year round the world trip? If so, please make absolutely sure that he plans out his schedule properly, consulting the consulate in Bangkok so as to get an 'embassy visit' paper which should ensure that he can get to see me. Should he be feeling generous then he can buy me something from the prison shop across the road.

Please tell Sam I am really happy to hear that she has been promoted and tell Emma that I said 'hi'. Also, I had nothing to do with Tom's earring, and he obviously hadn't shaved for a while prior to visiting me, so I had nothing to do with that either!

29 November

It has been a bad month what with me being ill for a fortnight (along with half the gaol) and two of my friends here passing away (suddenly in each case). I am beginning to lose count of the numbers of those that have gone, itself somewhat troubling. On the brighter side, my Persian friend Reza got a full pardon and Dharma from Nepal won his case (after over six years!) and was also freed. The latter even came back to visit a few weeks later.

I've seen trailers in the last few days for both the latest Harry Potter and *The Voyage of the Dawn Treader*. [...] The Dawn Treader was the first of these books I ever read. It totally gripped me, how magical it seemed. I refuse to watch a movie of it by Murdoch's 20th Century Fox, preferring to keep the memory unsullied. If you haven't already read it, I'd advise doing so before seeing any film they make of it. I am enclosing what may be the most basic, spartan cards for you all, apologies, they're all I had to hand.

Fondest regards to you and to all the children.

Lots of love, yours in some haste

Andy

Mother

Andy and Danuta, Austria, 1958

My mother wrote to me often, more often indeed than I wrote to her. Computer generated card and photos would arrive for Easter, my birthday, and Christmas. They would almost always contain some kind of religious motif, a Catholic religious picture, an icon, a depiction of the Archangel Michael or similar. The photos might be a recent snap of my son, or an ancient one of me, and at Christmas a family shot from the sixties of me, my three brothers and my parents in front of the Christmas Tree.

The actual letters would be exhortations to read this or that book that had grabbed her attention lately, almost always something of a spiritual, spiritualist or uplifting nature: she was unrelenting, upbeat and optimistic about everything, though she was uncertain about my acceptance of her suggestions in reading matter. When I asked her to send me a Bible, she sent me a small New Testament, rather than the whole book. I'd wanted the Old Testament, to check references to the expected coming of the Messiah. As for the book I actually got, its overwhelming reliance on St Paul and his acolyte Timothy, made it an object of revulsion to me. The zealotry of this convert was not something I had time for.

But I said nothing to my old mum about any of this. Whether I am naturally resistant to religious dogma, or just plain bolshie, I do not think I am in a position to judge. But mothers don't, as a rule, give up. I was irregularly peppered with my mother's beliefs, distilled in her letters or in short lectures delivered in person. An argument would develop, but because of our diametrically opposed positions, no satisfactory conclusions would ever be reached.

As the years passed, I found myself becoming more and more detached from the news my mother was conveying regarding family and friends. When I finally managed to arrange telephone privileges I virtually stopped writing to her, other than the usual Christmas and Birthday cards with a letter attached.

The phone system was ludicrously convoluted to get authorisation for. One had to get two numbers, landline only, for 'family members'. These were then given to the British Consulate, who was supposed to verify them. Only then would the prison authorities issue the prisoners with a card, on which were printed the numbers and the time and day to ring. I applied shortly after the system was introduced. It took a bloody year to get my card.

The card had its own individual ID Number, which had to be tapped into the phone in order to make a call. Credit for one's number came in 50- or 100-baht phone cards, whose numbers, under a strip on the reverse, had to be tapped in after the ID numbers. The calls to the UK were not particularly expensive, about 80 pence for the maximum of five minutes we were allowed per call, but getting the cards proved problematic. A 100-baht card bought from another convict when the prison shop didn't have any, could cost as much as 130 baht.

The actual phones were plugged in at about nine or nine-thirty in the morning by the blue shirt assigned to the job and only he was allowed to dial any numbers. This constituted their principal security measure. We were given to understand that they could listen in to any call made from those phones, either live or on playback.

There was an extremely narrow window for me to make calls. I wasn't prepared to risk my 'excellent' conduct category through arranging to use a contraband mobile phone.

The five-minute calls with Mum were a welcome addition to my usual avenues of communication. The slow pace of the postal system meant that it was often too late to make arrangements for, say, the consulate to acquire this or that item from the visitor's shop. If we needed to arrange a dentist visit – cash up front for those – it could take so long that a man had lost the tooth by the time he actually went to get the work done; this happened to me twice.

I usually phoned home on Wednesday afternoons so as not to clash with potential visits. One Tuesday, Bill came to see me and brought me some bad news. My mother had had a stroke on the last Saturday of March 2010. The next day I made my call, but got no answer, so I rang the other number on my card. This was my brother Martin who lived two doors up from my mum.

The news was not encouraging. She had become paralysed down her left side and was still in hospital. She would remain there for some time, as she had come down with MRSA. She was confined to bed at precisely the time she should have been undergoing physiotherapy. It was not until more than two years had passed, that she began, almost spontaneously, to regain some measure of movement.

I heard this in dribs and drabs. My youngest brother, Nick, following the break-up of his marriage, had moved into my mother's house. When she got out of the hospital, he took over the carer chores, at least until the local authority had organised a permanent live-in carer. This was Gosia[37] a cheerful Polish lady. I began to get letters from my mother again after a few months, tapped out on a computer keyboard and with a short hand-written postscript. I was relieved to see she was at last improving.

Danuta and Quinlan 1996

Corsica 2010

When I arrived in Corsica in the spring of 2010, the building team, this time organised by an Englishman, Fred, had been there a week and the ten rooms to be refurbished were now shells. The budget was so tight on this occasion, that, other than Windy the tiler and Ian the plumber, there was hardly anyone on site over 23-years old.

The two decorators, paranoid about not being paid, did a runner overnight within three weeks of my arrival, taking all my expensive dust sheets, trays, in fact anything lying around. Luckily, the night before, I had decided to give all my own brushes and trays a mid-job clean and had them all in my room.

I asked a young carpenter and electrician to stay on another week as painters. I also asked Eric, the hotel owner's son and an expert decorator, if he could join me to form a second pair, because we now had one week to paint and stain all ten rooms. That Sunday I painted from 6am until 10.30pm with the music blaring. Windy, one of the brightest, wittiest men I've had the good fortune to cross paths with, gave three hours gratis and 'cut in' with a steadier hand after seven pints than I had sober.

Fred had gone back to England for ten days and now Windy was to all intents and purposes in charge. I was really impressed by his handling of these young lads, both as teacher and boss. A lot of the summer staff had arrived and the temptation for them to party was becoming even greater, while all I could see was the clock ticking.

The fear of not being paid loomed because Fred had a history of debt and I knew if everyone was to work even harder, they needed confirmation that they would receive the final two weeks' pay. I rang Nick with the situation and he told me to tell the boys that his company would pay them the last two weeks' salaries, if Fred did not. It did the trick and the bad air cleared.

The plasterers and carpet layer were on a fixed price and so were working all hours God gives. I couldn't guarantee they were paid, and heard afterwards they didn't get a penny. It makes me mad; such lovely Lancastrian lads. I have used Danny the plasterer for two more polished plaster effects since and can't fault his work. 'Shrek', the carpet layer, organised golf with me and I had the embarrassing situation of apologising before teeing off. "Shit happens" he said and told me to forget it. It wasn't my fault.

Three days before the guests arrived, the remaining builders began panicking again about being paid. I rang Nick saying I had everybody's bank details and please could he transfer their money.

"No", was his reply. "I've paid Fred. He must pay them."

"But in that case you lied to me before, because you knew the lads would believe me. You knew Fred had no money."

Silence down the end of the phone. I hung up.

I found Ian and Windy and told them the situation. I suggested they finish the job and then refuse to move out of their hotel rooms and have a holiday in lieu of pay. They agreed. I then marched into Andre's office and told him what would happen if the money wasn't in their accounts in the next 48-hours and gave him their bank details. The builders on site got paid by lunchtime the next day.

At 6am on the morning of the guests' arrival, I heard a car's engine in the forecourt. I rushed out to find Fred leaving. He said he'd booked a cheap ferry to England and was giving a lift to some of the lads. I told him the snagging list was a mile long. He shrugged his shoulders and drove off.

I never saw Fred again. Apparently his debts caught up with him and he had to sell his house. He was lovely to work with when I joined forces with him in those early years. This was the man who, four years before, had helped me to transform a bar in the French Alps, not only had he helped line the walls and ceiling with leather but single-handedly laid the carpet himself at 2am in the morning.

When it came to fabrics there was nothing he didn't know. Sadly he had overstretched himself.

In desperation I woke Windy and the electrician who were leaving at 9am and begged them to put in two hours' work on the rooms for nothing, which they did. Now there were eleven hours until the guests arrived and only Nick, the handyman and myself to complete the snagging list. "Right Nick, which do you want, stain or paint?" He chose paint and the two of us went painstakingly over every surface, room by room. At 7.55pm I was backing out of the last bedroom with ladders, pots, brushes and dust sheets (Nick had already finished), when Andre came bounding down the corridor. He swore, grabbed me and my materials and bundled us onto the fire escape. The guests were downstairs in reception.

I wasn't prepared to leave without doing one more thing. The staff canteen was a dingy affair in the basement. On quiz night I knew the place would be empty. I got the remaining paint and decorated the walls in pale greys, taupes and chocolate brown. I mounted Emma's old paintings on the walls and got Shrek to use the left-over carpet, along with the surplus furniture, to create a snug. I was finished by 7.30am the next morning when the staff came in for breakfast. They were astonished. I told Andre not to tell me off as I'd done it outside working hours as a present for the staff. He just stood there laughing. My theory is, if the staff are happy, the guests will be happy.

It wasn't all doom and gloom – far from it! I was surrounded by wonderful people, from the hotel owners and managers to the plongeurs and kitchen staff. Francois, now site manager, took it upon himself to buy materials for all the trades on a daily basis. I asked him if he would get me some 70% chocolate.

"Vicky, what are you, a Princess? I am buying nuts and bolts, timber and screws and you say your chocolate is essential!" (Said in a sexy French accent.)

Two days went past before I asked him if he had spent my ten euros taking out a beautiful girl for coffee. That afternoon, while I was up a ladder painting the hotel landings, he pretended to be the action man in the advert for, "All because the lady loves Milk Tray." He crawled up the last flight of stairs and, as he collapsed, slid seven bars of chocolate towards my ladder along the shiny floor. "All because the Princess must have her 70% chocolate!"

Every Saturday night, the boys would have three glasses of champagne lined up along the Pizzeria Bar because word had got round that I didn't drink anything else.

2011

Andy to Vicky, 9th Letter

31 January

Dear Vicky

[...] I clean forgot to send cards to people I really, really should have and wanted to, to let them know I was OK.

But the legal business must have priority. It is absolutely essential for Steve to get a ruling against the cretins at the Cross Border Transfer section [...] failure would be a disaster. With this in mind I put in an enormous amount of energy, uncountable man-hours of thinking time and writing time [...] to Steve's would-be solicitor in Staffordshire. Steve should be back anytime between the beginning and the end of summer this year, whereupon he has ninety days to lodge his application with the court, if his barrister has done his homework and legal aid is granted. I will have already asked the consulate to arrange for my own transfer papers to be in my hands by 5 December this year, when an amnesty marking HM King Bhumipol's 84th birthday, is awarded.

As for our Christmas, we were fortunate to have Gale, [...] long resident in Bangkok, get for us thirty pre-cooked bangers and two packs (eighteen slices each) of best back bacon just before she flew back to the UK and the snow [...]. The meat went into our shop's freezer until Christmas morning. With it we cooked up fried eggs and tomatoes, fried onions and button mushrooms, three hoarded tins of baked beans and had a Malay

Chinese expertly do us four kilogrammes of thick-cut chips – all this for six of us. We were absolutely stuffed to the point of near immobility, in addition to being 'well-oiled', so it was just as well that I'd delegated the washing-up – I was in no state to do such complicated manual labour!

And not much has really happened since, though it seems that two more of the chaps in my cell will transfer, [...] probably before Steve manages to do so. One goes to Holland (immediate release) the other to Israel (ditto); he's a South African but just recently acquired an Israeli passport after seventeen years here. I'll have to get a Nepali to fill the vacancy in the cell, else they'll put someone in I might not want.[38]

And so I close for now. Do please contact my Mum when you get this. Give my regards to all the family. Ask Will for his gap year plans and the very best to you Vicky in the year of the Rabbit which starts tomorrow.

Yours from sunny Siam,

Andy

*

Samantha and I do go and visit Danuta and Niki, Andy's mother and brother. Danuta is able to get up so we all have tea in her upstairs living room. The stroke has reduced her to a shadow of her former self, although her brain is crystal clear. It is great talking to Niki who fleshes out my image of Andy.

*

I appear to have perked up a little when writing this 9th letter. We had managed to get through another Xmas and New Year without any major upheavals and had treated ourselves to a major fry-up on Christmas Day. There was even a quantity of prison-brewed wine made from sticky rice and some brewer's yeast and, for those willing to risk their taste buds, some distilled hooch. The latter tasted vile but could be kept down if mixed with cola. One bottle was still hot from the distillation process, which served to speed its effects.

News of Steve's transfer came on Bastille Day, 14 July, eight years exactly after his initial detention. Yet another of my friends was gone, but I was still there.

Junk

There are times when I feel uncomfortably aware that my moral and ethical integrity have been compromised. Since my teens, I've always maintained a steadfastly anti-heroin position, to the point of open hostility, yet here I am serving a preposterous gaol term as a result of my attempt to transport the one drug which I'd previously spoken against so vociferously. No convoluted reasoning, no sophistry can be summoned to square this circle.

I managed to hold this position at the same time as I expounded against the global blanket prohibition of so many pharmaceuticals, organic and synthetic, not to mention the World Health Organisation. If the purpose of such prohibition is to provide gainful employment for cops, courts, correction departments and of course criminals, then it could not have been better designed.

For Bang Kwang is the place housing not only those with the biggest sentences in the land[39], as I mentioned before, it is the only legal place of execution. The rate at which the fixed machine-gun in Block 19, the execution chamber, chews up its victims is running at 25–30 per year, most of them for drugs.

So here I sit with the other drug offenders along with a sprinkling of murderers, rapists, kidnappers and the occasional paedophile.

The drug offenders fall broadly into two groups. There are those for whom the drugs business is just that, a business, a way of making a living. They do not use their own product and have a barely disguised contempt for those who do. The only real difference between them and legitimate businessmen is a heightened awareness of the possibility of double-dealing or fraud. They know they have no recourse in law if they are cheated or robbed.

The other group start from the other end of the equation. They begin as users of the product and try to cover their costs by entering into the retail end of the business. While some drugs are traded on credit, this is not the case with heroin. Spot cash is required. Junkies are also far more likely to be inveigled into transporting the drug, since they are generally strapped for cash and/or heavily in debt. It seems to be the ground-state of their existence.

The sentencing being what it is, a person can see one man with a life sentence for a few grams, walking past another man with the same sentence for 45 kilos of the same drug. The first is a junkie, the second a businessman, but they will both be in here for a couple of decades or more.

For a place intended to be a punishment for crimes committed, there seems to be an awful lot of drugs about. Rapists don't get the chance to carry on raping or kidnappers to keep on snatching people, paedophiles to molest children and only occasional murders disrupt the routine, usually <u>not</u> committed by those inside for murder. Yet those who were drug 'businessmen' and those who were drug users, can, if they wish, continue as before. It really is a singular state of affairs.

The casual corruption of the screws make supply a relatively simple matter and the same goes once the stuff is safely inside. The businessmen continue their business, making enough money to fund their food, drink, clothing, footwear, electronic equipment, TV's, videos, DVD's, use of satellite stations, etc. The junkies carry on nodding off, occasionally eating prison food and wearing their tiny wardrobes of clothing until they are little better than scraps of rag. The screws meanwhile are getting handsomely paid to bring the stuff in, then paid again not to see what's under their noses. Add these sums to those accruing from not seeing the quite open gambling games of various types and it's no bloody wonder that they're driving latest model up-market cars, with two or three more in the driveways of their large and comfortable houses. They sure as shit didn't get all that from their monthly salaries.

And that is rather the point. None of this would be happening if the powers-that-be had not caused it to happen by first introducing, then expanding the prohibition of drugs. It's as though the lessons of the utterly failed attempt at alcohol prohibition in America have been totally ignored. It doesn't do a damned thing to prevent the adverse health and social consequences of drug use; if anything the adulteration of narcotics greatly increase the number of fatalities. The enormous profit opportunities are irresistible, and the consequent strife increase the death toll still further. It's utterly insane.

Better to treat physical and mental problems as might arise from drug use, as medical health problems. Deaths by overdose would plummet and it would be dramatically cheaper for society than this pointless 'War on Drugs'.

Those working at ground level in penal institutions have ambivalent attitudes to drugs. Their position is analogous to that of herders of cattle, or sheep, or goats. Whatever keeps the herd calm and quiet is good, what makes them agitated and noisy is bad. In Thailand, the convicts outnumber the guards by more than twenty to one. In the daytime there can be as little as six screws guarding 1,000 prisoners. The dangers of any disturbance to the tranquillity and equilibrium of the gaol is the single biggest concern. Minor, individual acts of violence are immediately dealt with and anything further up the scale, involving larger groups of prisoners, is met with a massively disproportionate response, sometimes involving firearms discharged into a body of convicts. Death can result even if guns are not used – a hardwood club across the head or neck or back is just as final as a bullet.

So, broadly speaking, screws don't give a tinker's damn if the cons are smoking ganja, or using smack, because the effect of these is to make them so laid back as to be pretty much horizontal. On the other hand the aggressive behaviour caused by amphetamines, both 'Ya-Ba', or Thai speed, and later an explosion of crystal meth, or 'ice', make screws nervous. To a lesser extent prison-brewed hooch pisses them off as well; the drunken brawls are a pain, plus it's hard to squeeze any cash out of the business, so they feel deprived of their due.

But all of this aside, the fact remains that in the convict-constructed internal hierarchy of the prison population, junkies are firmly rooted at the bottom, below the merely poverty-stricken. They have no credit, no friends, no possessions, and no one believes a word they say. If not for the walls and bars that confine us all, they would be outcasts, lepers. To see and understand this, is to truly know what both heroin, and its prohibition, are responsible for.

Loss

Between the autumn of '09 and '11 there are no letters from myself to Andy that I can find, though he mentions receiving one and of course I sent Christmas Cards. During that time three people who were particularly close to me died; Lauren, Suzanne and Stephan. My world, as a result of their passing, shrunk.

*I met **Lauren** for the first time when I was looking for a swimming teacher for the children. As I entered the main pool, an almighty wolf whistle rang out, stopping everyone in their tracks. "Ah, that's Lauren!" and I remember thinking, a woman after my own heart.*

The word that I heard many people use to describe Lauren was 'remarkable'. Despite a childhood of abuse, and a life of untold physical pain, I never heard her complain.

One day, while in her teens, Lauren was standing outside the bakery, when she was tapped on the shoulder and a voice said, "Don't I know you?" As she turned round, Lauren knew she was looking into the eyes of her husband. Lauren and Frank married when Lauren was eighteen and they had eleven blissful years together. Frank was working for British Airways and Lauren was then an auxiliary nurse. Time off was spent enjoying battles on the badminton, squash or tennis court, riding their motorbikes and most of all bringing up their beautiful daughter Yolande.

At twenty-nine, after multiple miscarriages, polyps were found lining the whole of Lauren's uterus. It was a miracle that she had

had Yolande. The hysterectomy that followed permanently damaged her spine and bladder and for the rest of her life she was in constant pain.

Lauren turned all our children into really decent swimmers but after one too many medical setbacks, she had to stop teaching. One of the lowest points in her life was being told that the daily spasms she had developed, were psychosomatic; there was nothing they could do for her. Eventually, a consultant at Kingston hospital noticed that two of Lauren's pills (and she had a metre-long toolbox of them), should not have been prescribed together. She was told not to take them and in forty-eight hours the spasms stopped. By now though, Lauren was irreparably paralysed down her left side.

Yolande and her husband Gareth never found a suitable moment to marry because Lauren was in and out of hospital. However they did have two beautiful boys, Byron and Denny, and Lauren found great joy in being a grandmother. Yolande would place them when babies, on Lauren's stomach. When she came back an hour later, one or other would be fast asleep. It was their favourite place.

On the many occasions I took Lauren out in her wheelchair, we turned this to our advantage. We went through 'no entry' signs when in National Trust properties. At Hampton Court, I jumped down into a 17th century sunken garden and nicked two pears off a tree for us both.

My most magical day with Lauren was as her carer at Wimbledon on finals day. Shouting, "Make way, make way, wheelchair coming through!" I got Lauren courtside for a mixed semi-final, followed by Court One where we had tickets for a men's and women's final. We then got, thanks to a very helpful steward, the last wheelchair slot on Henman Hill to watch the final two sets between Roger and Rafa. At this point Lauren was exhausted. I settled her with St John's ambulance and while the morphine kicked in, ran to the ticket office for wheelchair returns. The final coup was getting the last pair of tickets on centre court to watch Jankovitch and Jamie Murray win the mixed doubles finals in a nail-biting three sets. As Lauren gave me the biggest hug in thanks, I asked if she would suffer over the next few days from overdoing it?

"Yes," she said, "but it would have been worth it."

Frank once said to me that he felt he could have done more for Lauren. Well, I've never seen love and devotion like it. No man could have done more. He and Yolande were the reason Lauren lived as long as she did.

Lauren, you are the epitome of stoicism, patience and humour, a standard that few achieve. Thank you for being such a dear friend.

Suzanne was Swiss French, (imagine the sexy voice, 'attend', 'alors', etc.) and married to a Scot with one daughter. She was my best golfing buddy. We got to know each other when playing in a team for Royal-mid-Surrey golf club. She had a wonderfully calm manner and came off the course with the same philosophical attitude whether she had won or lost.

However, there was so much more to Suzanne than golf. Making use of her fluent French, she volunteered five times a year, to clothe, house and mother a sick child sent from Africa to have an operation at St Ormond Street Hospital. This usually entailed meeting the child at the airport ten days before the operation, taking the girl or boy to see the specialists, visiting him or her whilst in hospital and then, after a few nights back at her house, seeing them safely onto the plane.

She became a trained hypnotherapist and offered to give me a session. She got me to imagine a place where nobody could hurt me, where I felt completely free to be myself. I visualised a real frozen *lake I had been to several years before in Canada. On that occasion I had crossed its five kilometres alone, walking or running between the serrations. Halfway, I screamed all the frustration of a loveless marriage to my Indian ancestors. I had crossed wolf tracks but wasn't bothered. When I returned, it was dark and the whole party I was with were fearing for me. They had stopped being able to see me in the telescope. The owner's wife, a Dutch Canadian, gave me a pendant of a real bear's claw mounted on silver. She had been told to pass it on to the next Free Spirit.*

"It is now yours to pass on in turn," she said. What Suzanne had done was to give me this ideal place of retreat. I go there in my mind whenever I need to.

When Suzanne was diagnosed with breast cancer, I was so distracted renovating various hotels, that I wasn't there for her, as she had been for me. Thank goodness we had three months together, the summer before, doing up her flat. The only time I had a presentiment that all might not be well, I spotted a tired, old woman walking away from her car. On seeing me, the smiling Suzanne snapped into focus.

The following November I was giving the Austrian pizzeria another makeover, when Nick rang to say that Suzanne had died. I collapsed against the wall. I had hardly seen her since the summer and had had no warning, probably because I was still in my selfish, self-pitying bubble. Suddenly I felt Suzanne nudging me; "finish the job and then cry as much as you like." I don't know how I got through the next two hours decorating the latrines on my own. Afterwards, as I opened the door to my room, there was my Royal Mid Surrey membership card, lying on the floor, square onto me so that I couldn't miss it. I felt Suzanne was saying, 'Don't worry, I am here with you.'

Suzanne and Lauren have been my companions in spirit on every mountain climb, every walk, on the GR20, especially on the

Road to Santiago. I had a vision recently, that Suzanne, Lauren and I were dancing in the air above the lake with childlike abandon. How wonderful if we met up like this in the next life! God bless you for watching over and guiding me. I love you both.

The first time I met **Stephan**, he was 23-years old, with curly brown hair to his shoulders and an earring in one ear. He had an infectious smile, with twinkling blue eyes and a wicked sense of humour. As a boy he had tended the sheep and goats on the Tyrolean mountains and with this knowledge of the terrain, coupled with a burning desire to be the best, he became the youngest ever qualified ski instructor and then the youngest ever qualified mountain guide.

That first week he led us off-piste[40] became twice a year for many, many years. He had us skinning[41] or climbing up ridges, to get to untouched snow. No day was the same as another. We were frightened but never bored. I made the mistake once, of telling Stephan I didn't like heights. From that moment on, he had me scaling every summit.

He was the stuntman for the lead in 'North Face', a gripping tale of the ill-fated climb by the Austrians up the North Face of the Eiger before the outbreak of the Second World War. He told me that only the night before climbing the last section to the summit, did it come to him how to do it. He pulled it off, wearing authentic 1930s plus-fours and woollen mittens. However, Stephan and the production team didn't know that two climbers were summitting from the other face. They nearly passed out with fright as they saw what they thought was a ghost running towards them, gesticulating to them to get out of the picture. A helicopter with the film-crew appeared a moment later.

Stephan got married at 21 to his polar opposite. He was leading parties up Kilimanjaro and teaching mountain guides in Bhutan. His wife, a hairdresser, hardly ever ventured out of her village. They had two beautiful children, Johanna and Bernhard, but the marriage could not last. A domestic pet with a wild animal.

One of my biggest regrets is that the last day I skied with Stephan was the worst we ever had with him. I had just found out about Nick's affairs, was in a filthy mood and left without saying goodbye. If only I could turn the clocks back and thank Stephan for giving me some of the most wonderful skiing moments ever.

We heard the following summer that Stephan and another guide had died in an avalanche. A cornice on Mont Blanc, the size of two football pitches, broke off, taking half the climbers and both guides with it. I was told that Stephan and the other guide were shouting a warning to their groups before they were taken, selfless and professional to the last. Stephan's pack was found but no body.

He was 39-years old and it seems fitting that he died in the place he belonged, rather than in a hospital bed that he loathed. It is also serendipitous that he had his children early and could see them well into their teens.

When I have to dig deep, Stephan is one of the people I turn to. All three of these exceptional people are my inspiration. Every time I see a pair of birds I'm reminded of Lauren and Susanne, and when a third bird joins them I imagine its Stephan.

Confinement

When asked to describe prison conditions I usually reply 'crowded.' The norm is that there are always people within feet of you and in the cells, this shrinks to inches. The background is a murmur of human voices in many tongues, rising and falling and occasionally flaring with rage, along with the clatter of pots, pans, plates and cutlery. A loud noise of any kind from behind you makes you jump and turn fast – it might be an altercation with or without weapons and you might be in the way. The racket only begins to subside after about 9pm back in the cells as the cons (and the screws!) settle down for the night.

Privacy anywhere other than in your own head is a thing of the past. Outside, the eight squat toilets sit side by side, totally open, with a small trough in front from which you scoop water with your bowl to clean up. In the cell the single toilet also doubles as a shower, the trough filling with river water as required. There is a courteous, unwritten rule among the prisoners to only shit outside. A plastic curtain provides the only time you can screen away everyone else, other than a spell in Building 10. The Thais are gregarious and really don't like it in solitary. They have been brought up from birth to live in one room with their families and are comfortable with the close proximity of others, unlike those in the west. In my case, a combination of peripatetic family life and boarding school prepared me to take this confined living in my stride.

CHANGE

'When you really want love, you will find it waiting for you.'

– Oscar Wilde, *De Profundis*

2011

June

Back in 2008, taking Nick aside, I told him that if things hadn't improved between us by the time William finished school, we should call it a day.

Now, three years later, it was the very day of our youngest son's Leavers Ball, and Nick and I were attending. As Pam, my hairdresser, was doing my hair, I confessed to her that I felt my life had to change, but that I had no idea how to go about it. She suggested I meet her Austrian friend Isabella, a spiritual healer who, she said, would give me, "a sense of my place in the world".

Little did I know on our first meeting, a week later, what a powerhouse Isabella would be. I rang the bell of an elegant, early Victorian house and a smiling blonde vision answered the door. I swear she was glowing from inside.

"You have asthma," she said, as she lead me to a pure white bedroom adorned with candles, incense and feathers.

"I take on the person I am seeing a few minutes before they arrive, and I have been struggling to breathe."

She then sat us both in chairs facing each other. She stared unblinking at me with this beatific smile. Five minutes passed. Ten minutes passed. Gradually I stopped worrying about paying for silence and decided to use the time and this beautiful room of peace, to pray. Isabella suddenly pulled her chair towards me, looked deep into my eyes and, still smiling, said, "Your marriage is over. Did you hear me? Your marriage is over."

After a long silence the words that came out of my mouth were, "How sad."

Isabella didn't alter her expression. She then connected to my deceased grandfather who was an Admiral in the Second World War.

"Your grandfather has come forward. He is saying 'chin up girl, head up girl.' He is proud of you. He loves you like his own daughter. He is smoothing the path in front of you. He is at his most powerful, in his fifties, in a suit with a waistcoat. He has taken out his fob watch and it reads three minutes to midnight. He is showing me a ship under sail and passengers boarding with their luggage. He says that, if you don't hurry, you are going to miss the boat".

She then asked, "What is it you want to do?"

"I don't know?" I replied.

"What is it you want to do?"

At the third time of asking, I was annoyed and without thinking I blurted out, "The GR20, The Road to Santiago and Tibet."

She beamed, saying, "Your grandfather is nodding. He says you've understood and he's putting away his watch."

More silence, then she asked, "What does Albert mean to you?"

"I know someone in IT called Albert."

She frowned impatiently, "no, no! What does Albert mean to YOU?"

"Well" I replied, "Albert was the loving and faithful husband of Queen Victoria. Their love was legendary. They had nine children but sadly he died young."

She beamed again. "Well my dear, you are going to meet your Albert and he will not die young."

Another pause and then she said, "Your Grandfather says you are going to soar."

She took my business card, dismissed it and designed another one. She told me that I had a gift for creating healing spaces, that I was all about balance and harmony.

The session over, I said goodbye and realized I had to take responsibility for my life. My children were now adults; they didn't need me for survival. I had used them as an excuse to sleepwalk through life. When I got back, I began from that moment to organise the GR20 and the Road to Santiago. Tibet would have to wait.

Vicky to Andy, 8th Letter

11 October 2011

Dear Andy

I am sorry not to have got in touch before. I think of you often, talk about you a lot, pray for you and hope you pray for me. Still a letter counts for a lot. I love getting your letters. Anyway, William (my youngest) has finished school, so after 22-years, no more fetching, carrying, doing homework etc. I set myself to do three things (GR20, Road to Santiago and Tibet) to mark that event:-

The GR20

This is the toughest trek in Europe, beginning on the northern coast of Corsica and ending in the south. I went with Gail, a Yorkshire ex airhostess and fitness coach. We were each carrying 7–9 kg on our backs. You follow red and white stripes of paint daubed on rocks and trees every thirty to forty metres. You walk seven to nine hours a day, arriving at a refuge that provides basic food (carrots, potatoes, pasta). We soon realised that it was better... hiring a two-man tent than staying in the refuge, sleeping side by side with 25 others and fleas jumping around the floor. We would be in bed by 8.30pm and would have left by 7.30am the next morning.

The scenery is rugged and absolutely breath-taking.

At two stages there was a hotel with HOT WATER!! Had a humorous moment on day one when I went into the kitchen of the refuge to ask if they had any cheese for the pasta. Was given a look as if to say, what planet are you on?

I never had a superficial conversation, or met a superficial person. Everyone was fit and searching for answers. A doctor in his 60's, Joseph, told me that (35 years earlier) he had found his three-year-old son dead in a nearby stream when he had meant to be babysitting. Everyone had forgiven him but he hadn't forgiven himself. I may have helped him[42] because the next day, he came to me and said thank you, that I had given him some pieces of the puzzle. He seemed lighter, sprightlier, so I told him that the next stream, pond, mountain-lake he came to, to jump in without a stitch on, nothing less would do. He had avoided water ever since that tragic accident, but now he laughed and said he would do it. He said that when God made me, he had thrown away the mould. I'll take that as a compliment! [...]

[...] Emma has given me a book co-written by the Dalai Lama and a psychiatrist, called 'The Art of Happiness'. Apparently, Happiness is a mental discipline, so every night I am trying to make my last thought happy and the first thought as I wake happy and stretch that out as long as possible. You are not going to believe it. For the last two weeks that I've been doing this, I have slept through the night, every night. I no longer obsess about Nick and what women he may or may not have slept with. I am now focussed on my next goal. That is; walking for six weeks alone over the Pyrenees to Santiago de Compostela. I know I can survive with very little to eat during the day and I have never been happier or felt more free than those nine days on the GR20. Talking of which, we finished the hardest part but still have six more days to go, which we are doing at the same time next year with a growing band of followers.

Another girl wants to do the road to Santiago with me but I think I want to be alone for that walk, to meet people along the way and go at my own pace.

Right, enough about me, all the children are thriving. By some miracle William got a B, C and D and so has more than made it to Ealing Film School. He's done some carpentry, painting and decorating for me and is now working in the marketing department at Nick's head office. "From exhausting to boring," he said. He's going to do a ski season and then hopefully travel and get to see you next year. Of course he's got to earn enough money. He's worrying about his spots. He spends a ton on cleansing products and then cooks himself a fry up!

[...]

Better news [...] Samantha has handed in her notice at Academy Films and will leave in a week's time. Already a number of people (directors, agents, producers) have approached her. Ben my bother-in-law, also in the business, says she needs to find her 'tribe'. Anyway she seems much happier all round.

Emma is full on with her music career. She is performing this evening with her boyfriend and has bought out a single. She's focussing on their duo, 'Shuga'.

They are all living at home, which is delightful. They can't afford to live anywhere else. Long may it continue.

Tom is taking a sabbatical, after two years at Uni. He's intending to complete his degree if he isn't offered the dream job. In the meantime he has organised placements with different sports/TV stations, BBC, ITN etc. [...]

31 October

Andy, I want to get this letter in the 5.30pm post. [...] Samantha was unemployed for just half a day, is getting paid four times her previous wage and is being sent to Mumbai for two to three weeks as a producer's assistant. She is in seventh heaven. Best thing she ever did leaving her other company.

[...]

Andy, hopefully you'll get the two books I've ordered for your Christmas present by Christmas – not spiritual I promise.

Lots and lots of love,

Vicky

*

This letter marked a change in my focus. I had always written to Andy about other people and how I was helping them, whether family, friends or Nick's business. The GR20 and Road to Santiago were purely for me and now there was an energy and purpose to my writing. By contrast Andy, who had been buoying me up for the last five years, now seemed to be the one struggling.

2012

For the last six years, roughly the same time Vicky and I had been corresponding, I had been investigating the possibility of transferring to the UK. To begin with, I couldn't bring myself to sign my transfer papers, having heard first-hand of the harsh environment of an English prison, where bullying and isolation awaited me. A creature of habit, I found Bang Kwang a relatively safe and happy place, described as 'easy street' by those who had previously served time in a UK prison and I had now made friends among the inmates.

Once my friend Steve had transferred in 2012, I again considered going through with the transfer. According to British law, if I transferred now, I would have to spend another seven years in an English prison rather than the eighteen months that I was originally promised. Therefore I would be 62 years old by the time I got out. I feared that any decision I made might prove to be the wrong one.

Andy to Vicky, 9th Letter

1 February

Dear Vicky

It's been an age since I wrote, for which I apologise. [...] I find myself paralysed by a feeling of helpless indecision, with frustration and unnatural – for me anyway – depression. Should I sign up for transfer, I might go back to the UK with yet more years to serve and the probable loss of any chance of some measure of Royal Clemency. Should I delay, I might have stayed longer than was needful [...]

[...] On parole there is no possibility of a passport and thus no travel to Poland, the only place I have any reasonable possibility of earning a living (teaching English) until my sentence expires. [...]

My pardon had reached the absolute top of the pile [...] when the amnesty was announced in December. But now I find myself back at the starting gate [...] while the warrants of imprisonment are updated. [...] It is so frustrating it makes me want to scream out loud. [...] Oh well, enough of that.

I do hope that either Will hasn't left yet or that you are in regular contact with him. The reason being, the rules regarding visits have changed drastically, for the worse from our point of view, naturally. Now we only get a 45-minute chunk of time [...]. The visitor must arrive [...] a minimum of 30 minutes before the time slot during which he/she wishes to visit. [...] Best if he comes with nothing in his hands, you get through faster. If he wants, he can get me a carton of fags – the universal currency – and some toiletries from the prison visitors shop. [...] I'll be the chap with the stick, a cap and a beard – no earring. Tom got that idea with no input from me! If he plans to go down to Koh Phangan for the full moon party, my advice would be to give it a miss. [...] Local vendors sell buckets of a lethal combination of cheap spirits and Red Bull or similar. [...] If he's on his own and does pass out, he risks waking up with empty pockets; if he's really unlucky, his passport will be gone too. [...]

[...] Now I must prepare my threadbare 'indoor' bag for another fifteen hours in the cell. A nice English lady bought me a replacement. First she sent it as a parcel – returned to sender. Then she tried to bring it to me – the foreign section desk rejected it. It's just a bloody empty bag for gawd's sake, which they check manually and X-ray. This is as mystifying as it is infuriating.

3 February

[...] Woke to some commotion at around 4.30/5am, a large squad of cops and screws were searching the ground floor of the block: sure enough, we were ushered out, minus our bags etc., just after six, and the Cossacks went at it upstairs as well. Since the block had been most comprehensibly searched two months ago, there wasn't a lot to be found, and I think they were focused on two things; drugs and mobiles, with cash found a bonus. Luckily for us, the tornado touched down in a different locker section of our block's exterior compound, where padlocks were cut through and lockers searched even before the block search started. C'est la vie, or 'that's the way the croissant crumbles.'

I probably forgot to thank you for the photos you sent, of you looking extremely fit, hiking in what looked like hill country, somewhere warm. There was a particularly good one of you apparently flying horizontally, presumably in mid-dive into a body of water. I last swam in the Gulf of Thailand – in the waters off Koh Samui. [...] It was December but the water was still quite warm. The coldest water I had to swim in was a Polish lake I was attempting to cross in a kayak; not a true kayak despite its name, far more open top. It, er, capsized in a collision with a similar craft and I ended up dunked in the middle of the lake. [...] I managed to swim back to the boat, get it right side up and clamber in. I even hung on to the two-ended paddle (which a real kayak has) and made it back to my starting point, exhausted. [...] I swear that lake never got above 3°C or 4°C at its warmest – it probably froze over in winter for all I know.

There's a district (Mazuria) in the north-east of Poland with hundreds of lakes, plagued by mosquitoes throughout the warm weather. I've avoided it on the grounds of hating mozzies. Can't sleep in a tent if I hear that distinctive mozzy whine, I have to find the damn thing and put it out of my misery! They are attracted to the colour blue because of blue sky reflecting on the water that is their breeding ground. Almost every surface in this nick is painted blue, of course. I may as well be in Mazuria. Even the ill-fitted mozzy screens are blue. Now that's what I call planning – by a sadist!

5 February

Another cooler, raining night, followed by blue sky and fluffy white stuff in the air this am. The latest new directive following the parcels ban (ostensibly to prevent drugs and mobiles being smuggled in, actually to ease staff shortages) has now [...] been followed by a ban on visitors bringing food (cooked or fresh fruit and veg) to prisoners. The parcels ban showed no sign of lowering the seizure rate of phones and drugs. I'll now predict that the visit food ban will not do so either. The implications [...] that neither were the principal route for contraband, will doubtless not result in the restoration of parcels and visitors food. [...] I'd long since resolved never to be surprised by the latest damn fool thing a given regime might do, but this is just too much. A cardinal rule in prison management if one wishes to avoid unrest, is: NEVER bugger about with prisoners' mail or prisoners' food. This lot have done both in the space of about three months. And, since the objective will not be achieved, to no purpose. Quite depressing, really. Having said that, Thai prisoners are far more docile, in the main, and accepting of authority (the amount of bowing and scraping, [...] would totally mystify English prisoners), but they do have a snapping point. When reached, the results are deadly, far more so than prison unrest elsewhere. Live ammunition is, often as not, the final resort. I do not want to be here if, or when, such a thing was to happen. [...]

8 February

Gordon Bennett, is there no end to this folly? On Monday, our new block chief [...] announced that henceforth only family would be allowed to visit. I chewed my nails over this one; bad enough that my ex-pat visitors would not, [...] be allowed to bring food from outside (rye bread, ham, cheese, fruit, all from Villa Market or Foodland or one of the other supermarket chains); now they wouldn't be allowed to visit at all. [...] Yet the following day, I got an afternoon visit (a rarity these days) from an English chap [...] whom I didn't know from Adam. [...] I then heard that the visit goods ban was not...only on food, but on everything, [...] including books, magazines, and [...] clothes. We wear our own in the block and a blue 'visit' shirt does duty for any foray outside Block Six's gate. [...] Eventually we will be in tattered rags. Prison issue blues are made of a material so shapeless, heavy, itchy and one-size-fits-none that one cannot conceive of wearing it full time; certainly not to sleep in.

And yet, apart from the parcels order, none of this has gone up on the noticeboard. The British ladies and some Australian fellow Samaritans, are acting as our families' representatives, holding money sent over, for us to make purchases or deposit in our accounts should the necessity arise. To bar them (whilst allowing missionaries, who convert no one, to continue to manage the financial affairs of others) is discriminatory in the extreme. [...] There is even talk of conducting some visits with a monitor and camera and watching imprisoned Kith or Kin on screen, not seeing them face to face at all! I fear some officers on a jolly to the US have been awed by the technology, and it's cost, with the opportunities inherent there, and convinced themselves, their masters and their ultimate masters in the Justice Ministry that all this 'sound and fury signifying nothing' is actually worth it. Since they are yet again in the early stages of another 'crackdown on drugs', with ludicrous targets voiced, they've actually gone for it! The mind boggles. A 'supermax' is to be built, or rather is being built/refitted, where bad boys get sent and get no visits, no mail, nothing. It bodes, well it just bodes, that's all! And what effect will this have on the drug trade, that drug prohibition alone makes so profitable. [...] Why, none whatsoever of course, except perhaps to encourage the perpetrators to buy heavier weaponry in order to evade arrest. Already a greater readiness to shoot it out rather than say 'it's a fair cop guv' or the Thai equivalent, has been noticed. If you know you'll spend twice as long inside for a drug offence as for murder, shoot your way out and ditch the evidence. Or shoot anyone remotely suspected of informing.

This is exactly what came about with higher drug sentences in the US – suddenly street punks with knives and the occasional pistol sprouted an arsenal of Uzis, Mac 10's and other automatic weapons, with no hesitation in indiscriminately using them. Prior to this, emergency surgeries for gunshot wounds [...] in Washington DC, Baltimore and Philadelphia would save four patients out of five. Afterwards the proportions were reversed, due to sub-machine gun wounds. Of course this is the country with a constitutional right to bear arms, or arm bears, whatever you want. And DC and Baltimore are right close to Virginia where you can buy a second-hand weapon at a gun fair with no checks whatsoever! As for Texas, it has more firearms than citizens – by three to one. Thailand is a major hub for arms as well. No one has the slightest idea how many weapons there are in this country. Not an earthly.

So, all in all, not a safe place to be. For Brits, indeed, a survey a few years ago showed it to be the destination most likely to result in the death of a UK Subject. [...]

Frankly I don't know if I am on foot or on horseback, with all these different problems colliding like rogue asteroids in my head during my more contemplative moments. I must try not to lose sight of my guiding principle, not to worry over what I can't change and to try to change what I can and consider that my best done. [...] God give me the strength to survive, and the patience not to wallop these half-wits, jobsworths and amateur management sadists.

16 February

[...] Still no sign of my own transfer consent forms, now three months late. My hope of arriving in the warmth of summer is rapidly deteriorating. [...] I am also trying to ensure my clemency petition, with its new warrant, moves asap back up to the palace, just in the hope that I can get a cut or at least an answer (it's been six years) to it, before I transfer.[43] [...]

I rang my mother yesterday, a brief conversation but at least she said she was feeling better than ever since she had the stroke. I meant to ask if she got out much, a wheelchair perhaps or a walker – but not in the weather the Northern Hemisphere's temperature zones have been having lately -36°C lower than here – eek! Lord, I hope I don't have to go back into the freezing cold from this sweatbox.

19 February

[…] I really hope that, since the last chick has flown the coop, you are enjoying your new freedom to the fullest. You deserve it. I likewise hope that my next letter has something more definite, more positive in tone, to impart. Re-reading letters from my ex-cell mate, it sounds as if, while being considerably cleaner and better organised in his UK prison, it is more of a lonely existence: the camaraderie, shared experience, the outdoor existence, these are things he obviously misses (also food sounds incredibly bland!). […]

Affectionately yours,

Andrew Hawke

PS Or Andy to my friends, which you all are.

*

I used to run past a burnt-out pine forest where the leaves were still green in the uppermost branches. The bark was blackened and there was a strange sacred feel about the place. I always stopped there to pray for Andy's release. One day as I began to meditate, I felt as though bands of energy were streaming out of my hands. The current was so strong, it enveloped me, pushing me down into a praying position, with my palms outstretched but turned upwards. I was pinned down for some minutes until the power was 'turned off.' It happened that at the time I had a medium staying with me. She said that Andy was at an all-time low mentally and physically and the best I could do, whenever I thought of him, was to visualise wrapping him in a pink blanket. I did this almost daily, never forgetting to tuck him in, particularly round his feet. She said that he might die but I was determined that if prayers could keep someone alive, mine and Danuta's would.

Vicky to Andy, 9th Letter

27 April

Dear Andy

I hope by now your mother has spoken to you. I probably won't know because I am doing the pilgrimage to Santiago de Compostela with a pack on my back, no mobile phone or watch on me.

Your last letter, with the knowledge of this impending trip, fired me up to do what I should have done long ago and that is HELP you. I have spoken to two judges, one MP, and a friend who extradites political prisoners, but finally I got lucky and received a message on my answerphone from Edward Fitzgerald, probably one of the most high-powered, proactive, human rights lawyers in the country. He promised personally to take on your case, but explained that 'we' needed to work under the auspices of a group of which he is a trustee called the 'Death Penalty Project'. As the name suggests, they deal with prisoners on death row but they do take on other cases, and the head of this organisation is called Parvais Javar. He [...] said that once they had your agreement, they would kick the whole system into gear, get you back to an English Prison as quickly as possible, B for a short period and then, with Edward behind you, OUT.

They have personally said they will help you from start to finish, but only if you help them 100% your end. Andy, please trust me as a dear friend of yours and say yes. I have had a letter back from our MP Justine Greening, Minister for Transport and she has spoken to William Hague, the Foreign Secretary, personally, and he is now looking into the deteriorating rights and conditions of UK prisoners in

Thailand, on the strength of what you described in your letter. If you could just get back to England, with your brain and eloquence you could champion this cause. You have the voice and I have got them listening.

I am dedicating this pilgrimage to you and it would make my life worth living to know that you had let me help you.

A friend of mine's boyfriend has just come out of a Cat B prison and written this manual, 'How to Survive Prison'. I am sending this letter separately in case the manual is confiscated. If that happens, let me know through your mother or by letter and he will write to you on the subject instead.

I feel sure now that you and I will meet. Samantha, Emma and Tom are taking up the baton while I am away. I should be back sometime before 11 June. It is time for you to come home.

I and the children will be waiting.

My love and prayers

Vicky

27th April

(Fragment of a letter from Samantha)

Dear Danuta,

Vicky was very concerned about Andy from his last letter… He sounded depressed and as if he was losing heart. My mum is doing the Road to Santiago on Monday and, a few months ago, in desperation for his plight, began trawling through her contacts. She spoke to two Judges, one MP, and many others before striking gold with one of the top defence lawyers in the country. His name is Edward Fitzgerald, and he is prepared to help Andy through extradition to release from an English

*prison as fast as possible through the auspices of the group
'Death Penalty Project' led by Parvais Javer.*

*All Edward and Parvais need, to fast track his case, is
Andy's assurance that he is willing to help in every part of
the process. They will give him a lawyer and a doctor to
check up on him [...]*

*

Three days after I'd written to Andy, I was standing in the
hall, backpack and passport ready when I got a phone call from
Niki, his brother. I quickly reopened Andy's letter and added a
postscript.

P.S. 30th April – I am leaving in half an hour. Have been in
touch with Niki. He has briefed me on your reduction in
sentence and your possible release this year and he is
liaising with Parvais and Edward to look into that aspect.
They will do nothing without your say so.

I hurriedly licked down the envelope, and ran to the post-box.

Lek

I started spending some time with an older Thai prisoner who
went by the name Lek. Short, squat and asthmatic, he, like
me, favoured the wearing of hats. Unlike most Thais, he
spoke quite reasonable English, and had insinuated himself
into a permanent daytime spot in the library.

There were six stacks of six shelves in there, and the
Thais jealously reserved five of them for Thai use... when
only five percent of their shelves were utilised. The "farang"
bookcase, on the other hand, was absolutely packed two

deep... Lek was methodically working his way through them, as I had already done. He kept an eye on them and stopped them being chucked out.

His attitude was decidedly stand-offish regarding the screws. Even though he had access to funds from outside, he did not flaunt this like the flash gangsters. He did not smoke, drink, take drugs or gamble. He did seem to have a large extended family, and one of these, an uncle, became of interest to me and Steve. He worked in the Pardons Office. More particularly, he worked in the King's Palace: the last link in the Pardons Office chain.

To this day, I do not know if my friend Lek's efforts on my behalf made any difference to my own submission for Royal Clemency. I had to chase that thing through several stages of the bureaucracy that processed it, and Lek's uncle couldn't really have had any influence on the steps prior to the palace. Nonetheless, once in the palace, the decision over plea submittals is shrouded in secrecy.

The fact remains that, unlike the overwhelming majority of applicants, my plea and that of Steve's, <u>was</u> acted upon and we received a substantial cut in sentence. And so, not long after, did Lek himself. His sentence, already down to forty years (!) after a general amnesty, was cut to fifteen years. This was almost unheard of for a Thai convict. The local screws and lags were open-mouthed in astonishment.

The Road to Santiago

May, 2012

For 25-years I had longed to walk the 900km 'Road to Santiago', inspired by reading Paulo Coelho's book, 'The Pilgrimage'. I had come to a crossroads in my life. I had done all I could to save the marriage but finally acknowledged to myself that it was a lost cause. Nick had 'left' decades ago but neither of us for our own reasons had wanted to admit it. I knew that now was the time to walk one of the most famous pilgrimages in the world. 'The Camino' as it was also known, would give me the strength to ask for a divorce. I got into training and did all the necessary reading. I'd already bought and tested the kit and walking shoes when doing the GR20 in Corsica.

I knew I was going to ask for a divorce the moment I came back, but I wanted to give us one more chance to stay together. On my last night I waited until Nick was in bed and then, standing in the doorway, I asked him if he had been unfaithful since confessing five years earlier. He froze. We eyeballed each other in silence for five minutes. I eventually turned on my heel, thinking that at least he'd had the decency not to lie this time.

I was dedicating the Camino to Andy and I intended to place a prayer stone on all the kilometre markers as a way of praying for his release.

A month before I set out, I found myself in W.H. Smith at Gatwick airport, asking God and the angels for a book that would prepare me spiritually. I found myself holding 'The Magic', by Rhonda Byrne, author of the world-renowned 'The Secret'. The book is a month course on gratitude. I quickly counted on my fingers and realized I would finish it on the day of my departure.

The Road to Santiago is, in fact, a series of roads throughout Europe, leading to the shrine of St James on the west coast of Spain. The 'Camino Francaise' that I was on, is marked every fifty metres by a yellow ceramic shell or a painted arrow. At night, if like me their budget doesn't stretch to a Hotel or Parador, the pilgrims disperse to 'Refugios', hostels ranging in size from converted churches housing 300 beds to tiny eight bed cottages. They will cook together or find a cafe that offers the ten to twelve euro

'Peregrino' menu, before going back to their bunks. Before dawn I would set off alone, to walk peacefully in prayer, until I found a place for breakfast. After that I would go with the flow, talking to fellow pilgrims and eating almonds and dried apricots. I made a point of visiting every church I passed. Once, I entered an 11th century church with no Renaissance embellishments. The purity and grace inspired such a feeling of awe that I prostrated myself in the form of a cross. If my children are reading this and squirming with embarrassment, don't worry, no one else was there!

I realized that I would do better looking with my eyes and listening with my ears than reading a guide book. I was not used to my backpack and at the beginning it felt really heavy, so I left my two treasured books, Paolo Coelho's 'The Pilgrimage' and Shirley Maclaine's 'The Camino' on a lost property table, and took a little rucksack for my valuables instead. I kept my diary and my wonderful Archangel Michael cards – short prayers providing gentle spiritual guidance. I had left my iPhone at home and have never owned a watch, so gradually I began to trust my intuition and 'know' where to go or stay, when to eat and whom to talk to or walk in silence with.

Significantly, on the first day of the pilgrimage, I only walked and talked to Françoise, an English divorcée. She told me not to be afraid. Divorce is bloody, but I would end up much happier and become freer to be my own person. This precious time with her rubber-stamped my resolve to ask for a divorce on my return. Thank you Françoise.

My wonderful physiotherapist, Stephanie, had told me to make the pilgrimage one of 'joy', so I asked Tom's girlfriend Louise, to prepare me a shuffle of my favourite tunes from Angelis and Josh Groban to the Rolling Stones, Guns N' Roses and Paulo Nutini. When there was a relentlessly straight, hot and dusty section, with a busy road nearby, I'd don my earphones and sing and dance my way along. I met an Irish priest on the road, Peter, who said a prayer sung was worth two said.

I got into conversation with a Swiss girl, who complained about the relentlessness of walking alone on this particular stretch. I told her I dealt with it by listening to music. She told me that I should be working through the boredom, frustration and negative thoughts, not blocking them out. I replied that I had never wanted this pilgrimage to be of the hair-shirt variety – I was done with suffering and she could keep it. I was going to tap into the huge positive energy that is 'The Camino'. She looked at me as if I were insane.

Throughout this month-long pilgrimage, walking seven to ten hours per day with a pack on my back, I had no aches, pains or blisters. I attributed this to joy and trust in a higher power. On the road, I realized that the word 'belief' was empty if there was no 'trust'. My mother is an out-and-out Catholic but she seems to worry all the time. I heard many people on the pilgrimage despairing, "I knew this hip would play up, this knee would give me jip, that I would get blisters." Where was their trust? However, everyone I met completed the Camino, and those who struggled physically were the ones with tears of joy at the end when they collected their certificates.

Three days in, I found myself in front of the most beautiful alabaster statue of Our Lady. I felt cold and, as the trail was deserted, it seemed the perfect place to stop and change into my leopard print leggings. I whisked the cycle shorts off and had just got one leg in, when I heard an American voice behind me.

"Excuse me ma'am, could you tell me who that statue is of?" I spun round to see a smiling, whiskered face.

"Excuse ME!" I spluttered, as I hastened to pull up my shorts,

"You have GOT to be kidding me. You are on the Road to Santiago and you don't recognise that statue? 'Maria Virgine' is written underneath."

"Well I am Jewish, I haven't got my glasses and it could be Mary Magdalene."

I knew, that with this grinning face and Billy Cristal humour he epitomised the joy I was seeking. He introduced himself as Michael (like my Archangel – what are the chances?) – and declared himself to be a semi-retired lawyer and agnostic, with no belief, but open to persuasion. He was walking the Camino, to thank a God he didn't believe in, for saving his life. It transpired that, before he originally set out, his wife had persuaded him to have a medical check-up, being in his sixth decade. It turned out he needed a quadruple bypass and so delayed his pilgrimage by five months. From beginning to end, it was a pleasure when our paths crossed.

The next day, an Italian pilgrim called Paolo invited me for a drink and quickly we became friends. He had been the singer in a two-man support act for rock bands on the US circuit before chucking it in and becoming a forester. His job was to travel the world checking that eco-friendly certificates were genuinely deserved. He wore safari gear and played the harmonica. I have fond memories of singing for hours with Paolo, Michael and Roloph, a Dutchman, to get through a particularly gruelling section.

Our feelings for each other deepened a few days later as I approached the bridge of Puente la Reina alone, and found Paolo waiting there. When he said, "I knew you would come;" without hesitation I replied, "I knew you would wait". Naively, I felt Paolo might be my soulmate and potential life-partner. I had had almost no experience with men before Nick, and the affection and courtesy he showed me provided a lifeline.

Michael had been walking with an Austrian mystic called Martin when I met him. Now the two of them left Paolo and I to walk alone. Eight days later we arrived at the city of Burgos. Michael had dinner with us and then left the following morning, saying, *"you'll find me in three days" – what's with these men and their biblical prophesying? – while I stayed on with Paolo as he was to leave the next day.*

As we were having our farewell breakfast in a café next to the Cathedral, Paolo said, "Don't you want to let your family know you are safe? Use my phone".

I texted Samantha, saying I hoped the family were all well and that I was loving the Camino. As we were getting up to go, Paolo's phone beeped.

"I think you should read this..."

09.08 Mon 14 May

> Hi mum, glad you are enjoying yourself. By the way, have you heard? Andy has received a full pardon and will be released shortly. X

At that I jumped up, tears pouring down my face and ran in front of the Cathedral with my arms outstretched. "Thank you God, thank you Jesus, thank you angels, thank you, thank you, thank you!"

*

25 April 2012

Six years to the day after I'd gotten the heart-breaking news of Denise's death, my world changed again. I was told that I'd been given a substantial cut in sentence by an individual act of Royal Clemency, to an arbitrary sixteen years. I had already served just over thirteen years four months. Four months later, following another general amnesty, my sentence was cut again and I now had only six months to go before I'd be released and deported.

*

The pilgrimage was dedicated to Andy's release and the impossible had happened. But now, did I have a reason to continue? Paolo was leaving at lunchtime and there was no one to share this joy with. Or was there? I decided to find Michael, the Agnostic-Jewish lawyer or 'Archangel Michael' as I called him, and to use the remaining two weeks of the pilgrimage to thank God for Andy's release. I knew Michael was a day ahead of me on the road, so I decided to get two days (forty-five km) walking done in one, to catch up with him.

I had started to look more and more like a pilgrim. I had acquired a beautiful staff, bought off an old man who had carved on it the name of every town and village I would pass through. He also carved a poem on the stick, declaring that he, Pedro, would guide me, 'Victoria', safely. Paolo had given me his 'Out of Africa' Robert Redford style hat and a large, pink, shell was dangling from my pack, so I was now, externally at least, a pilgrim.

I passed a bundle of Archangel Michael's blue plastic rope, discarded by the side of the path and had my first laugh of the day as I draped it round my neck like a feather boa. Of all the angels, he is the one with the sense of humour. Chelsea blue is my pet hate colour and I loathe artificial materials, so he reveals himself to me with this infernal plastic rope. It's also to remind me how far I've come since the days of my deepest depression, with its suicidal thoughts, and to remind me never to think of going there again.

A few hours later, I bumped into Françoise and Joan coming out of a greengrocers. We hugged and cried. Joan, a vibrant American, had been telling everyone she encountered, to meet at 4pm on her thirtieth birthday outside Santiago Cathedral. Now, as we sat together in the tiny village square, she told me she was about to quit because of her painful hip. "Absolutely not! This is your dream!" I said. "Whether you end up taking buses and taxis, complete it. See you on 6 June", and with that I left before she could change her mind.

It was now 3pm and I still had a day's walking to do to catch Michael. As I emerged onto a huge wheat plain, the skies darkened and soon I found myself drenched, rain, lightning and thunder all around me. I discarded the blue plastic boa by the side of the road. Just as self-pity started to get the better of me, the storm died away and a double rainbow[44] appeared. I knew then that the cycle of unhappiness was ending. I remembered Shirley MacLaine in 'Sweet Charity,' dancing and singing "if they could see me now," and skipped on with gusto, using my staff as a baton and Paolo's hat as a top hat. At the end of that number in the film, the camera pans away until Charity Hope Valentine becomes a little dancing figure in the distance. I imagined myself as a tiny dancing speck among wheatfields; above me, huge rainbows in a dark blue sky, the sun for the first time piercing through.

Shirley MacLaine walked the Camino alone, developing her psychic sense among other things and towards the end of the journey had powerful visions. At this stage in my spiritual development, I had not experienced visions. I felt like someone who has turned on the radio but can't tune into any channels. My ears hummed with the sound of angels and when meditating, the pressure would increase. At key moments, loud buzzing in my ears would remind me to focus carefully on my intuition.

That evening Archangel Michael (not Michael the lawyer), made his presence felt. I hadn't eaten more than dried apricots and almonds all day and had now come to a dark and deserted village. Just as I despaired of finding a place to sleep, I got the loudest piercing whistle in my ear. At that moment I heard an engine, and a few seconds later, a farm van appeared. I flagged it down and asked the driver to take me to the nearest Refugio. He drove 200 metres at high speed and pointed to a steep flight of steps. I ran as fast as I could, given the heavy backpack, and rang the doorbell at the top. A beautiful woman answered, said she was about to lock the door and that I was really lucky because there was only one mattress left. I asked if there was any food. She looked at me strangely. "Yes, I was just about to throw away a ready meal left by a pilgrim". Thank you Archangel Michael.

Hitching

I've hitched four other times. Once, in 1979 when my taxi broke down in sight of Luton Airport. Smoke was pouring out of the bonnet. I leapt out and persuaded a man in a digger by the side of the road to give me a lift the rest of the way. I thanked him profusely and then nearly killed myself getting out, because I forgot I was over a metre off the ground. Very undignified; very Bridget Jones!

Second in 1981, on Hammersmith roundabout, when my twin sister Sarah and I had been to an Arabian nights' party and were dressed as belly dancers. An open-topped sports car screeched to a halt. A man with dark sunglasses told us to jump in and then proceeded to drive in the opposite direction to our family home, saying he needed a drink as he was depressed about his marriage. Two hours later, he dropped us home, but insisted on coming in for a nightcap. Well, we soon had him shitting himself, as we pretended to hear creaking floorboards, saying we had a professional boxer for a father who had a terrible temper and was sleeping upstairs. He soon left.

The third time I hitched in 2011, I was racing to Lots Road Auctions to bid for a faux snakeskin coffee table for my son's girlfriend, (now wife) Louise. I was walking there with my backpack, to get fit for the GR20, but had underestimated the distance. As

I started running over Wandsworth Bridge and into Sands End, I knew I wouldn't make it unless a miracle happened. My ears were resonating loudly, a sign to listen up. From a sideroad, to my left, the biggest open-topped Bentley approached, the driver wearing designer shades and stubble. I ran in front of his car and begged him to get me to Chelsea Harbour where I could then take a short cut. The initial look of horror – I'd forgotten about the pack! – now relaxed into a grin and with a deep, sexy, Russian accent, he said 'Get in'. I had only seconds to register the cream leather interior and rich chrome, before we were heading down the wrong side of Sands End at breakneck speed with me pinned to the seat by the G-force. In 3.4 secs he had dropped me off at the barrier. I told him he was an absolute angel and had saved my bacon.

That evening when I came into the house, the boys were glued to the TV.

"Hi boys, I hitched a lift today."

No response.

"Hi boys, I just hitched a lift with Roman Abramovich."

They heard this time. Both didn't believe me. Tom turned on his laptop.

"What was the car?"

"Something like a Bentley."

He shows me the very same midnight blue car. "Yes, that's it."

"Does he look like this?"

"Yes. Identical."

"Ok, but why would he be driving alone without his bodyguard?"

No sooner has Tom said this, than he reads, "when in London, Roman likes to drive alone without his bodyguard or chauffeur."

The following Wednesday, Chelsea are playing. They score a goal; the camera picks out Abramovich and there is the very same smile playing across his face.

Vicky, Klosters, 1979

I once hitched in 1979 on someone's behalf and I do believe it changed my life. I was 21 years old. Newly graduated, the only way I could afford to ski was to rep for the Ski Club of Great Britain. I was working in Klosters and amongst the skiing party that day was a boy in his early twenties. As we were all crossing the road to an Alpine restaurant, he remembered that he was meant to be having lunch with his mother at the top of Klosters cable car in fifteen minutes. It would be the last time he saw her before going to work in South America for two years.

The group leaders studied their timetables but it was lunchtime and nothing doing. While they were faffing, I threw my hair back, unzipped my jacket provocatively and stood in the road with my thumb out. The first car coming round the corner screeched to a halt. I leant in invitingly and asked the driver if he was going to Klosters. "Of course!"

"Oh thank you because my friend needs to be there right now." He gave me a wry smile.

That evening, during my office-hour, a glamorous Swiss woman in her fifties walked straight up to me and said she could not thank me enough for getting her son to their lunch. She said her name was Kirsty. She was leaving in three days time but, until then, she was happy to take me and my group skiing. A brilliant skier, she was as good as her word, showing me local off-piste routes as well as giving me skiing tips. On the third day she introduced me to her friends, Hans and his girlfriend. She said they would guide me for the next two weeks with my group. It was in that fortnight that I made 'The Great Leap Forward' in my off-piste skiing. I was introduced to all the locals of Klosters and I never looked back. Four years later, on the night Nick proposed to me, a hundred people turned up to my ski club cocktail party.

The Road to Santiago (cont.)

Out of the hundreds of pilgrims walking each day, I was bumping into the same 25 people and felt sure this was not an accident. I called them my 'MAY 1st TRIBE.' One day a young Austrian boy fell into stride with me. He told me about life on his parents' farm, that it was his first time away and that he saw life as "half-empty.

"Not true," I said. "You are smiling and chatting to me and your way of walking is confident and expansive. You are definitely a glass half-full person."

"Thank you, thank you," he said. "Do you really think so?" He beamed and said goodbye, adding by way of explanation: "I walk faster."

One day, when walking up a hill with an uncommon number of pilgrims round me, everyone's pace quickened including mine. No, I thought, this is not a race. The only progress worth making is inwards. With that I veered off to the left, climbed a hill and lay down in the stubble until my heart rate had slowed right down. When I joined the path again, it was empty. I eventually arrived at a bar set up against some ruins, run by a very good-looking hippy. I sat down on a hammock next to a nondescript middle-aged Japanese woman, wearing a bonnet against the sun. Suddenly she broke into song and I listened in awe as this professional soprano sang 'Panis Angelicus'. How lucky that I had held back.

It was day three in my search for Michael. The guidebook said that for the next two days there were alternate routes. Two yellow arrows pointed at 90 degrees from each other. I stood silent, until I could feel a pull towards the right. "Ok angels. I trust you." That afternoon, I entered a deserted village. Feeling uncomfortable, I didn't stop but at the next village, I was done in and ready to sleep anywhere. As I approached a tiny Refugio, the door opened and there was a smiling, bearded Michael.

"I told you three days."

"Do you have any idea Michael, what I've gone through to find you?"

I got the last bunk and who was sitting opposite and completely exhausted but the lovely Austrian lad, Claus. "Half-empty, half-empty," he muttered. He could not even manage a smile.

While I rarely walked with the faster-paced Michael, I tried to see him in the evenings. We were often joined by three Canadian women. The oldest, Victoria, had her sister and 19-year-old daughter with her. They travelled separately but had a telepathic way of meeting up. Whenever I saw them, more often than not, I'd ask, "Where's Michael?" Eventually Victoria took me aside, saying I *should give the poor man some space. So for the next two days, if I passed Michael, I simply gave him a brief nod. Next time I saw Victoria, she said, "I made a big mistake. I think he's missing your company." I knew Michael was happily married, so felt completely at ease in his company. He was clever and challenging. He made me laugh and I realized it was manna from heaven to someone like me who had not had too many laughs in recent years. He was my friend in the purest sense.*

On the Road to Santiago, I continued to practise the energy healing I had begun on the GR20. A South Korean girl came up to me, almost in tears. Her friend translated that her ankle was swollen and she was worried that she would not be able to continue. She let me put my hands on her. I then asked Archangel Raphael, the angel of healing, to work through me. After a while she said something to her friend, who told me that my hands were boiling hot and currents of electricity were pulsing through her ankle.

I saw Victoria dangling her inflamed foot in an ice-cold stream. Walking away, Michael whispered that he had seen that injury before and she would not be completing the Camino. I was shocked. We were two-thirds of the way there. For the next two days I did absent healing and put down prayer stones for her. She would be finishing if I had anything to do with it! The following evening I caught sight of Victoria approaching me from the other end of a village street. "You have been healing me, haven't you?" she said. She got better and finished, but how did she know? I hadn't told a soul.

The next day, at an old monastery, I was preparing a meal together with twenty or so pilgrims. Once seated, our host asked if we could say our name, where we were from, why we were doing the Camino, and requested we sing a song. I sang the refrain, 'Into your hands O Father I commend my spirit.' I told them that I had been walking for Andy's release and since the news of his 'full pardon', I was walking in gratitude. Afterwards, the host gave me a badge with the St George cross on it and told me, "Take it to the Last Knight Templar you will meet tomorrow. Tell him I gave it to you." He also said, "I am a friend of Paolo Coelho and when I next see him, I will tell your story."

At 9:30am the next morning, we arrived at an encampment: a series of makeshift rooms made out of corrugated metal. An old man, dressed like a medieval knight with a sword, led prayers in Spanish. I understood next to nothing. A young Mexican kindly translated for me, "The Camino is a river of love which has been in existence since before Christianity. It exists to counteract all the pain and suffering in the world." Afterwards the Mexican introduced me to this holy man and I showed him my badge, explaining why I had been given it. He told me, through my translator, that I had a great heart, full of courage, and that St George and the badge would protect me. However, before I became too big headed, he told me that everyone who walked The Camino had courage and protection.

Ten days before reaching Santiago, Michael and I arrived at the 'Cruz de Ferro.' This iron cross, just under two metres high and supported by a stone column, stands on an ancient pile of stones and can be seen for miles around. Pilgrims, for thousands of years, have each carried a stone on their journey, representing their burdens, which they place under the cross. In the unbroken silence, clambering over thousands of stones, scattered with garlands and photos, I placed Paolo's as I had promised, and my own. I had been walking with Michael but my heart was so overwhelmed by the centuries of pain and sorrow gathered in this sacred place, that for the rest of the day I travelled alone.

Like the serrations on a scallop, all paths from Europe begin to converge on Santiago. Mike Brierley's guidebook suggested taking a different route for a day, away from the alternative bustle of main roads. It had been the Camino two hundred years before and *wound its way over passes, through tiny villages, providing shade and pumped well water but nothing else. I followed my nose, while Michael and Johnny, a young English boy, followed behind with the guidebook. A woman in black, led cows and an enormous bull past us, the beast's horns almost touching me. Another old woman, also in black, was riding side-saddle on a donkey. After ten hours, we arrived at a village. I knew intuitively that the last house, with washing hanging on the line, was our destination. However I had to bite my tongue while Johnny and Michael asked for accommodation at every place along the way. Only this last house had rooms available.*

A few days later, tired and dusty, we arrived at Santiago! I felt a bit flat as I went to collect my certificate, but my spirits soared when, queuing up just behind me was Martin the mystic, and a much slimmer Roloph. Martin told me that when he had laid his prayer stone under the iron cross, he had had an epiphany. He felt, through every fibre of his being, all the sorrow and pain that had been laid at Christ's feet over the centuries. Ill and weak, he was forced to rest for a few days which was how I had caught up with him.

We went to the Cathedral at noon for the pilgrim's mass. Who should be standing outside but Claus, the Austrian. He looked at me astonished, and lifting me high into the air, shouted, "Full! Full! Full!" The atmosphere was electric. Inside, I recognised many of the pilgrims and went and hugged each one. At the end, the huge incense burner was swung by the monks from one side of the transept to the other, seemingly about to crash into the rafters. The smoke and strong scent filled the cathedral. Afterwards, to celebrate, many of the 'MAY 1st TRIBE' ate together. We reminisced and laughed, but I felt a little sad that nearly all the group were now finishing.

Saying goodbye is never easy, so I slipped away before dawn, not without waking a groggy Michael and, with tears pouring down my face, told him: "If you want to see the face of God, look in the mirror."[(45)]

It was 2 June, so I had time to walk to Finisterre, and be back in time for Joan's birthday. Only ten percent of the pilgrims continue on after reaching Santiago. This section is wild and barren, passing through four villages in as many days. The god of this path predates Christianity and attracts younger pilgrims, agnostics and those spiritually hungry. The idea is to burn your clothes at Finisterre, 'the end of the world,' and take on your new self. On that first morning I didn't see a soul. After some hours, I sat on a fallen tree trunk and tucked into my almonds and dried apricots. A lone figure appeared, in his fifties, sporting a limp and twinkling blue eyes. We walked together for an hour or two. He told me his name was Uver. He had grown up in East Germany and had escaped over the wall one month before it came down! He had wanted to give something back to society and so joined the prison service. After 20 years he had developed stomach ulcers and was invalided out. I asked him about his limp. He had used his early retirement and compensation funds to explore the world. Trekking down from the mouth of a volcano, his front foot slid forward as his footing on the shale gave way. Unfortunately his back foot got caught between rocks and his leg almost came away from its socket, all the sinews overstretched. Despite operations and specialists, the damage appeared to be irreversible and he was now in constant pain. Perhaps he hoped for a miracle cure on the Camino. He is in my prayers. I loved his company but I felt the need to walk this section alone and so hurried on.

On the following evening a whole load of the 'MAY 1st TRIBE' were already at the Refugio on my arrival, including the three Aussie nurses, 'The Three Graces.' They were very distinctive because they carried smaller packs than anyone else, with their washing hanging off the back buckles. When they walked side by side, they looked like a Chinese laundry. I had my angel cards and gave them all readings. We went to a café together and I realized that everyone around the table was in some sort of caring profession. I told them about Lauren, got quite tearful, and I think they were very moved.

The next day I walked alone. It seemed fitting as it was the last day of the pilgrimage. When I had my first glimpse of Finisterre from a rise in the path, I stopped to thank God for this remarkable experience. I had journeyed 900km to find a peace that five years ago I would have sworn was not possible.

I thought of all the wonderful fellow pilgrims I had journeyed with. The woman resting by the side of the path with the most beautiful and serene face, that made me catch my breath. The American honeymoon couple sharing my bread and honey and us raving about the local hot chocolate, causing a run on it and a British writer exclaiming that it was indeed the best hot chocolate on the Camino. Two retired firemen walking to thank God 'who we don't pray to but who we support', for keeping them safe during all those years. Sitting outside an ancient monastery in the afternoon sun while Meta, a beautiful Dutch girl, told me about being alone in a wood for three days and nights, and a rabbit talking to her. Her mystical eyes were mirrored in the faces of almost all the pilgrims in their final week. I was struck by how calm and gentle everyone had become.

I was nearing the end of the road. On the outskirts of Finisterre, an overwhelming loneliness hit me. I sat down at a picnic table and tears started to fall. I looked up and in the tree above me hung an old rope tied into a noose. For God's sake Vicky, look how far you've come! You've completed the Camino and, in the process, found an inner strength to look after yourself, be more content in your own company, share the experiences of so many different people and find joy in living for the moment. It had been liberating to have nothing more than a back-pack, which I could now hoist effortlessly onto my back. I was now much fitter physically, mentally and spiritually. My faith and trust in God had increased. For the first time in my life I had only myself to worry about. I'd been through the mill, but I'd survived.

That evening I set off alone for the lighthouse four kilometres away, to burn mine and Paolo's headbands. I'd also been given some sandals by an Australian girl I'd walked with. She had run out of time. I offered to burn them for her and so she threw them to me out of the departing bus window.

I hadn't thought about how this burning was actually going to take place. When I got to the lighthouse, there were many of the 'MAY 1st TRIBE,' all in their twenties, who invited me to join them, wine and nibbles aplenty. A German boy, who had irritated me throughout the pilgrimage because of his extremely loud voice, redeemed himself by opening his pack and producing lighters and paraffin. He found a hole in the cliff rock, started a roaring fire and we burnt our various articles of clothing. The flames leapt up as if trying to kiss the setting sun. A helicopter flew overhead and the sky darkened. A beam from the lighthouse circled round us. Jacob, a beautiful Danish boy, told me that he had found out, two weeks into the Camino, that he had failed to get into the music college he had set his heart on. Worse still, the year before he HAD got in, but turned it down to have a gap year. In England you can defer your place, but not so in Denmark. He said that in completing the Camino he had found a way to accept the situation.

It was not his loss, in my opinion, but that of the college. As the German boy and I began to walk back, Jacob turned to us and said that we should sing a round in Latin. Pitch perfect and patient, he made us go over and over our parts. When we finally put the harmonies together, what a sound! We didn't dare stop. Unknown to all of us, a husband and wife in their sixties were walking behind. The woman must have been a professional singer. She used our round as a background for the most beautiful of arias.

The next day the heavens opened. Having experienced only five hours of rain in the whole month, it now bucketed down. I decided to have a baptismal swim in the sea. The beach was deserted, with the exception of a lone fisherman and a woman dressed in a long black cagoule, looking like something out of 'The French Lieutenant's Woman'. I was wearing my lilac waterproof top and the palest blue waterproof golf trousers. As she approached me, I caught my breath. It was none other than the beautiful woman I had seen sitting by the path almost a month before. It turned out that she was an American writer called Jenny. This was her fifth Camino and she had come ahead of her lover, in order to get down to writing. She had been waiting on the beach for him to show up. Although she had met him on her third Camino, she was beginning to wonder if he was the man for her after all. She had just asked God to send a sign, when I had walked onto the beach in my angel colours, to her like some apparition. "Who is this man? I may have met him", I said and she replied, "Uver." "You and Uver? You and Uver?", I kept repeating, "You two are a marriage made in heaven." At that I whisked off my clothes and ducked and dived amongst the churning grey foam. She took photos of me as I danced for joy at the thought of these two beautiful souls together. She asked me if he had mentioned her. "No, but we didn't talk for long," I replied, thinking: Men, really!

That evening I found Uver and Jenny sitting outside the pizzeria. They laughed as I shook my finger at them. "You could travel the whole world and never find someone so suited."

The next morning I got a bus back to Santiago. I went straight to Zara and bought some pale-blue jeans and a turquoise cardigan. I bought a silver scallop pendant and chain which I have worn to this day. I booked in at the Seminario Minor as a treat to myself. For 28 euros, this old monastery sports vaulted 12th century dining rooms and individual monks' cells with en suite shower!

The next day was Joan's Birthday. As I came down in the lift, I heard two Americans discussing a rendezvous with "Joan" at 4pm, in front of the cathedral. There was a crowd of at least 20 people, including Françoise, who I hugged tearfully. Her eyes, I saw, had grown as soft and gentle as a deer's. Finally, Joan appeared. She was with her boyfriend (now husband) who had flown all the way from the States. How healthy and happy! No pain at all! When she saw me, she burst into tears, and ran to greet and hug me. "Archangel Michael's rope healed me," she sobbed. She explained that the day after I had seen her and Françoise in the square, she had spotted my blue plastic boa lying in a heap where I had discarded it. She cut off a strand and tied it to her pack. She said she knew from that moment, she would complete the Camino.

The next day I left for the airport. At Stansted, Tom and Samantha were standing at arrivals with a homemade banner sporting: 'Welcome Home Pilgrim'.

Unfortunately our joyous banter came to an end when I told the children in the car that I was going to ask for a divorce. They had organised a surprise party back at the house and were very upset by the news. When everyone had gone, I told Nick, and knew in that moment that life as I had known it would never be the same. The Camino Francaise had built back my strength and confidence but I didn't know how deep I would have to dig to cope with what was to come in the months and years ahead on the 'Camino of life'.

*

The last and youngest of the Oak family to make the trip to Bang Kwang was William. Like his siblings, he arrived in Thailand on his gap year. He had trouble from the start which might have been due to his hangover from the heavy night before. His cabbie took him first to the big facility at Klong Prem, in Bangkok proper. He was then ferried to two or three other nicks in the city, before finally he grabbed a motorcycle taxi upriver to Bang Kwang.

When he got there he had a further difficulty. Since he had not given me warning of this visit, I hadn't cleared my busy schedule, and my regular visitor Bill was already talking to me. He roamed the visitors' area with no idea what I looked like. More puzzling to me, when I later heard of it, was that he didn't ask anyone who I might be. I found out much later that he eventually rang the British Consul, who confirmed that I had a ponytail and was in the visitor's area, rushed back in, only to watch me being led away. He had come 6,000 miles and was less than six feet away! I had to marvel at this when he later told me of it.

Vicky to Andy 10th Letter

19 July 2012

Dear Andy

By now you will have probably heard about the fiasco of William's visit. He was standing three feet from you, had finally guessed it was you but didn't want to barge in on your conversation – and then the visiting hours were over ....so disappointed for you and him. However, everything can be put into perspective by the fantastic news that you have been given a, "full pardon and will be released shortly." (Samantha's words) I cannot wipe the smile off my face.

(Fragment unsent)

2013

I am only three weeks away from being released from Bang Kwang, sentence completed. I am anything but calm. People are asking me, "are you all packed?" Good grief, I've accumulated so much stuff.

I started with one locker, tile topped, about the size of a washing machine, in a 'house' of 10 lockers arranged in a square, leaving the central area and an 'exit' free. The 6 or 7 farang occupants gradually shrank as men transferred back home. Eventually I was the sole possessor of all the lockers and somehow I managed to fill them all, bar one that I gave to my 'boy', The term was widely used for anyone who cooked (or did laundry) for another, in our case usually an ethnic Chinese – they tended to be the best cooks.

The front two lockers are for kitchenware, with an extra one as overflow for foodstuffs including a dozen or so cartons of Krong Thip cigarettes for cash emergencies (I smoke roll-ups). Another couple I use for clothes, towels, linen, etc.

One locker holds all my stationery and correspondence, boxes of stuff in there. The rest are FULL of books. I read all the time and am very fortunate indeed that so many were gifted to me by so many good people. But just properly sorting through it will take scores of man-hours. Assorted paper products alone must come to almost a hundredweight. What to do? I dither. I engage in various kinds of displacement activity.

Andy to Vicky, 11th Letter

8 January

Dear Vicky

First, let me apologise, hopefully for the last time, for taking so long to write you a proper letter. [...]

I am in a state of constant, exhausted tension and anxiety over my release and return. You'd think euphoria would be the emotion, but it just isn't so. A chap I met in here donkeys years ago used to work for the California Department of Corrections. He reckoned that prisoners kept longer than seven years were totally institutionalised. I've been in for twice that long. Whether the statistic can be applied to me remains to be seen. The majority of my time was spent under a regime relaxed by Western gaol standards [...] But the ultimate purpose of the place is the same as any other of its type, so I am not sure. The test of it is yet to come.

I thank you for your offer to take me clothes shopping. Pride says I should refuse, or politely decline. Poverty says otherwise. My most pressing needs on arrival will be firstly, accommodation and secondly, financial support. What's left of the welfare state is all I can rely on for both of these. Ideally, I would like to find, immediately, a housing association that would take me on. They make the best landlords, so I am told. As to other benefits, well, initially I was frightened by something called the Habitual Residence Act, which stipulates that a UK citizen who has lived over two years abroad cannot claim any benefits for at least six months, which would have seen me in a cardboard box underneath the arches (cue music). Happily, the recently retired Kate from the consulate told me that this exclusion specifically does not apply to people returning from detention abroad. Phew!

So social security, on which I must perforce rely to keep body and soul together, is on. But, absent of an address, I am still in trouble. I can't live at my mother's place: no room, my brother Martin is a no-no (sister-in-law would object vehemently): and my other option, Kay, an old girlfriend who wanted to marry me, passed away. I shall be coming back, but not home, as I don't have one, and this is my biggest worry by far. My brother Pete has said he would come over from Poland to be there when I arrive and sort out somewhere for the first few nights, but helpful as that is, it is only a stopgap and not a solution. I really am almost paralysed with anxiety on this point. It looms large in my mind every single time I think about going home.

You'll see from the above that perhaps the Californian was right, I must be institutionalised to be feeling like this. Knowing that this is the cause of my worry, doesn't do anything for the effect, though Valium might, in a large enough dose.

I try to think of things unrelated to the process of 'sorting myself out' when I get back [...] Apart from finally getting to see my son Quinlan, whose seventeenth birthday is a couple of months after I land, I have one obligation I must fulfil. I promised Eric McGraw, the editor of *Inside Time*, that I would write eight hundred words on the whole experience of coming home from such a long sentence abroad.

I read your little note inside the card and was saddened for you, that after so many years, you are divorcing. First everyone loses in a divorce. You'll be hurt by a gradual falling off of friendships with other married women: you will be single again, therefore ever so slightly dangerous in their eyes. [...]

I am glad to hear your offspring are all doing well. I'll always have a soft spot for Sam, the first to visit me. She seems to have her head screwed on right and is a thoroughly good-hearted person besides. You can be justifiably proud of the brood you've raised. I would be.

Despite my worries over what will happen when I get back, quite frankly I can hardly wait to be gone from here in, what, fifty days' time. I am just so tired of being around drug pedlars, murderers, kidnappers, bank-robbers, conmen and thieves. The prisoners are nearly as bad. (This is a joke on the screws, in case one of them has learned to read English and is in charge of censoring our mail!) [...] The fairly relaxed regime that was in evidence when I arrived, has been progressively tightened, to our detriment, over the years. It is a statistical certainty [...] that some will not survive [...] I suppose I should count myself lucky that I am not amongst their number.

It's gotten warm again, 33°c and sunny blue sky. [...] What sort of weather will I be coming back to? Silly question: England in March!

I'll close now to catch tomorrow's post. All my best wishes to you, to Sam, Emma, Tom and Will. I promise I'll ring as soon as I am back. For now though, I'll bid thee adieu.

Yours ever

Andy

*

Samantha and I are now in regular contact with Niki regarding Andy's release and arrival in the UK.

Andy's letter of 8 January is full of fear for the future instead of joy at freedom after so long. The day after I receive it, Niki calls, also full of fear. He tells me that there is no room in his mother's house as originally promised. He, Danuta and a full-time carer have commandeered all the bedrooms. He tells me that Andy can stay for three days and then he's on his own.

I put down the phone and immediately pick up pen and writing paper. The situation is untenable. If I had flown from the Far East, I wouldn't be over jet lag in three days, let alone ready to face life in what will seem to Andy, after fifteen years, a foreign country. It's going to take months to become part of the system – social security, GP, housing. He will arrive back to laptops, iPhones, oyster cards, and a transformed London skyline for pity's sake. How many friends will he be able to track down? Kay and Denise are dead, his two-year-old son is now seventeen and living in Norfolk. How is he going to be reunited with him when he hasn't got a penny to his name, and really this reunion with his mother and son Quinlan are the only things that matter. I write fast and furiously to make the evening post.

Vicky to Andy, 11th Letter

1 February 2013

Dear Andy

Delighted to get your letter, and I am hoping against hope you get this before your release sometime in March.

Not to beat about the bush, I would love you to come and stay with me indefinitely until YOU feel you can stand on your own two feet. The best way I can put this is as a list.

1) *I am now on my own, living on a building site, talking to four walls so your company would be really welcome.*

2) *Tom is in his last year at Leeds reading Broadcast Journalism. He is really keen to make a documentary about you [...]*

3) *Don't worry about money/food/roof over your head. I will always have enough to share. What is much more important, once you have found your feet, is your wish list... It doesn't matter how trivial. Clothes are on the list and taken care of. Give them a big tick along with roof/food/friends. I can't guarantee heating/hot water as the plumber keeps turning it off! Possibly by the time you get here, nearly all the plumbing will have been done.*

4) *Have you learnt from the Thai prisoners how to meditate? Samantha, Tom and Emma are into it big time. It will be far more use to you than Valium.*

5) *This is the hard part Andy. [...] I think you should make a promise to yourself that you will not touch drink and/or drugs. If you do, you will have to leave.*

6) *You have so much to offer with your brain, eloquence and experience [...]. It's great writing this article for 'Prisoners Abroad'. They said that if you were up to it, they would like you to give some lectures.*

7) *The main thing is to get sorted/acclimatised. We can get a medical for you. A course of vitamins etc. If in any way you feel I am behaving like a bossy older sister (even if I am a year younger), just tell me to back off.*

8) *If you want privacy/quiet, just say.*

9) *At Easter I would like to go to the house in Portugal. If there are no restrictions on travel, the children and I would love you to come with us and have some TLC. Probably about ten days.*

10) *I'll get you an oyster card (half-price travel card) which you can use for buses/underground and overground and just top up. Go and visit your mother*

as often as possible because she has waited so long to see you (bossy again!) [...].

Lots of love

Vicky

P.S. My neighbour down the road has been involved with the plight of prisoners her whole life. She says she wants to talk to you about all the options, including getting a degree.

*

Mail call, and a letter from Vicky. There is, in response to my telling her of my raft of problems to be solved on my return, an answer to one of them. She's offering to put me up for as long as necessary at her house in Putney. But there is a thorn buried in this offer, the sharp point of which now pricks me. She says I'll have to deal with my "drink and/or drugs" problem or I'll have to go.

I get out a writing pad and start to pen a reply. I don't even know whether or not I am going to gratefully accept this offer, or regretfully decline. I put the letter aside and, in the event, will never finish it. I shall go with the flow and trust to luck. I cannot really think of anything better to do.

*

Reading back over this letter I am embarrassed, as all I needed to say was, "Don't worry Andy, there's a bed for you here." I sound bossy, controlling and am under some misconception that Andy will hit the ground running and do, do, do. Perhaps, when I had no control over my own life, I was throwing myself into his. Well at least my heart, if not my head, was in the right place.

I've always worried about the adverse effects of alcohol. I had a wonderful grandmother, highly intelligent and artistic, who I watched, while growing up, secretly drink until dementia set in. At one moment Grandma was paranoid that my mother and sister were stealing from her, and in the next she'd be found walking naked down Sloane Street. One day Boozy and I found her unconscious in her flat; horrifyingly we'd entered her hall to see an arm lying lifeless on the floor. She was lying in her nightdress among shards of china and glass. It seems she had drunkenly lost her balance, grabbed her dining table and, being of a pedestal design, pulled it over, along with a china bowl and a pair of silver cockerels. Then she must have tried to stand up using her glass shelves, with prize china arranged on them, and brought the whole thing on top of her. She was taken to St John and St Elizabeth hospital, at death's door, and yet a few hours later was rummaging in her suitcase for a bottle of gin! As she was dried out, the nuns showed me their scars where she'd scratched them. I got a call from one sister:

"Mrs Booth is refusing to take her medicine; her brother Mr d'Abreu prescribed it."

My grandmother snatched the phone off the sister and in a baby voice said, "Frank says I don't have to take it."

The sister came back on, "she does"

Grandma snatched the receiver back: "I don't"

It sounded like they were having a tussle, and then the line went dead. I hoped my grandmother hadn't strangled this poor nun with the phone cord.

My grandfather and uncles were also 'heavy drinkers'. Uncle John, a child prodigy, ended up with dementia as well, going to the races impeccably dressed, although he had overlooked one thing: his trousers.

A few of my in-laws were alcoholics. I had watched my brother-in-law, before he joined AA, descend into bankruptcy, and the misery that caused my sister and children. I had worked my adult life on building sites and seen drink cause no end of mishap. Two of the team had served time for GBH while under the influence.

My youngest sister had struggled with drink and drugs and I worried that my own children might carry this addictive gene. The last thing I wanted, with the divorce starting to get underway, was to be taking on more problems.

The Second Discovery

In that rushed last 11th letter to Andy, I had added a final paragraph almost as an afterthought...

Vicky to Andy, 11th Letter cont.

1 February 2013

[...] Three weeks ago today, Nick followed me upstairs. I said, "You're going to tell me something serious."

"Yes," he said.

He told me that he had been having a 10-year relationship with a Russian woman, sixteen years his junior. He bought her a townhouse in Marbella 9 years ago and they have a five-year-old son. Having found this out, our children won't speak to him. Samantha is engaged but won't let him lead her down the aisle or make a father of the bride speech. Tom told him that he had stolen ten years of my life by not telling me and said he would not speak to him again if I was not happy with the settlement.

As you see, we are both in our own ways at Ground Zero, with not a clue as to the future. Can't wait to meet you! [...]

*

This bombshell revelation of mine passed Andy unnoticed, understandable considering he was experiencing major upheavals of his own.

Nick had moved out at the beginning of 2013, although I'd told him there was no need. He said his lawyer thought it was for the best. Each night, however, he kept returning to have supper with all of us and then watching television until nearly midnight before leaving. This was out of character, but I just thought he was finding it hard to leave the family home. On the fourth night he followed me upstairs, when the children had gone to bed. He told me he'd been having a relationship with a Russian woman for the last ten years. There was a five-year-old boy. His next words were, "I know how you must be feeling. She has two or three other lovers."

Nick had finally found the courage to tell me. At that moment I felt released from a 'cloud of unknowing'. I finally had the missing piece of the puzzle. The next morning, his divorce documents, Form E, landed on my doorstep containing all previous income and expenditure transactions. They also revealed the existence of a girlfriend, Anna, and son.

I must have been in shock at this revelation, but my immediate feeling was relief. A weight had lifted from my shoulders. Finally I knew the truth. Nick rang each of the children the next morning to tell them. I felt I had, after all, made the right choice in asking for a divorce. I knew I had to get the hell out of this marriage.

How had I not known about this other family? It was mind-blowing that Nick had managed to keep this secret not only from myself and the children but also from his friends and relatives. Despite having a secretary, he booked his own flights and kept his own diary. She once broke down in tears to me, saying she never knew where Nick was when asked, and she felt it made her look incompetent. Tied to the home and children, I couldn't be with him and also had no idea where he was. My Godmother, who used to work for the Ministry of Defence, said that Nick would have made a brilliant spy.

Following a fitful night's sleep, I rang Nick, my mind buzzing with questions about our marriage in the light of these revelations. After answering two, he said in the coldest voice I'd ever heard, "If you ask me one more question, you will never hear from me again."

Later that year I went to the Edinburgh festival and there listened to a TED talk on 'Lying.' The speaker, a lecturer at the university, told us how, when a teenager, her mother became obsessed with the idea that her husband, a dentist, was having an affair with his assistant. Her father denied it but the mother wouldn't let it go, began drinking and their rows became unbearable. After six interminable years, her father sat her and her siblings down and said, with despair, that maybe it was time to have their mother sectioned – she was clearly delusional. Luckily, not long after this, her mother received a call from a stranger saying that his wife was having an affair with her husband. The speaker defined her father's manipulative behaviour as 'gaslighting'.

This was the first time I had heard the term used and I wondered if I had also been gaslighted? I began to read up on the subject and immediately identified with 'the victim'. In Theodore Doopat's, 'Gaslighting', the author speaks of the "manipulation of (the) victim's honesty and love." I was trusting, naïve and gullible. Having witnessed my parents' incompatibility, I so wanted a perfect marriage. I had seen my mother try to control my father's every move and vowed not to do the same. My mother pried into my twin-sister's things when she was nineteen, found the pill in her cupboard and threw her out of the house in the middle of the night, screaming, "You whore! You prostitute!" I swore at that moment that I would NEVER snoop through anybody's belongings. Therefore I didn't snoop into Nick's things. I could never have picked up his phone or rifled through his wallet, cupboards or drawers. One of the children said I would never have needed to get a private investigator. I just needed to open his drawer in the bathroom more than once to see that his stash of condoms was being replenished regularly. They definitely weren't being used on me.

One after another, instances of deception surfaced in my mind as I tried to piece together the last 28 years.

In court Nick said he first met Anna in 2007. As we uncovered more and more facts, he finally conceded that he'd met her early in 2001.

A friend admitted to me, once she knew I was getting a divorce, that in 1999, she and her husband had bumped into Nick and a glamorous, much younger, blonde woman on the stairs of a beautiful beach hotel in Thailand. He introduced her as a work colleague but it didn't fool my friend. I now wondered if this was Anna and therefore they had met even earlier.

I remember around 2003, Nick told me he was going to a health farm in Turkey.

"I'd love to come!" I said, having heard how beautiful the country was.

"You don't need to go to a health farm and anyway, who would look after the children?"

"Who are you going with?" A pause and then,

"My manager in Turkey."

I now realized he had taken Anna. The children say he's been going with her every year since then.

One morning in 2003, Nick approached me as I was getting Tom, age 12 and William, age nine, into the car for school. He asked me to sign some papers. "I haven't got time to read the small print and shouldn't I be signing in front of a witness?" The look of annoyance became a shrug and he drove away. A fortnight later, again as I was rushing to get the children to school, Nick asked me to sign, this time saying he really had run out of time as he was about to leave on a 10-day business trip and anyway these were just standard insurance papers. I don't know to this day what came over me. All the warning signs were there, ears buzzing, tightness in my chest, hairs standing up on end. I went ahead and signed. As the divorce got underway, I figured out that my signature had authorized Nick to re-mortgage our house in order to purchase a house in Marbella for himself and Anna.

During the summer holidays Nick would come to Portugal with us for the first ten days, then go 'on business' for two weeks, and return for the last fortnight with us. Now I realised he had probably been going to Marbella, and not to Paris as he had said.

When Nick first admitted to his affairs, I asked him if he'd had any children as a result; he replied, "not that I know of". Now I calculated that 12 days before this conversation, he had been at the birth of his son.

Memories like these kept on surfacing. Why had I not realised their significance earlier? Had I chosen, subconsciously not to see what was under my very nose?

*

With the release date confirmed and looming large in my mind, it would be fair to say that my most powerful feeling was one of apprehension. A life technically free, but actually severely constrained. If not for the offer of a place to stay from Vicky, I would be in the severest of difficulties. Even with that unasked for kindness, I was going to be in trouble. As it was, it would be a leap into the unknown. I was in a state of permanently high anxiety, even though my expectations for the future were really quite low. I was simply not equipped to deal with what was to come. But what choice did I have? I now understood why extreme cases of institutionalisation sometimes lead to re-offending immediately so as to get caught and incarcerated once more. It is the only life they know. Despite this, I was determined not to be one of their number. The very last thing I could cope with, would be to go back inside. 5,200 days were more than enough.

RELEASE

'With freedom, flowers, books, and the moon, who could not be perfectly happy?'

— Oscar Wilde, *De Profundis*

2013

"How do you know he isn't going to rape and murder you? You don't know anything about these types. I do. You can't trust a word that comes out of their mouths."

Rich, I think, coming from an ex-addict. I'd rung Brad, who had been a member of AA for 10 years, in case Andy went back to drinking. I thought he might offer support, but instead he is shouting at me. Andy has been with me for two days. I'm loading the car with rubbish for the dump, when Brad turns into the road on his bike, fully lycra'd and helmeted up.

"Why do you think I'm here?"

"I have no idea," I say snootily.

"Because I'm concerned about you."

Oh sure Brad, so concerned that you advised my husband to use your female divorce lawyer: one philanderer coming to the aid of another. Instead I say, "Come and meet Andy. He's just gone round the corner to the bread shop."

Wheeling the bike, we head for the main road. Coming towards us is a small ageing, hunched figure, with stick in one hand and paper bag clutched in the other.

"Does rape and murder come to mind Brad?" I ask.

As Andy walks up I introduce them. Platitudes follow and then Andy asks if he can go because he's bought a cheese filled croissant, *the first for fifteen years, and he wants to eat it while it's still warm. We watch him walk hurriedly away.*

"You done good, girl. You've given him a dry roof over his head."

In thirty years of working on building sites I never felt remotely threatened by 'the lads,' many of whom were ex-offenders. In my opinion, once you've done your time, you've done your time. They were very stand-offish with me at first, but when they saw me grafting as hard as they were, every single day, they began to relax. Once the banter flowed between us, I knew they'd accepted and trusted me. Over the years of working with them I realized they were an exceptionally trustworthy, honourable and hardworking bunch despite the stereotype. So when I decided to invite Andy to stay with me, fear for my safety was the last thing on my mind.

*

The house is a mess; rooms with no power, no light, the kitchen gutted, an Aga dismantled and rusting on the stone-flagged patio, a two ringed Baby-Belling to cook on. The washing machine is due to be dismantled. In fact the bedroom and shower that I've been put into, in a sort of annex above the laundry room, are about all that does work properly. Vicky is in the other annex on the opposite side of the house and it feels like the comic representation of a lord and lady sitting at opposite ends of an immensely long formal dinner table, empty place settings stretching between them, a butler trudging from one end to the other to serve them breakfast. The dust, the rubble and assorted detritus of the builders efforts are everywhere. There is a heater in my room and I leave it on 24/7. I am so not used to this.

*

When Andy says everywhere, he is dead right. For five months dust was on the towels, bathmat, bedlinen, plates, cups, soap even the water. After a week I gave up the battle. I'm told by my children that I was always covered in dust but didn't seem to notice. They thought I'd given up washing my clothes. They weren't far wrong. Actually, I'd stopped taking my clothes off at night because it was just so cold. In fact I usually put on my coat and sometimes even my beanie before I got into bed. I really wondered if Andy was considering a transfer back to Bang Kwang.

*

5pm Friday 8 March

A few days earlier I had cleared customs with my meagre luggage. After a twelve-hour flight from Kuala Lumpur, another of two hours or so just prior to that from Bangkok, and more than 48 hours without sleep, I was exhausted, dishevelled, grimy and monosyllabic. I was too tired to be cranky. At the gate I saw not just my brother Martin, whom I was expecting, but also Tom, almost four years older than when he came to see me in Bang Kwang. With my brother is my cousin Marek, over from Poland, with whom I've always been especially close. With Tom, and operating a camera that was recording me even before I'd heard or said a word of greeting, was his friend Jon. This young chap took up station in the car, filming the while as we headed into Ealing and my mother's house.

The door was answered by mother's full-time carer, Gosia. I noted the stairlift as I went up to see Mama. She was sitting up in a power-assisted armchair. She looked small, shrunken somehow, after her stroke of three years before, but was radiantly happy to see me, and that trumped everything.

I went on to Vicky's house in Putney, Tom now driving with Jon still filming. We arrived at about nine in the evening and by now I was really wilting. Vicky herself was clothed as though to go outside: in fact she was wrapped up because there was no heat. Smiling, she demanded, and got, a hug from me. Other than my mother, this was the first woman I had held in years and I held on tight. She then insisted on a tour of the house. So groggy and confused was I that none of it sank in. I was led to a bed in a little annexe to one side and fell asleep listening to an England versus New Zealand test match from the other side of the world.

I was doing the laundry when I heard Tom's voice and turned round to see Andy for the first time. The initial impression was of a man with a white ponytail halfway down his back and a matching beard trimmed to a Chinese rectangle. He was shorter but less haggard than I'd imagined. My first reaction was to look into his eyes. I saw a good person there and breathed a sigh of relief. It would be fine.

Saturday 9 March

Andy appeared at breakfast-time and asked if he could have some toast. "We're out of bread. Here's some money. There's a bakery in the shopping arcade, right at the end of the road." I wanted him to know that this was his home but I wasn't his Thai chef.

I'm sent down the road for bread and am frozen into immobility by the traffic. It's loud, it's noisy, the exhaust fumes are choking me and above all its tons of metal that could mow me down 'cos it moves faster than I can. It took me ages to cross the damn thing.

Sunday 10 March

Vicky takes me, Tom and Jon to lunch at the Hurlingham Club, just north of the river in Fulham. She has been a member since infancy with her childhood home only a road away. I'm pleasantly full when Vicky suggests we visit her mother who lives in a block of flats nearby. We are introduced, I as being recently returned from Thailand. Her mother enquires whether I am a missionary and I am momentarily stunned. Vicky is grinning like an idiot as I mutter under my breath, "it's not even my favourite position." Has she even seen the foot-long ponytail, the bushy beard, the... oh wait I get it now!

"I don't want your second-hand shirts Grandma", Tom says airily as she proffers one as a gift. "I want your cash. Where have you hidden it?"

He starts rifling through her kitchen drawers and then peers into the oven. She's loving every minute of it.

Monday 11 March

James, Samantha's ex-boyfriend, rang to ask how things were. He said he was in the high-street and suggested Andy meet him there and he would sort him out with a pay-as-you-go mobile. I gave Andy money and an oyster card, told him where the bus stop was, which bus to catch, where to get off and where to meet James; "Watch how the other passengers tap their cards." He pulled it off. Feeling a little braver, he then took a bus to Wandsworth that afternoon to sort out his social security. Andy would have to wait six weeks before the first payment from the DWP was made, but after four days he was in the system.

I'm in Wandsworth High Street, still in thin clothes, while the swirling wind is blowing snow in my face. This time I'm trying to cross Armoury Way, the one-way system and an almost continuous rush of big, fast fume-belching chunks of heavy metal. I'm overwhelmed with indecision and frustration. In fourteen and a half years, the only traffic I had been exposed to was the odd pick-up doing three or four miles an hour down the prison's central avenue.

Tuesday 12 March

Took Andy to M&S and TK MAXX and kitted him out with a basic wardrobe, including a leather biker jacket.

Wednesday 13 March

We went to the medical centre and Andy got the ball rolling there.

Thursday 14 March

The two filmmakers came with me to the Finsbury Park offices of *Prisoners Abroad* – an organisation which had been of some assistance to British prisoners in Thailand and which I hoped would be able to help me now that I had come home, sentence served. However, on the single most important area they were of no help at all; they said that, in the matter of accommodation, I was on my own.

*

Over fourteen years a prisoner in 'Amazing Thailand'[46] had thinned out my blood. 20-degree mornings there were considered quite brisk, anything cooler a veritable cold snap. Re-acclimatizing during the tail end of a brutal winter north of the 50th parallel was hard. I had a permanent cold for weeks and the building dust in the house didn't help. The freezing temperature made me loth to go outside.

In late April, the weather finally turned. The impatient trees began to bud, then flower. The birds returned from their winter hideaways, and squirrels started appearing in numbers. Along with the world outside, I started, finally, to come alive.

Quinlan

May

It's Spring Bank Holiday weekend and my 17-year-old son Quinlan comes down from Norfolk. He's staying with Denise's old school-friend Pauline in West Ealing and we meet at my mother's house.

They are there when I walk into the room and I see a slim lad, a little taller than I, in colouration now favouring his mother. When I last saw him as a toddler he'd been blond with cornflower blue eyes; now he's much darker and the eyes are a paler blue. We lean in for a long, almost wordless hug before we sit and start talking.

I'd been worried about this for years. Quinlan had no memory of me except as an absent sender and recipient of letters and cards, though Denise always kept me alive for him and did not make of me an ogre, for which I shall be eternally grateful.

He is excited to see me and chatters away happily. I see I'm getting many years of him telling Dad about his day rolled into one and I don't mind a bit. I cannot stop smiling as I listen to him. I touch on his mother and sadness comes over him when he speaks of her. He still refers to her as Mummy as he did during her life. He'd been just shy of his tenth birthday when we lost her.

After some three hours sitting in my mother's back garden we part, Quinlan on a skateboard to Pauline's and I to get three buses back to the other side of the river. I think we are going to be OK.

*

Andy now has his social security stipend rolling in, new glasses, and prescription painkillers in place for his hips and knees. With his oyster card, he has visited Danuta almost every Sunday. With his fluent Polish, he has acted as interpreter for some of the builders on site who speak very little English.

The taciturn man of those first weeks has gone. He never seems to get bored and, though he needs time on his own, he also loves company. I imagine that, looking like Father Christmas and with a quick, dry wit, he was armed with the perfect tools to disarm aggression and provide entertainment for the prisoners.

Andy has an innate sense of respect for other people's space. He used to jump a mile if I came upon him unexpectedly or crashed a lid on a saucepan – what unspeakable things had he witnessed to cause this? His jumpiness is now minimal. He smiles and has begun to strut like the Chinese rooster he is. In fact, given his spectacles, an embroidered tunic would complete the Mandarin image.

He'll be in his trademark black leather biker's waistcoat, his bandana worn jauntily round his neck or around his head Apache style with his hair loose. Yes, he has got style but what I see is his grit to survive 14 and a half years in one of the most notorious prisons in the world. I promised his mother I would help him to become independent. I can already feel the metamorphosis.

After twenty weeks, the house is almost finished and it is a pleasure to have all the rooms back again, to have a kitchen and hot water.

*

I think that bloody woman wants to kill me. She keeps finding me jobs to do. The latest is to transfer all her clobber from the other annex to the master bedroom, and all her books and papers to the office. I'm puffing and panting fit to bust a gasket. My knees, my hip and my back are sending urgent messages to the control room. After the fifth or sixth trip, these messages twin into a rapid staccato noise, 'SOS, SOS, SOS'.

They say that what doesn't kill you makes you stronger. Cobblers, it's going to put me in a wheelchair if I'm not bloody careful. Finally I'm done, and done in.

"Thanks for that. Could you do just one more thing…" Aargh!!

I rise with the sun. Vicky crosses the road to get Anni, her neighbour who lives opposite, and off we go to Richmond Park. A few minutes of hiking, after parking the panzer, and we reach the Isabella Plantation. We've timed it just right. The plantation is a riot of colour, bank upon bank of flowers, a profusion of species that I don't know any names for but appreciate no less for that. It's a veritable feast for the eyes. Vicky tells us how she arranged a treasure hunt here for William's 9th birthday party years before, planting clues at dawn, then giving out maps and the odd hint and turning the kids loose to get on with it. My admiration for her enterprise knows no bounds. At the same time, when the searchlight of her attention is directed at me, it is abso-bloody-lutley exhausting. I know she does it for my benefit and not her own. What's worse still, she's right, dammit! And so I must go with the flow, yeah, like a fallen leaf in a mountain torrent. I just hope this waterway broadens out somewhere – that calmer waters lie ahead.

I had seen a few photos of Vicky by the time I made it back to London. The one that Below:

Vicky on the GR20, 2012

The photograph caught her in mid-dive horizontally, into a mountain pool, encapsulated her essential nature. Fit, athletic, unselfconscious and entirely unafraid to go into something head-on; a quality she shows over and again, all the time.

She does not LOOK like a middle-aged, middle-class housewife at all. The only time her hair is combed or brushed, is when she goes to get her hair done – she never does it. It should look awful, yet it does not. Her genetic heritage has given her olive-green eyes and a light brown skin, which tans richly and deeply. The years of physical activity and exercise have kept her body trim and fit. Her choice of clothes is almost always jeans, boots, sporty-type halter top and perhaps a piece of Indian gauzy fabric as a further top garment. She loves Indian gear.

Dammit, sometimes she makes me feel so OLD, so tired; her energy makes me feel dizzy. She is perpetual motion. She is a force of nature, a storm, a flood, a tidal wave or sometimes a volcano. She is unstoppable. I marvel at this woman, truly.

August, 2013

The divorce proceedings are dragging along and, although the house has been done up, there have been no decent offers. I guess it was inevitable that my job as interior designer for Nick's company would end as the divorce began. The children have now all moved out, other than William. It dawns on me that if I don't want to slide back into depression, I need to stay occupied. What better way for Andy and I to fill our days, than to compile a book around our seven years of letters to each other. I find him in the garden, in a patch of sun, smoking.

*

When Vicky proposed the idea of a joint book, I was torn in two. I didn't want to do it and certainly didn't want to write some breast-beating, tell-all, prisoner-as-victim attempt to solicit sympathy. However, simple gratitude on my part would have ensured my assent to the idea, but there was more to it than that. She had told how she had prayed for me constantly and how, on her pilgrimage to Santiago de Compostella, she had received the news of my pardon, and wept for joy. I wanted to hug her to me but settled for holding tightly onto her hand.

*

Today I am being taken to Richmond Park, or more specifically to Pembroke Lodge, as a 'change of scene' is in order to address my poor productivity rate. Vicky goes off for a run.

I part with £3.25 for a cup of lukewarm coffee and a croissant and take it onto the restaurant terrace. Even after eight months, I'm still not used to these prices, but it is worth the trip just for the view out across the valley where the Thames is hidden by an extraordinary riot of colour. Autumn seems later this year; it is already mid-November, and while some trees are in various shades of red, yellow and brown, the foliage on others is still green. It requires an effort of will to tear my admiring gaze away from the lodge's panoramic vista and to focus on the task at hand. I'm sitting on a cold metal chair at a metal-mesh table, in the pale sunlight, scribbling my narrative. Some extremely forward and cheeky birds, black from claws to beak, come looking for crumbs. I put my plate down by my feet and a biggish specimen starts to peck the remaining flakes even before I have removed my hand; it's inches away, unconcerned. An occasional ripple of wind sends the dead leaves tumbling away from a nearby tree. Where I had been almost the only person sitting out here, a steady influx of people has begun, if not to fill, then at least to make less solitary this little piece of heaven. I wish that I'd known about the place months ago. I love it. If only the leaf-blower man would bugger off.

The Circle of 20

Once I had asked for a divorce, I contacted **Isabella**, my spiritualist friend and mentor, for guidance. Her first suggestion was to gather a circle of twenty people around me for strength and protection. I wrote twenty names on bits of paper, including hers, and stuck them on my bathroom mirror around my own name.

A few months later Isabella rang me, wondering if she could stay for a week and do some sessions at my house with her English clients. Is the Pope a Catholic? She was a whirlwind of positive energy. She gave Andy a brutal massage and healing on his knee. She told him that his birth mother had never wanted to give him up and had thought about him whenever she was alone. She had now passed on but was by Andy's side.

While Isabella was staying, she met **Marek**, a wonderful Polish builder. He came to my rescue when no one else was available to do up the house before we sold it. Marek is always smiling, always cheerful, and loves to find solutions to problems. Apparently, he says I used to say to him, "everything is possible". I'm sure that's what he used to say to me! Only once did he come in to find me crying. "What is this show? Come off it. Don't let me catch you crying again. You need to be strong Vicky." Marek was in his late thirties but I always felt I was talking to someone much older and wiser. In the first two weeks, freezing with snow flurries, he got his carpenter to remove the gothic windows of the conservatory and replace them with large, clean panes of glass. "No more bars. No more cage. You can now see your life clearly."

Andrew, 'the Rock', is also a builder. This Lancastrian never loses the plot, meeting all disasters with: "It is what it is." He is precise, ordered and considerate as all good carpenters are. He has a huge heart and has come to my rescue even when jobs have not worked out or clients have been a nightmare. While doing some bespoke flooring for me, he and I would have to eat every night in Andy's bedroom around his desk as it was the only table not in storage. One of my more bizarre meals: Andrew with a plate of spaghetti on his knees, seated on Andy's bed, Andy at his desk not looking up and saying little, and me perched on the only other chair I'd bought from my room, trying to make polite conversation. In fact I resorted to impolite conversation, just to get some reaction.

Andrew is always on the other end of the phone. We have climbed the Three Peaks in Yorkshire twice together.

The first time Andy came out of his shell was when the three of us joined forces in a pub quiz. It was in no small measure due to Andrew's easy-going nature.

Maggie is my business partner and dear, dear friend and confidante. Her level headedness, love of paperwork and number crunching kept our interior design business afloat. We share a similar sense of humour, which has been a Godsend on jobs where there hasn't been too much to laugh about.

What has been beyond and above the call of duty is Maggie's support throughout this marital breakup. She has been a tower of strength, a shoulder to cry on; has offered me unlimited supplies of wise advice. She has fought for five years to get our outstanding payments from Nick's company. She has put together my financial portfolio for the lawyers. They always breathe a sigh of relief when she is at meetings.

All my builders and suppliers adore her (she has the Northern Brit and Polish humour off pat.) She lightens the lives of everyone around her, a sentiment my children endorse.

Maggie purchased a Dachshund a year ago. I don't coo over dogs or babies, but I would quite happily kidnap Bruno. Maggie wears him like a throw over her neck when she's on the computer. Does that constitute ill treatment? Should I rescue Bruno before she also uses him as a tea towel?

***Pam**, my New Zealand hairdresser, is the problem solver of the circle. As she was the one who had put me in touch with Isabella, I asked her if she could find me a lawyer. "Easy" she replied. "I have cut Richard Collins' hair for five years and can vouch for him."*

*How right she was! The first time I met **Richard**, he came striding down the corridor like a knight in shining armour, strong, direct in voice and eye, to shake hands with me.*

"You must be devastated," he said consolingly.

"Five years ago, yes. Four years ago, yes. Now, no. I've just come back from the Road to Santiago so I would like this divorce to be as quick and amicable as possible."

Since then, I do believe Richard, like his namesake, is on a crusade to get me justice and fairness. People love to say that lawyers drag out proceedings to make more money. I haven't seen anything of that. He encourages me to deal with his second, Sarah-Jane, to keep down costs.

***Sarah-Jane** has a brain that fills Andy with admiration. Her letters to Nick's lawyers are always clear, even when the subject is complex. Her 'blondness' belies a razor-sharp mind. Her correspondence to me is always reassuring and unhurried. She doesn't speak often, but when she does, it pays to listen – just like **my father**, who is in the circle as well.*

Guy, or 'Dad', is undemonstrative but has always been there for me. He has never let me feel guilty about not phoning or getting in touch, or even saying thank you. Even though he'd paid for my wedding, he told me I could still change my mind on the way to the church. I remember replying, "I've never been so sure of anything in my life". Throughout the divorce, he has rung me regularly but has never passed judgement. He taught me to do cryptic crosswords and Sudoku. In the middle of the night or in the bath, I work though book after book of the 'Deadly Killers'.

Boozy is my younger sister. I always think of any third child as the peacemaker. In a household of women constantly flying off the handle, she was the North Star. Like my father, she provided a healing presence. Having done thirteen ski seasons, she became an action-shot model, with her Farah Fawcett-Major blonde hair and perfect smile. She was expected to leap off a jump, one hand in front of the other, one ski in front of the other. This perfectly revealed relevant logos on skis and jacket but pretty much guaranteed a bad landing. You try holding a brilliant smile under those conditions.

Boozy introduced me to Nick. She has been a tower of strength throughout the divorce, despite going through difficulties of her own. I hope one day I can repay her.

Three women with the name 'Ann' came forward to help me during the divorce.

Annie, a fellow golfer, sensing that I was in no fit state to play competitively, started to ask me for friendly games. A committed Christian, she suggested I come with her to a vibrant Anglican church, Holy Trinity, Brompton. Two years later, I finally plucked up courage. At the end of the service, those who wish, are invited to the front for healing. I went and found myself crying as a kindly woman laid her hands on me. I went up every Sunday and finally, after six months, the tears ceased.

Anni lives across the road from me. Everybody adores her. She radiates warmth and love. She moved in eight or nine years ago.

She knew I had insomnia and would leave a light shining in her kitchen window every night, to let me know that she was always there for me.

The first time Anni and I met, she declared, "you and I have met in a past life." She is my soul mother. I learnt from her that she didn't push enough in her divorce for a decent settlement and in the early days struggled financially. She is one of many women who have convinced me to fight for what the law says I am entitled to as my right. She has battled with cancer and is a vegan. We both love organic food, so I try to do her shopping for her when I can. In her seventies, she can still be found up a ladder, decorating, making curtains, or cooking cakes and that's when she isn't visiting other cancer patients in hospital or with her beloved family. The surgeon asked Anni what the secret of her recovery was so he could tell all his patients. "Taking my pills with holy water," was her answer, which left him floundering.

Anni sees Spirit Guides. She says she is always taken aback when I come to see her, because she says there are two people sitting on her sofa. Eventually one day, when she answered the door and said, "he's so handsome!", I asked her who 'he' was.

"A Native American of course."

I pumped a fist into the air, Hallelujah! Since I was little, I have always felt akin to Native Americans rather than cowboys. Like me, Anni wears her hair long and has postcards of several Lakota chiefs above her door. I suspect she too has an Indian spirit guide. I think we share the same tribe.

*Last but not least is **Anne**, my oldest, best buddy. We became firm friends in our first year at boarding school. She knows her mind and is not afraid to speak it. Her sparkling sense of humour is reflected in her mischievous eyes.*

During my teenage years, Anne invited me every summer to France and Spain and I was welcomed as one of the family.

Anne studied History of Art and has grafted her way to the top of the art world, even being headhunted as Curator of the Washington Museum. She turned the job down to get married and, ever resourceful, set up a nursery. The school is still thriving, and she now has a part-share in an auction house, 'The Potomac Company'.

When Anne heard about her goddaughter Samantha's wedding abroad, she didn't hesitate to come, though God knows what it must have cost in time and money. She always leaves me emails and texts to cheer me up. She has the chutzpah to take life by the horns. God Bless You Anne, my friend for life.

Gail *is my extrovert, lion-hearted and loyal friend. When I mentioned my plan to do the GR20, Gail was ringing me with her diary out and ten days in September were ear-marked.*

On the day of departure, I figured that if I couldn't carry my backpack to Gatwick, I couldn't carry it across the Corsican mountains. Off I set from Barnes station, looking the real deal. At East Croydon I had to change to another

Vicky GR20, Corsica 2012

platform via a ramp. The incline tipped me backwards and I had to grab the railings for dear life, looking round furtively to make sure nobody had noticed. That night, staying at the beloved San

Lucianu hotel in Corsica, Gail and I tipped all our possessions onto the bed and ruthlessly discarded anything not essential. Thank goodness! Nick's long-suffering French agent, drove us at 3.30am to get to the start by dawn and the immediate thirty-degree incline nearly sent me running back to him. The poor man had only just finished teaching us how to abseil.

Three days later, we plateaued and the northern coastline was now no longer visible. On day four, we faced the infamous Cirque de Solitude. The guidebook's consoling words were, "if you thought the first three days were tough, think again." Already two other girls has been airlifted off the mountain with vertigo, and that was only on day one.

Gail was in a filthy mood the next morning, so reminding her that I hadn't made her come, we ascended to the first col in silence. The scene that greeted us was the most desolate I had ever witnessed; too steep, high and exposed for a single blade of grass to grow, miles of shale with the painted markers disappearing into it. I began the first abseil descent, lying through my teeth to reassure Gail, as I grabbed the metal chain. Suddenly she shouted, "we can do it Vicky!" I began blubbing with relief because I knew this Yorkshire lass was not for turning but I couldn't take my hand off the chain to wipe my streaming eyes and nose.

Unfortunately, what goes down must come up. We eventually reached a natural platform with a metal ladder disappearing into thin air. Gulp! Having fortified ourselves with chocolate and dried apricots, we gingerly ascended the rungs and at the top were again faced with an endless series of chains ascending out of sight.

"What did Bernard say in the car park?"

"Lean out!"

"Pull! pull! pull!"

We survived and were met with huge applause from the other walkers as we reached the final col. Gail burst into uncontrollable sobs in my arms and afterwards told me that she had never cried since Daniel, her first born had been diagnosed with a brain tumour. When I had first mentioned doing the GR20, she knew she had to do it, despite hating heights. I really believe a huge weight lifted off her that day. The Cirque de Solitude bound us together for life. She has been a huge support throughout this divorce and we have remained soul sisters to this day.

__Brian__ is a psychotherapist and dear friend of mine, who successfully treated Tom for bedwetting when we had tried for seven years to find a solution. He taught Tom to meditate when he got into bed, to completely relax and then go to the loo just before falling asleep. Within weeks, Tom was dry.

Before long, Brian and I were battling it out to the 18th green on various Surrey golf courses. Only once did he beat me on the 13th hole, during my depression from the failing marriage. It was years later before I challenged him to another round. I told him I was getting a divorce, and since then he has buoyed me up with regular games and encouragement.

__Sao__, a wonderful Portuguese woman, has been cleaning for me for 26 years. I cannot imagine life without her. She has remained a constant. She is strong mentally and physically, and through all the twists and turns of the divorce she has hugged me, bossed me and empathized with me.

The most precious of the circle are my four children, __Samantha__, __Emma, Tom__ and __William__. They wanted to know why I married Nick in the first place. Simple answer. I was in love. Would I go through it again? For them, yes, yes, yes.

I wish to God though that they weren't having to go through this. They've been caught in the middle of a vicious feud, with new information from the courts daily. None of the children are talking to Nick at the moment.

Looking back, the 'perfect family' image that outsiders saw never fooled them, so I don't think they were surprised by the split. However, as the family was being torn apart, the pain and insecurity for the children must have been immense.

Emma withdrew from the family in her teens. She spent a lot of her holidays at other people's houses and only came to speak to me for money or a lift. I don't know when she got into drugs because I couldn't see any of the tell-tale signs in her that I'd seen with my sister Itsy – non-existent time keeping, the munchies, no desire to work. Emma, by contrast, was up and doing every morning. Her skin was perfect and her mood swings I put down to hormones. Nick had experimented when a teenager and told me not to worry. It was just a phase. It was through working on this book that I found out the extent of it from Emma herself. She couldn't approach me or Nick because we were wrapped up in our own selfish and unhappy lives at the exact time she needed help. Thank God, Emma's godmother Penny stepped forward. She guided Emma and her eldest son to work with international spiritual healers in order, in her own words, to "plant a seed." I will be indebted to her until the day I die.

On his gap year William travelled around South America and developed a cannabis habit. He came back to find out we were splitting up. It didn't help that when he began his film school course his flatmate had a constant supply of weed. He developed paranoia and obsessive-compulsive tendencies and in the end quit his course.

I wasn't capable at the time of providing either of them with the love and understanding they really needed and they had to find help elsewhere. In fact if anything our roles reversed and they were the ones offering help and advice, hugging me, ringing, checking up on me. Our house was on the market and it couldn't have been easy helping me dismantle the only home they had known and loved, and ferry the contents to auction houses, charity shops, and recycling yards, to drive back and forth to the storage unit, to help man stalls at Ardingly and Portabello market. It was no mean feat after accumulating thirty years of stuff. Thank you guys for being so helpful and caring. I simply couldn't have got through it all without you.

One positive is that it has brought the children closer to each other and they will have that bond for the rest of their lives. My parents' break up had the same effect on my sisters and I.

Andy *himself completes my Circle of 20. I was living alone on a building-site when he moved in, and had just embarked on what proved to be a lengthy divorce. During that testing time, Andy was a godsend. Without his companionship, sympathy and understanding, I would almost certainly have spiralled back into depression. His sharp mind cut through the endless barrage of legal documents, to give me the facts in plain English and allow me to use him as a sounding board on a daily basis. He is a still person, aware of everything around him and never misses a trick, while I rush around, forgetting to smell the roses. I'm not sure I will ever get used to his drinking and smoking, but he is never boring and has this wonderful razor-sharp mind to spar with or against. He makes me laugh and unknowingly has the most wonderful smile, unknowingly because he's very sparing with it.*

My days for the most part are positive and full of purpose. On the bad days he is there with the scrabble board or a recorded radio four comedy half-hour to cheer me up. And when the tears come, there is always a hug and words of comfort.

Scrabble
(Dear reader, skip this if you are NOT a scrabble player.)

By September, the Putney house was completely finished. I didn't have to go to court until September so it seemed like the perfect moment for Andy and I to decamp to the villa in Portugal. I had found out that Andy played scrabble daily in Bang Kwang prison, so I dug out the board and an old Collins dictionary. It became our reward after a day's writing. Andy would be armed with a beer and cigarettes in shorts and T-shirt, I with a cup of hot water in a cossie and sarong.

Why do I have this daily compulsion to challenge Andy to a game I have little chance of winning? If I beat him, it's when I get great letters and he's had too many vowels. When he beats me it's too sickening; with an encyclopaedic knowledge of words and their meanings, he conjures forty points out of nowhere. One seven letter word or three is 'de rigueur' in any game with him. On the rare occasions I put down a seven-letter word, I have about fifty seconds of gloating before he follows it with his own. After every game, I vow I won't put myself through such hell again, but with my proverbial goldfish memory, the board is out the following day.

Worse still, if I win a game, I don't feel as pleased as I should. What in God's name is that all about?! Andy played several times a day in Bang Kwang, I'm lucky if I play eight or nine times a year.

I should have listened to my angel tarot cards that I consult on a regular basis. "Avoid situations where anger and/or competition are expressed"... He has just straddled two triple words and scored 126 points! And HE'S the one who's moaning. For one moment, I thought I had snookered him but not Andrew Hawke.

"You're going to hate me," he says with a glimmer in his eyes and a smugness to his tone.

It's at times like these I wonder if he isn't safer back in prison. Can you credit it! Two goes later, when the bag is almost empty, he pulls out a letter and growls because it's not what he wanted. I am sitting looking at 'u's 'r's and 'n's; I am over 200 behind. In the end *he finishes eleven shy of 500. I mean, I used to be considered a good player at Uni.*

Today is a milestone in my battle on the scrabble board with the vainglorious Mr Hawke. I have finished seven shy of 400; well who wants to be an anorak and I have beaten him by 64 and NOT REALLY TRYING. Two seven letters in three goes and he can't find the wherewithal to riposte. Said words were 'asinine' and 'writers'. Do I read anything in that?

*

As we set up the board I am INFORMED of some new rules. I raise an eyebrow at the possibility of swapping a played blank for the letter it represents, so long as that blank is used immediately. She has a Collin's dictionary of uncertain vintage which may be used to check a word BEFORE it is played.

I'm duly spanked by fifty or sixty points in our first game. Vicky has a look of satisfaction on her face and says that we should play again on the morrow.

In our subsequent daily encounters I average two, then three, then four games to her one. My winning margins are somewhat larger than hers and she begins to exhibit a sense of frustration. I get over 300 every game, and crack 400 a couple of times. Once I almost make 500 and that seems to be the high-water Nick. The win ratio stops being so unbalanced and when she wins twice on the trot, she is jubilant.

The day she's victorious and keeps my score below 300 for the first time, about a month after we began to play, is a milestone. The day she wins by 98 points with a personal score in excess of four hundred, is a red-letter day. She says she has never done this before. I may still win by slightly higher margins, and a tad more often than she, but she no longer begins a game believing that she will probably lose. If games are a metaphor or a microcosm of the battles faced in life, Vicky is now good to go; well set to face whatever the future may have in store for her. Om Shanti.

*

The woman sometimes infuriates me. I'm done writing so I'm pottering a bit. I notice that she has been gradually moving from one lounger to another as she writes, trying to stay in the sun. I go to move one over to the lawn so she can catch the last rays. She accuses me of peeking over her shoulder at what she is writing. Que moi? I'll be seeing it in a couple of hours at our daily swap of written material, and I wouldn't be so utterly crass in any event. Grr!

But it is the laughter in her voice that robs the accusation of any malice, and that laugh, that smile, are utterly infectious. She is happy in the moment. That is something I cherish.

*

Yesterday, Andy called me to come quick. I rushed outside and saw him looking up at the sky. The biggest and most brightly coloured rainbow was curving in front of us. Arched above it was a fainter rainbow. We linked arms and watched in awe. "A pot of gold at the end for both of us," I said. "Is mine the left or the right?" Andy asked.

The last time I saw a double rainbow stretching out in front of me was on the day that I received the text from Samantha:

"Andy has received a full pardon and will be released *shortly*"

The rainbow is a promise from God that he will never send a flood again. Andy and I had survived. It would never be as difficult for both of us from now on. When I saw the double rainbow yesterday, I knew for certain God was confirming this promise.

Rain

I'm watching the rain here in the Algarve on the last day of September. It is so fine, the drops seem so small, that when it starts to fall it's almost like an optical illusion. I have to focus, look closely, to be sure it's there at all.

I've always loved the rain, it's like a transfusion of life from the sky. It washes clean the streets, gurgling down the drains with its cargo of debris from the careless litter of trees and people, and leaves the air so fresh and new and alive. The furious driving rain of a storm is even better. I would be transfixed as a child, watching the swirling, squalling curtains, face wet, hair whipped about in the wind. I'd search for the lightning, wait for the thunder: the louder the clap, the longer and more drawn out the roll, the better.

I would stand in open ground, next to a tree already shattered by lightning, not once but three times, heedless of the danger, until a dozen bolts tore across the sky from horizon to horizon and I would be screamed at for being a lunatic and for not knowing enough to come in, but nothing could wipe the grin from my face, joyous at having seen such glory on high.

Tropical rain is a different kind of animal altogether. In England it may rain cats and dogs: in SE Asia it rains tigers and elephants. The raindrops are huge and they hit hard and fast. Water comes off the corrugated roofs in cascades, joining the deepening pools and lakes already on the ground; the force of impact creates a splashing, fountaining, leaping and bouncing water feature that stretches as far as the eye can see. The drumming of the rain, on trees, buildings, vehicles and on the ground, the road and the pavement, drowns out all other sounds, except for the crack and rumble of thunder. To stand in this, to see it, to feel it, is to be alive to one's fingertips. I love the rain.

Hail, on the other hand, is just a giant pain in the arse.

*

Today I persuaded Andy to get into the sea. The waves were rough, so we held hands as they broke around us. Andy's hair, beard and glasses were glistening with salt spray. His face was a picture of concentration; fear and exhilaration playing over it. The last time he'd bathed in the sea was in Thailand sixteen years before.

The Wedding

Algarve, October 2013

Samantha and Will had first met when they were 11 years old, in Portugal, so they had set their hearts on getting married there and had organised a four-day wedding. Samantha had forgiven Nick enough for him to walk her down the aisle and make a speech. I was hoping the divorce wasn't going to mar the occasion as my parent's separation had at mine.

The process of 'uncoupling' had now dragged on for fifteen months. My lawyers had advised me not to speak directly to Nick but only through them. I hadn't spoken to him for over a year since the night he told me about Anna and their son. I wondered how I was going to maintain this distance as well as my dignity over the next four days. The vitriolic lawyer's letters, the revelations in court, the fact that I was trying to live off my house-keeping allowance and pay my lawyers, all this was churning round in my head. I was dreading having to face him.

For five years, Maggie and I had been trying to get paid in full for all our interior design work for Nick's company. In the end, faced with lawyers' fees, I resorted to threatening to boycott the wedding if the money wasn't forthcoming. I found out much later that Gareth, Samantha's father-in-law, had taken Nick out for lunch four days before the wedding and persuaded him to pay us rather than sully their childrens' special day. The money was in my bank account that afternoon but this whole episode had upset the children and looking back now, I feel heartedly ashamed.

Tuesday 8 October

The grinding machine that is the timetable for Samantha's wedding to Will steps up a gear. People arrive first in ones and twos, then in a great tide. Sam's sister Emma cannot locate her passport but manages to secure a new one on Tuesday morning, flying out that evening. Her young man, Luis, comes out the night before as scheduled, with Polly, one of the bridesmaids. Tom and Louise arrive on Tuesday morning. Emma is in a mood, and the tension between mother and daughter is palpable.

Wednesday 9 October

William arrives on Wednesday. His trip was anything but smooth. He's been at the Oktoberfest in Munich, even wearing lederhosen, managing to get a ticket under cover and drinking with the Germans. When he tried to get a plane to Portugal from there, he found there wasn't one for three days. Into someone's car for a 10-hour trip to Paris, plane to Lisbon, two buses to Faro, then a thirty-pound taxi to the villa. At least he remembered his morning-suit.

What should have been the unalloyed happiness that goes with the wedding of the first-born, has been slightly soured for Vicky by the concurrent saga of what looks to be a long drawn out, and increasingly expensive, legal tussle in the divorce courts. The worry is taking it out of her and I hope that she gets through it all as unscathed as possible.

Thursday 10th October

On Thursday, the first official day of the wedding festivities, Samantha and Will had organised a golf competition for their guests, putting together two teams to play 'four ball, better ball' a la Ryder Cup. They had thoughtfully put Nick out second and me last so that we wouldn't meet. As I went up the 18th fairway, I had a premonition that Nick would be on the clubhouse balcony watching. Without saying goodbye to my teammates, I slipped away. One day down. Three to go.

Friday 11 October

On Friday, a hot, cloudless day, we drove with great excitement to the cathedral, but my stomach turned over at the sight of Nick chatting with ease to Will's parents, Gareth and Juliet. I was finding it impossible to hide my misery. The young priest, Father Pedro, wanted to talk alone with Will and Sam, leaving the rest of us to mill around for nearly an hour. When Matt, Will's great friend, practised the Trumpet entrance, everybody was in tears. I felt such a well of loneliness that I went from side-chapel to side-chapel in an effort to regain some of the Road to Santiago tranquillity. One statue of Our Lady seemed to look at me with such sorrow and love. I fought back the tears because they were ones of self-pity, rather than those for the beauty of the moment that everyone else seemed to be shedding.

In the end there was no time for a rehearsal – Emma and Luis rushed through a refrain of their song, Luis playing far too quickly, Emma singing flat. I suggested they sing another song, unaware that it had been requested by Samantha and Will months ago. It was the straw that broke the camel's back. Emma exploded, releasing all the rage pent up in all of us. Screaming and crying, she tried to jump out of the moving car, then tried to pull my hair as I was driving. William, seeing how dangerous the situation was, deflected all her frustration, pent up for months with this bloody divorce, onto himself. In the ensuing fight, it was a miracle I got the car back to the house without crashing.

Only William and I drove to the beach. I thanked him for trying to help and we hugged. He sobbed into his hands, grief-smitten and helpless to turn this situation into anything approaching joy.

*

The family, bridesmaids and ushers are seated according to a table plan at one of two large tables. Nick is seated with his back right behind us, Vicky is unwittingly heading into a conversation that touches on her divorce. I silently point out Nick's close proximity which shuts off that flow completely.

*

I tried to block out Nick's voice. My dark glasses, I hope, hid the blotchy, tear-stricken face. I relayed in a whisper to Tom, sitting to my right, what had happened in the car. "It's all so fucked up," he whispered back.

Suddenly Emma appeared coming down the road. She got near to the restaurant, was obviously in tears, lost courage and turned round, back again, lost courage again. Andy appeared at the far end of the car park smoking a fag, offered one to Emma and I saw their heads together. Please God Andy, with all your training at disarming situations in prison, find the words to reach into the heart of this darling, wounded child of mine.

I left with Andy the moment Gareth (father of the groom) had made his speech. It was welcoming, simple and heartfelt. If he had only known that to see Emma laugh, despite herself, was the loveliest gift he could have given me that day. Maybe, just maybe, this was the Leonard Cohen, 'crack for the light to get in'.

*

A cocktail party is scheduled from seven until ten this evening. We arrive back to find preparations at the villa in full swing.

The swarm of caterers have set up shop, using the big table under the vine leaves and commandeering the kitchen to prepare the nibbles. The place fills up rapidly after seven pm, mostly with young guests.

I can see a few trying to work out just who the hell I am, what I'm doing there. I know I must jar on their sensibility with my long beard, long hair, black leather waistcoat over a white T-shirt. This is the closest I can come to the 'smart/casual' dress-code of the invitation.

I amble slowly through the throng of guests, occasionally introduced to people whose names escape me within seconds, and drift out to the edge of the milling crowd. They look so young, well-fed in a measured, healthy way, so sleek, athletic and self-confident. They unconsciously exude an aura of wealth and privilege and, above all, of belonging to the same tribe, one which I will never be part of. They are aliens. My tribe is long gone, dead or scattered to the wind, and I am a stranger in a strange land indeed. I even get that feeling in London.

Saturday 12 October, The Wedding Day

Next morning, both Tom and young William slope off sharpish to do something or other regarding their duties as ushers. Phillipe, the hairdresser, arrives at the villa and with his young female assistant, gets a production line going. He has the bride, her mother, two maids of honour and two bridesmaids to prepare for the wedding, all but the mother being kitted out with hair extensions, and they are generally wandering around in curlers and underwear. A tall, willowy young American girl is doing all their make-up and the wedding photographer is snapping it up for posterity. I'm about as much use as tits on a bull, and in the face of Phillipe's offer, 'I have scissors,' try to make myself invisible.

Every adult male is to be in a morning suit. I sigh and begin putting on this relic of a bygone era. Time was, I'd have thought anyone in such an archetypal fat-cat suit would 'be first up against the wall come the revolution', and here I am actually wearing the damned thing. I am told how smart or how good or even how cute I look. I feel like the most over-dressed chimp at the tea-party.

*

Nick arrived and complemented me on my hat, and I thanked him, which broke the ice. After photos at the front door, the two bridal cars set off for Faro Cathedral. Emma and I had hugged and made up earlier. We said we loved each other and were sorry. The clouds were breaking up and the sun shining through. I could feel the red carpet of a special day being unrolled, already such a contrast to the day before.

This sense of magic in the air was heightened as I stood at the Cathedral door. Down the aisle towards me came my two sons, looking tall, handsome and with such sweet expressions, I was lucky not to be floored there and then. They escorted me up the aisle and I felt proud as punch. Octavia came next, the cutest one-year-old you will ever see, walking and beaming, hand in hand with Will's brother in law, Leo. This was the cue for Matt to trumpet Samantha in. By the time Samantha, looking utterly radiant, had reached the altar, with Nick by her side, a third of the congregation were in tears. The lace and diamante dress clung to her with a transparent veil revealing the coiled cluster of hair and pearls underneath. Her four maids of honour were in figure-hugging lace mini dresses, beige with a hint of pink. Juliette (Will's mother) was in an elegant beige-and-white striped suit. I was in beige as well, with a fuchsia pink jacket and a huge hat in beige and pale pink. 'OK' and 'Hello', readers, are you satisfied?

At the kiss of peace, I moved along the pew to hug Tom, William, and Emma, and then found myself face-to-face with Nick. I gave him a long embrace and he wept in my arms. I hadn't realised we were standing in the aisle and I heard afterwards that all those who had kept it together until then, gave way, it later being referred to as the 'Eastenders moment' (cue theme tune).

*

It's a Catholic church and I was raised in the faith, but it's been more than forty years since my father was buried and I've hardly been to mass since then. I've long forgotten when to stand, sit or kneel, and I can't for the life of me remember any of the liturgy, not even the Lord's Prayer or the Hail Mary.

I inspect the inside of the church, the side chapels with their ornate gilt finishes and the vibrantly coloured tiles on the walls. A pew, full of young men behind me, have begun to sound like a rugby club outing during the hymns, much to my amusement.

In the middle of the mass comes the wedding rite itself, which doesn't actually take long at all. It's over before I've fully grasped what is happening. After this comes the business with the bread and wine, followed by the bridegroom and witnesses signing the register. As this takes time, Sam's sister Emma, sings a song picked by Sam, with Luis accompanying her on a guitar.

A final prayer, a blessing from the sky pilot, one last hymn and then all rise and make for the cathedral steps. Eventually the newlyweds come out to a shower of petals from one side and a cry of dismay from the other as the strong wind blows them straight back in their faces. Tourists and locals alike stop to gawp at this strange tribe. I think it is the exceptional uniform of the men rather than the women's sartorial efforts which has them mesmerised.

*

The sun was shining. Official photos took place on the steps, wind blowing dresses and hats. There was a buzz of electricity as we all made our way across the square, through an arch to a private ferry. Heels caught in the pier decking, hats were clutched but champagne and tinkling ivories provided the perfect welcome.

Andy and Vicky in front of Faro Cathedral, !3 October 2013

Emma was now taking polaroids of all the guests on board. Little did any of us know she was going to compile a huge book of photos for the next morning, getting everyone to write in it next to their picture.

*

My shoes still have shiny soles, being as yet unworn, and I'm slipping and sliding my way across the cobbles. It's normally about three-quarters of an hour to our destination, but the ferry will take a lot longer than that, spending much time simply waiting in the roads at lowest prop speed. This is to give the only restaurant on Ilha Deserta, a chance to get rid of its lunchtime patrons and then set up the room for the wedding party. Eventually, the vessel picks up speed and we approach the jetty at the tip of the island. The restaurant is almost the only structure there.

*

Everyone made their way along the boardwalk towards the wooden restaurant. Looking out from the boat was simply beautiful as all the guests were sharply silhouetted against the fading sun – like a magic lantern projection.

Along the trestle tables lay rows of thick white candles and white roses in little jam jars. Glass baubles hung from the ceiling. Out on the shoreline, the photographer was busy taking photos of Sam and Will, with the setting sun and the two lollypop lighthouses behind.[47]

I had been placed on the top table and I could see Andy seated nearby. My 'minder', wasn't quite as near as I would have liked.

*

We have devised a system beforehand. If I think she needs to be hoicked out of a negative frame of mind, I am to raise my hands, palms forward, tips of index finger and thumb together in a circle, the other fingers together pointing upward in a nod to the Buddhist paintings I have seen and mouth the word 'Om.'

She turns to me, sees me in precisely this pose. Her face melts into a huge smile then laughter. It seems my timing is improving.

*

George, Will Clark's great friend and master of ceremonies, introduces the father of the bride with an admonition 'not to turn his speech into a puff-piece for his latest package holiday'. Nick steps up to the microphone and says, without missing a beat, that George has now vetoed half his speech. A long list of people to thank follows, then a potted history of the bride up until this day. He's striking the right notes, but it's not until it's over that both Gail and I remark, in unison, that in all the thanks, the mention of family and friends, he has glaringly omitted Vicky, the bride's mother. She has been airbrushed from his version of his daughter's life.

*

Now it was my turn to speak. As I began, I realised all would not be plain sailing. The spotlight was shining from behind me, over my left shoulder. The top table was to the right. If I turned to them, my shoulder cast a shadow on my speech so that I could not see the pensioner's print Tom had prepared for me. If I adjusted to the light, my mouth came away from the mike and didn't pick me up. Panic set in, but gradually I found a way and the speech began to flow.

*

My fingers are crossed as I watch this exceptional, wonderful, beautiful woman begin to speak. The knot of tension in my stomach dissolves as Vicky describes Sam as the forward, highly intelligent, utterly fearless and totally determined child she was, and how these character traits, along with her will to win at anything and everything, became defining hallmarks of the fully adult woman she has now become.

Then Vicky ambushes me. She relates the story of how Samantha decided to visit a British prisoner at Bang Kwang and went to the British Consulate to get a name and other necessary information. On being told that visitors had to be friends or relatives, she vehemently asserted that she WAS a friend or relative and to find her a prisoner. They gave her my name, which Vicky reads out, then tells all present that eight years later, I'm sitting here witnessing her marriage to Will.

"She ambushed me," I say out of the side of my mouth to Gail, as applause echoes around the room. There's no room to stand, so I do a set of half bows to the assembled crowd. No bloody wonder the blasted woman wouldn't let me proofread her speech before delivery. Even to my biased ear it seems to have been the best, the most considered, above all, the most loving speech of the evening. Tumultuous applause and cheering confirm this view, though it may have been the younger generation's relief at being freed to get down to the business of some serious partying.

M/C George announces that the boardwalk down to the beach leads to an open-air dance floor with a live band and a wet bar. After some major wriggling, elbowing and downright rudeness, I by-pass the dance floor and get to the front of the bar. Since I'm obviously at least twice the age of the rest of the scrum, the Portuguese head barman serves me up a beer immediately, for which I give him a heartfelt "obrigado".

Near the stage, Vicky is dancing with one of the young 'uns and she's giving him as good as he could hope to get — she's grinning her head off and having a whale of a time. The band is playing a U2 cover, which I happen to know is one of her favourites and her delight is radiating from her face. It is infectious and I find myself grinning as well. As the number ends I compliment her on her dancing, bringing on an even bigger smile. As the music starts up again she whirls off into the throng.

*

I did not stop dancing with anyone and everyone, particularly my crazy nephews and nieces, until the last ferry left at nearly 3am. I was particularly touched when my oldest nephew, the worse for wear, leant towards me and whispered in my ear "I love you so much."

*

Bone disease and a bike crash mean I'm not able to join them dancing, and forty-odd years of support for the tobacco companies says I wouldn't have the puff to last five minutes, so I join the rest of the milling crowd. I spot Luis, not too difficult as he's the only man to have completed his ensemble with a top hat. He's been mooching smokes off me for days, and I know he's got a pack or two of American fags on him, so I tap him on the shoulder and say "Cigarette me, Luis" in the manner of Burt Lancaster in the 'Sweet smell of Success.'

I'm approached by several of the young guests, all expressing interest in me, in my 'ordeal'. I'm like an actor in a long-running play: I've done it so often, so many different ways, to so many types of audience, that I'm bored with my own story. I'm becoming ever more irked that I'm not asked something — anything — else.

It's nearly time for this shindig to shut down. Those of the ushers who are still upright and capable of speech, begin the job of shepherding this lot back to the ferry. It's like herding cats and takes a seeming age, but eventually the vessel re-acquires its load of revellers, many of whom are worse for drink. Some are asleep within seconds of sitting down.

It is at least 4am when we arrive back at the Villa and Vicky goes up to bed immediately, with Emma following not long after. Luis and I share a companionable smoke or two, after I have first divested myself of the penguin suit. I mouth a prayer to any deity that may be listening, that I'll never have to wear one again. And so to bed.

Sunday 13 October

An informal Sunday brunch at Maria's restaurant on the beach is laid on for those not too hung-over. Will and Samantha, after mingling informally and playing beach games, are waved goodbye. The last of the wedding events is over.

Other than the 48 silk roses in their jam jars by the front door, the five bouquets hanging upside down from the iron chandelier, there is no evidence that a wedding which took nine months to plan, with 170 guests, ever took place. It is over. As Sarah Twist, William's godmother, put it, "I really think you had a crowd of angels looking over everyone on the day."

Writing

A few days later, Andy and I are back to the writing rhythm we had established before the wedding. While he catches up on the news and reads, I go for my run. The beach is proving very soft underfoot, so I decide to run close to the cliff, where the sand is old and hardened. Are my ears deceiving me? My right side is picking up the deep boom of the surf fifty metres away. My left ear is picking up a high tinkling, rushing sound that seems to suggest a waterfall INSIDE the cliff. It takes a few seconds for me to register that the sound of the waves is reverberating against this natural wall, but coming back as an echo in a much higher register. Angelic or what!

Six years ago, my runs would have been taken up with murderous or suicidal thoughts. Now I relish the deep red of the sandstone, the pale blue, shimmering haze of the horizon, the warmth on my face and the emptiness of a beach out of season. I run my tongue round the inside of my mouth and find gaps on the upper left- and right-hand sides. There was a time when my jaw had clenched so hard during the night, every night, that I had cleaved three perfect molars in half.

The first time I had problems, was about fifteen years ago. My jaw locked as I was biting into a particularly large, crusty roll. I could only talk like a ventriloquist and imbibe liquid through a straw and by that evening there was no improvement and I was desperate. Our GP Kenric, suggested I go and see the ear, nose and throat specialist at Parkside. The consultant looked at me bemused, saying that this was a bone problem and not his area of expertise. Seeing my disconsolate look, he prescribed two Valium, to take half-an-hour before bed. He suggested that, as I woke, to prize open my jaw, when it would be at its most relaxed. Nick was away, but his mother was staying, and on my return I found her in front of the television. I downed the two pills and parked myself beside her on the sofa, waiting for the prescribed time to elapse so I could go to bed. Suddenly a feeling of deep benevolence consumed me. Not only did I feel that we were watching the BEST film I'd ever seen, but that the television and its housing, in fact the whole room, was the most stunning I had ever set eyes on. I turned to try and mumble this to Vera and found myself looking at her with such love. In fact, if it wasn't for some inner voice telling me this was the work of two little pills, I would have invited her to move in with us FOREVER! I floated to bed and the next day remembered to force my jaw apart. The noise was horrendous but it worked.

Now as I run, I realise there is no tension at all. The tsunami has passed; the divorce is simply disaster recovery. I am happy and it is due in no small measure to this hippy, Chinese Mandarin Viking ex-con. No man has ever listened and encouraged me to the extent he has. If I am in a 'now is too late' mood he walks away, leaving me to fume alone and the boys to giggle. This habit of walking away, sometimes in mid-sentence, is so uniquely Andy's. He moves silently, so that it's a receding back or often only an empty space that's left. I suspect it was a very useful ploy to keep out of trouble in prison. Possibly former girlfriends when hysterical and/or hormonal as well.

When I sprint the last hundred metres down the side of the villa, I see Andy, his grizzled head down, writing. He is sitting at the large mosaic table under the trellis of vines and now, after six weeks, no one, least of all me, would think of moving him.

Sometimes he drives me mad, mooching around drinking. On other days, however, he will be cleaning and tidying the kitchen, loading the washing machine or just commiserating with my divorce. Better than that, I love it when he lowers his glasses to give me a wry smile, with that playful wit. Today he is writing away, lighter and tin with his homemade rollers beside him. He is a creature of habit, rolling twenty smokes a day in an elaborate procedure of cutting and drying.

Since we have been here, the yellow tinge to his skin is fading. He ate fish two days in a row and now eats olives and salad. He squeezed himself a fresh orange juice this morning. Lawks-a-mercy, he may be turning into a healthy specimen. God forbid, if he starts lecturing me on the benefits of a wholesome lifestyle. It's bad enough that he's an expert on everything else under the sun. I can honestly say I am happier for knowing this man. I wish that *we'd both prosper and, above all, stay firm friends for the rest of our lives.*

We are leaving in four days' time for London and the cold. The hearing is due on 26 November. All previous family court sessions have been delayed so I'm not holding my breath. If it wasn't for that, I would stay here where life is so simple. Andy and I have had some very deep conversations, which don't happen back in London with the distraction of radio, television and people coming in and out of the house. Normally my deep-and-meaningfuls take place while traipsing over dales and mountain peaks with other pilgrims or hikers. Andy, by contrast, is a very still person. He rarely leaves the compound here, unless to make sure I come back with beer and Rizla papers. It's too far for him to walk to the sea but I sense he is in no hurry to leave this beautiful and tranquil house.

2013/2014

Winter

We were now back in London and trying to adjust to the miserable weather when Andy had a visitor. John Harris, age 65, had been released in June after 20 years in Bang Kwang for being the interpreter on a drug deal between Thai and Laotian gangs. Because of his age and the length of his sentence, he was automatically given a flat in Tottenham. Tall, thin, with the face of an aesthetic monk, a non-smoker and vegetarian, John had always done yoga and meditated. He and Andy are like chalk and cheese.

Both Andy and John agreed that their buildings Six and Two, were full of life – 'happy' is the word they used – because everyone knew that a harmonious environment would make the time pass quicker. John painted a picture of Bang Kwang for me – workshops, stalls selling stuff, colourful clothes hanging out to dry, an outdoor gym, library, classroom, water troughs for washing and plenty of green grass and space. He told me that the death row block was adjacent and exuded a feeling of sadness, in marked contrast to their sections.

Andy had time to soak up knowledge and think – his two favourite pastimes. John was able to invent electronic gadgetry. Neither man was bored. There were others, however, who found the time unbearable. One man stuck his hand in a socket to liven up his day.

I asked Andy what John was doing for Christmas.

"Nothing. He isn't bothered as he's not a Christian."

"*Sorry Andy but he's not spending Christmas day alone having just done a 20-year stretch. See if he wants to join us.*"

Lo and behold, John jumped at the offer. We had fourteen round the dinner table, and all would have been sweetness and light but for the mortifying moment when my mother whispered for all to hear, "Are you going to invite these gaol birds every year?"

In fine tradition, Tom set us all a quiz. That Christmas of 2013, I have a fond memory of Andy captaining one team, John another, and Peter, my mother's boyfriend, the third. John's team won by a whisker, to Andy's eternal chagrin.

On returning to London for the court case and Christmas, so much was happening day-to-day, lawyer's letters aggressive and debilitating, the weather foul and I couldn't bring myself to write. I was in the middle of what turned out to be a five-year-long battle in the courts with Nick over money. I was struggling to live on my housekeeping allowance. Each email from Nick's lawyers felt more toxic than the last, the divorce process unbearably slow and painful.

Without knowing it, I was offloading my feelings of despair and frustration on poor Andy. I can only speculate that he, in turn, was having a very hard time; worrying about his mother, fragile since her stroke, having to put up with me, and trying to build up courage to write about the painful moments in his life, having written about everything else. He was drinking more and more.

January 2014

We've returned to a wet, cold, and deserted Portugal, hoping to get back into our old writing pattern.

I have resorted to writing in bed with my coat and woolly hat on because we can't seem to get the heating to work and Andy has commandeered the only warm place near the fire and television (so he can use it as a radio).

This morning I have been working for over two hours at the dining table while I watch Andy shuffle from bedroom, to living room, to kitchen, to terrace, for a cigarette, to bedroom, to living room. I watch him look at the pool for ten minutes outside with yet another cigarette. At 11am he's sitting in front of the still empty pad. Next thing, his head is in his hands and he stays like that for twenty minutes. Finally he tells me he's not feeling well. I give him Echinacea and vitamin B, tell him I'll make him some soup for lunch, and he puts himself to bed.

I think I know what's making him miserable. Totally isolated with no friends or family, unable to access his own funds, with me trying to control his drinking, he must feel like he's replaced one prison with another. He's served his time and he deserves to be free. I'm not sure I'm the right person to help him anymore.

Andy has now written extensively about every subject until only the two most painful are left to tackle; his marriage to Jean, and his partnership with Denise. He said to me yesterday that the hardest moments of his life weren't necessarily behind bars. The disintegration of both those relationships will be unbearable to relive. I wonder if he has the courage to write with complete candour or if he will refuse that final fence.

Denise

I first saw Denise one lunchtime in the Railway Arms in Greenford in 1985. I was on my fifty-minute break from working in the big warehouse complex next door, as was Roy, a younger lad who worked in the same section.

The pub was almost entirely peopled with men on their lunch breaks, from surrounding work places, and when this woman walked in, I wondered briefly if she was lost. About five feet four inches tall, wearing snug-fitting faded black jeans, highish heeled boots and a dark suede jacket over a mid-grey sweater, she looked way too cool to be with any of the already-boisterous Friday afternoon drinkers that were there. To my mild surprise she made a beeline for the table where Roy and I were sitting with a couple of other blokes from our 'Chelsea girl' Warehouse and said Hi" to Roy.

I couldn't believe it. The lyric from Joe Jackson's song, 'is she really going out with him?' ran through my slightly derailed mind while I looked at her face. Dark brown hair worn long, nice earrings, no rubbish, minimal eye make-up, an aquiline nose but on her it looked great. She flashed a smile as we were introduced and I really began to like this apparition. The reason for her presence became apparent as she explained that the pet insurance firm she had been working for, had just been sold for millions. Rather than getting a reward for her considerable efforts and dedication, she'd been summarily dismissed with a tiny severance package.

Over the next couple of years, Roy and Denise became regulars at my old haunt, the New Inn in Ealing. On any given Friday or Saturday night one might spend half an hour just saying hello to two or three dozen people, some ever-present, some occasional visitors, and often a new addition.

I liked my job in the Chelsea Girl's clothes section. For one thing we got a cold weather bonus to our wages which, in winter, amounted to about 25% of our weekly basic wage. For another, overtime was at time-and-a-half, double-time on Friday nights and Sunday mornings. If we did four hours on a given day, there was an extra eight pounds tax-free meal allowance as well. Some weeks I'd do five nights and Saturday mornings, which both greatly increased my take-home pay and cut into my spending time. Since I was only paying £20 a week to my deaf 90-year-old Polish landlady for my attic conversion room with bathroom, this left me a respectable sum as disposable income. I even managed to save some of it, which for me was something of a novelty.

My friend Ed was working in an office by the Hanger Lane Gyratory, and used to come up the Western Avenue to Greenford on Friday at lunchtime, to have a pint and a game of cribbage with me. Denise took to showing up then too, and would sit by me so she could see my cards as I played. I would then see her in the New Inn in the evenings. I liked having her there.

I was prohibited by the unwritten code of mate-ship from making any kind of attempt to prise her away from Roy. I wish I'd broken it when in 1988, Roy and Denise announced they were going to Australia. I thought I was saying goodbye to her for good.

A little over a year later, they returned but by then I'd gotten together with Jean, whom I'd known for a few years and who had spilt up with her partner not long before. We were living together in a quiet, roomy, studio flat in Acton, near the station.

Privately, Denise told me that while working in the fly-infested outback, she and Roy had almost split up. One day he had taken off without warning for Bangkok. He returned three weeks later giving no explanation. Her speculations on the topic only increased her frustration and anger. They arrived back in England as a couple who only looked each other in the face when they were arguing.

Somehow Roy and Denise stayed together for another five years, moving to Hounslow where Roy was employed at the airport. Jean and I got a place near Boston Manor. Three years later, in September '92, we were married, me in a double-breasted gangster suit, complete with turn-ups and Jean setting out her stall in a bright red trouser suit.

Denise got a job with the Electoral Registration for Hammersmith and Fulham, just off King street. Roy had been a biker for years. Denise followed suit and got herself a motorcycle, a very nippy Kawasaki Z650.

It was an old model and I took it for a spin. It went like the clappers, the engine was in surprisingly good condition and the acceleration was amazing for such an elderly machine. I felt though, as if the bike was pulling to the right. I mentioned it to Roy and Denise but they dismissed this as illusory. I let it pass; I wish I'd shouted at them or something, but I didn't, and I doubt if it would have changed what happened anyway.

In the early summer of '94 I got a call from Pauline, Denise's best friend since schooldays. Denise had been in a serious accident on the A4, on her way home from work. She'd hit a support pillar of the M4 elevated section and been airlifted to the Royal Free hospital in Mile End Road in East London. I groaned in despair. "No, no, not her, not her," I whispered. At the first opportunity I took myself over there. She was lying in a bed that had been pushed through the French windows so that she could smoke.

Denise looked like a ghost. She was propped up by a few pillows, with her left leg in a cast. The left side of her head and face were a multi-hued bruise and her left hand was heavily strapped, though not in a sling.

I gave her a bunch of chrysanthemums (the best I could find in the hospital's florist shop) and asked her what had happened. Her eyes were on my face, I think looking for some reaction that would tell her just how bad she looked. She'd been sailing along in the outside lane of the A4 westbound and came to a point where it curved to the left. A car on the inside lane began to drift over. As if in slow motion she saw a woman passenger in the car gesticulating, wild-eyed, in her direction as the driver continued inexorably to push in towards Denise. She lost control of the bike and flew off into one of the support pillars of the M4. She was sure she was about to die.

She regained consciousness, albeit in agonies of pain, as those around her called for emergency assistance. A helicopter was summoned and she remembered the flight in a hazy, surreal way, but blacked out on arrival at the hospital. When she woke next day, she was in the post-op recovery ward. Her first thought, she said, was that if she had lost her leg, she was going to commit suicide. She said this with a face set like stone, and I began to worry more about her state of mind than the battered state of her body.

Her left femur was badly broken, as were several ribs, and there was severe damage to the muscles, ligaments etc. of the left leg and knee especially. She had been wearing a very good quality full-face crash helmet. This was crushed and cracked like the shell of an egg struck by a heavy spoon. An inferior helmet would almost certainly have been the end of her. Three teeth were gone altogether on the left side and others, where the nerves had been severed, were already becoming discoloured.

As soon as they could, the hospital discharged her. It took over a month to get her rehabilitated to the point where she could get around, at first in a wheelchair, and then on a pair of crutches. She would never fully recover, and the physical scarring was matched by a mental one. The man who had run her off the road didn't stop and no one got his license plate, so Denise was left brooding and frustrated over this callous bastard. An idea took hold that it had been a deliberate act, and the rage, the impotence, consumed her for a long time. Perhaps it never truly dissipated.

Just before Denise's accident, in May of '94, Kay and Helen, another friend, went for a week to the Algarve, staying in a villa owned by Helen's parents. They were sitting in our living room a couple of months later, planning their return to Portugal. They had already asked Jean and me if we wanted to go with them and we had agreed. The next thing I knew, they'd resolved to ask Roy and Denise to come too.

I organised a stretched Mercedes to pick us up from our four separate locations and take us to Gatwick. On arrival at Faro, we had two rental cars waiting and we drove off to the villa in Carvoeiro. There were three bedrooms, one of which was en suite. Helen put Jean and me in that one on the grounds that we were married, Kay and Helen took another and Roy and Denise the third. A large and comfortable living room overlooked a decent swimming pool which was reached by a short flight of steps. It looked ideal.

I am a fair-skinned, blue-eyed, blond type so I'm always wary of the sun. A little sort of shack with a U-shaped bench around a solid little mosaic-covered table lay off to one side of the pool and I made straight for it. I spent the day sipping beer, rolling up smokes and trying to read the book I'd brought. Occasionally I'd be called on to slather sun-tan lotion onto Jean's back, or Helen's, with Roy doing the same for Denise and Kay.

The next day the girls were all out by the pool, setting up the sun-loungers ready for a day of serious tanning. Even Denise, so painfully self-conscious about the scar tissue running down the outside of her left thigh, from hip almost to knee, changed into a bikini, as did Helen and Kay. Jean only had a one-piece swimsuit.

Funnily enough we never made it to the beach, and I didn't even notice this until after we had returned to London. We did take a day trip out to an old sea-fort, Cape St. Vincent, [48] a wild, desolate place, the cliffs high and sheer, with the path sometimes inches from the drop, the waves pounding against the base and splashing high up in the air. I kept a close eye on Denise, whose utterances on suicide had left me very worried.

She did try to enjoy the trip, but her reactions to any set back, however slight or un-important, were snappish and irritable. The pain, sometimes dull, occasionally more acute, was a constant reminder of what she had been through and she would never regain full mobility, a walking stick always to hand.

The crunch came the next morning. A trip was proposed to some place called Monchique. As we were getting ready to go, Jean decided that we two would remain behind. I was non-plussed at first, then plaintive, then angry. She would not budge, so in the end I conceded defeat. The others drove off leaving us behind.

I could not fathom why Jean had done it. It wasn't the idea of being alone together that made me annoyed. It was the fact that she announced it at the point of departure. It was, not to put too fine a point on it, bloody rude. Jean arranged herself on a lounger and I sat indoors, fuming, and read a book. This was going to be a long day.

I resolved not to be drawn into an argument over it. After a few hours, the day-trippers returned, also subdued. It appeared that the atmosphere generated that morning had followed them as well, and it was a quiet group that sat down to eat that evening.

We decided to go out rather than cook for ourselves, as we had done the last couple of nights, and as the evening progressed, the mood brightened appreciably. When it came time to wend our way back to the villa, Helen drove me, Jean and Denise back in one car, leaving Kay and Roy to come back in the other.

On returning, we sat around the glass-topped coffee table in the large stone-flagged living room. We waited. Then we waited some more. And yet more. An hour after we got in, there was a knock on the door. I went to open it and saw Kay leaning against the door jamb.

"We got lost" said Roy to the assembled company.

I didn't buy a word of it. They'd been at it in a lay-by somewhere, that was plain to me. Jean, Helen and above all Denise, looked frankly disbelieving. We sat around the glass-topped coffee table and had a last drink before turning in. Conversation instantly turned to argument. Denise, who was infuriated beyond recall, grabbed the edge of the table and pushed it over. The glass top jumped out and landed on my toes edge-first. It shattered as it hit the flagged floor and I bled into the shards as Denise stormed out and confusion reigned.

The rest of our stay was in a state of low-level psychological warfare. Jean had been singularly unhelpful in papering over the cracks and I was bloody annoyed with her, and with Kay and Roy. Oddly enough I wasn't that angry with Denise. I could excuse her outburst on the grounds of provocation. Helen tried, as always, to be the peacemaker. Talk was stilted, or non-existent. By the time we flew home, the atmosphere was positively poisonous. Kay would later take to calling it 'the Holiday from Hell', which I thought a bit rich considering her part in its unravelling.

Roy and Denise's long partnership deteriorated rapidly after our return from Portugal. She was still on medical leave, and Roy was the one who had to deal with the fall-out. Physically unable to get in and out of a bathtub, needing assistance to do something as simple as stand up from a chair or the sofa, she became almost permanently angry at the world. Her injuries healed gradually, at least to an extent, but the relationship between them deteriorated almost in proportion to this recovery. After a few months Roy could take it no more and when she had at last reached the point where she could function without third party assistance – just – he abruptly left, giving up his share of the flat they were paying a mortgage on. Denise was alone but for Rocky, their black cat.

Jean and I were having more ups and downs than the Alton Towers roller-coaster. She'd decided that I was, had been, or WOULD be having an affair with Kay, and the atmosphere was either silently poisonous or noisily vitriolic, with some physical violence on her part. She never saw Denise as a threat. Quite the opposite. After her accident, Jean felt deeply sorry for her – "there but for the grace of God go I," – to the extent of inviting her over for Christmas Day. I answered the door and there stood Denise with a huge grin on her face. She looked absolutely gorgeous. She'd just had her hair permed. The day was over too quickly, the last utterly peaceful day that Jean and I spent together.

Our relationship had been juddering along in fits and starts for some time. It had begun six years before, a meeting of like minds despite the 15-year age gap. She contrived to live the hippie lifestyle while holding down a steady job as a solicitor in the 'straight' world.

Birds of a feather as the saying goes. Everyone I knew drank, smoked and partook of 'happy baccy' at the drop of a hat. A small number of these were what became known as 'poly-drug users': that is, they did not limit themselves to just the one prohibited drug. Their choices were restricted to bathtub amphetamine sulphate, prescription drugs such as barbiturates and valium, LSD, and of course heroin. Use of the latter almost always led to a parting of the ways with us ordinary potheads. Junkies made us very nervous.

The distinctive feature of dope smokers is that, contrary to stereotype, they are usually in employment or self-employed. They are not, as a rule, given to violence and do not, excepting the illegality of their drug of choice, tend to attract the attention of the forces of law and order.

To the reactionary right-wing media, we were lazy, left-wing, degenerate subversives. In our own eyes we were on the side of the angels, the voices of reason and of personal liberty. And we were legion. Lawyers and builders, office cleaners and estate agents, plumbers and doctors, postmen and teachers, stockbrokers and librarians and many others were amongst our number. I never met a member of the clergy who puffed a joint, but it would not have surprised me if I had.

It was from this milieu that I found all my friends and lovers. It was inevitable. I scarcely knew anyone who DIDN'T use hash or weed so it wasn't really much of a surprise. But there was one thing, which did not strike me until years later, which made this group different, and that was how few of them had children. Fully three-quarters, or even more, of those I've known, ended up childless. Perhaps there is a research paper in it for some psychologist somewhere. Probably a pot-smoking, childless one.

Jean was already at, or at least fast approaching, menopause when we moved in together, while I was then thirty-one. My experience with women, after the first wild and tempestuous teenage excesses with Kathy, had been irregular and generally brief. Jean had given up a baby girl for adoption, when I was only six years old, and had subsequently been married and divorced. She came to me after the break-up of an 11-year relationship.

I was enamoured of her, not just physically, but in her persona, her history, her attitude. We both enjoyed the same LPs, Radio 4, and cryptic crosswords. Needless to say, we both voted Labour and regarded Thatcher and her ilk as enemies of the people.

We had become friends quite early on, at first bumping into each other in the pub – where else? – where she and Pete would show up.

At this point, I was still working at 'Chelsea Girl's' Greenford warehouse. Around me were largely younger lads in their early twenties. When it became apparent to them that I had steady access to decent hashish, I ended up getting theirs when I got mine. In this totally random and almost accidental way, I developed a side-line as a dealer on the smallest of scales. I developed a reputation for probity and quality and a rueful supplier of mine noted that I'd returned more stock as unsuitable to him than all his other customers combined.

Initially I did some deals in pubs but soon I got too nervous about the high visibility of such transactions. When we got a flat near a Tube station all was done inside, away from prying eyes. Foot traffic outside the block was sufficient to make my occasional visitors un-noteworthy. Those who came to me were all from my circle of friends and acquaintances, and I never made any attempt to expand. I didn't want any trouble with the cops. We were all a pretty law-abiding bunch, daft drug laws excepted.

I only took employment which paid in cash. I didn't object to paying taxes or anything, just bank charges. The temptation to go into debt that a credit card offered was avoided. As a result it fell to Jean to pay our rent and me to pay for the rest of our outgoings. Neither of us had any interest in amassing possessions, though our one-bedroom flat soon became cluttered with books and LP's. We were not rich but we rarely had to worry about the pennies, which I suppose to the truly poor IS rich.

In hindsight it seems that I met all three of the most significant women in my life at roughly the same time, in '85 and '86. Our lives were variously linked and intertwined from then on. Kay was always there somehow and whenever she was having some crisis, it was me she turned to. This did not alter after I got together with Jean, and in the long run this may have been the main reason that our marriage foundered.

Since my friendship with Kay pre-dated my relationship with Jean, I felt that I could not simply cut her out of my life and because there was no carnal element to that friendship, I did not feel that I had any cause to do so. Evidently I was wrong, at least as far as Jean was concerned. The argument festered, bubbled and finally burst. It was over after almost seven years. I walked away from a comfortable, ordered and satisfying life.

The consequences took some time to play themselves out. I hauled some of my meagre possessions over to Ed's and found myself at a loose end for most of the time, staring at the walls of his maisonette over in Yeading. I went to see Kay, where the obligatory post-break-up discussion, dissection and deconstruction went on until I was too tired, in mind and body, to continue.

Whilst on Kay's houseboat, Denise came by as well. She and I had long conversations about my break-up and also her own. She eventually told me, somewhat shyly, that she had been interested in me as soon as she first met me, but hadn't felt able to tell me so. I told her that I'd felt the same way, but had been hamstrung by Roy's presence, and that, when they had gone to Australia, I'd given up hope of ever seeing her again.

Above: Andy with Sheba 1996

But now, here we both were, free or as close to it as made no difference. One kiss and I knew Denise was the one for me. I was smitten. Eventually I moved in with her. I spent some time brightening the place up, getting a damn sight more space and air into the apartment. Once finished, the place was barely recognisable. A visiting friend said it was the first time he'd seen me fully relaxed. I realised he was right. I had not fully disentangled myself from Jean, but the process was in train and I felt lighter of heart.

That did not mean that things weren't complicated. I was still paying the bills at my old address, and having to cover some of the bills for Denise too, as well as all the grocery shopping etc. Then came the really big news.

In December (1995), Denise told me she was a couple of months pregnant. I was, by then, 38 years old and had, when with Jean, resigned myself to remaining childless. Being a dad was going to take some getting used to, but I felt it was something I wanted. I was dazed but happy.

Denise's injuries made the pregnancy difficult. Giving up smoking and drinking for the duration made her cranky and irritable. As her belly swelled, she found it increasingly hard to find a comfortable enough position to sleep in. I did all that I could, with patchy results.

She was still working at the Electoral Registration Office off King Street in Hammersmith, from which she had been riding home at the time of the accident. The longer she worked, the more paid time off she would have after the birth. In early May, seven months into the pregnancy, I got a call from one of her co-workers. She had collapsed, bleeding, and they were waiting for an ambulance. I ran out to my motorbike and rode with no regard for traffic laws, straight to her office, where the ambulance was pulling away. I followed.

In the hospital, I found out that Denise's placenta had torn loose from the wall of her womb and the baby was going to be born imminently, two months prematurely. To my amazement, Denise actually apologised to me: I told her not to be daft. I nipped back to the flat for bits and bobs and then settled down to await events.

The doctor was keen that it should be a 'natural' birth but it was not to be. Denis's accident injuries were still too painful to allow it. So, at 2.40am on 9 May our son was delivered by Caesarean section as I held her hand.

"It's a boy," I exclaimed as he was lifted from her, "and he's hung like a horse." "That's the umbilical cord," said the doctor. After being placed, oh-so-briefly in his mother's arms, he was whisked off to be put in an incubator. He was only three and a half pounds in weight.

Next morning I took her up to the ward in a wheelchair. Our boy lay inside a Perspex box, lit and warmed by the lamps. Denise looked at him in wonder, saying, "He's so tiny". He remained in an incubator for another month.

We had to register his birth within three weeks of his coming into the world. Denise found the name Quinlan, which meant 'perfectly formed' in Gaelic. My surname became his as well. Denise wanted to breast feed. She tried to use a breast pump and became intensely frustrated at the meagre results. In the end he had to get his sustenance from a bottle, much to her unhappiness. It saddened me to see her so.

Post-partum depression is a fact of life for some mothers, and therefore for their partners. It was a roller-coaster ride, the mood swings coming without warning. She was already suffering from depression anyway, as a result of the trauma, physical and mental, from the accident, and was under the care of a trick-cyclist. I'd gone with her once to the offices of one such, up in the West End. She came out of his office weeping, but assured me that there was nothing to worry about.

She had older trauma affecting her psyche too. Ten or eleven years before, she had found herself pregnant. At first, her boyfriend had urged her to have the baby; then he did a complete U-turn and demanded an abortion, making him as nasty a piece of work as one might imagine. Given his lack of empathy and support, her mother also urged her to abort. Eventually, she gave in.

She told me she was totally naive and ignorant of what the procedure would entail. This was a 20-week foetus and abortion at such a late stage involves a degree of savage butchery including dismemberment in the womb. She was in floods of tears, both then, and when she told me of it over a decade later. The horror of it, and the guilt, returned to her in nightmares from which she woke, shaking and weeping.

For the record, my own birth to a nineteen-year-old, unwed mother, and my subsequent adoption, colour my thinking. Had abortion been legal at the time, I might never have been born.

I would only add that a decision to abort carries potentially heavy consequences for the woman, most particularly if it is her first pregnancy. The trauma and guilt can be life-altering, regardless of the rationality she may have thought she exhibited when making the choice.

Quinlan, two months old, came home one sunny day at the beginning of July, to a home filled with all things needful for a bouncing, blond, blue-eyed, baby boy. We spent all day and half the night looking at him, holding him, bathing him. The smell of a baby is a wonderful thing and we couldn't get enough of it. He slept a lot, and what is more, didn't wake up crying to be fed or changed. He was what's known as a 'good baby'. We were in our own little enclosed world.

Quilan, Andy and Denise, May 1996

Eventually Denise's maternity leave expired and she had to return to work. Since I was way too busy as a medical courier, we found a nursery nearby. Though it was a wrench, we consoled ourselves with the thought that at least there were many kids there. He was always so happy to see us when we came to pick him up and it gave us a warm glowing feeling every time. That Christmas the presents were all for Quinlan, and our hearts swelled fit to burst at the sight of his happy, little, smiling face.

Denise received a call one morning, informing her that her grandfather had died. Since Quinlan was only eight months old, we decided that I would stay home with him while she went to the funeral out in Kent. That evening I received a call to let me know that Denise had gotten drunk and turned into some kind of screeching harpy, hurling vitriolic abuse at all and sundry and was now sleeping it off until morning. I didn't know what to make of it but was worried sick for her.

When she returned, she had a face of stone. She demanded that I leave her, with no coherent explanation as to why. In vain I begged for answers. She was immovable. When her mother showed up as moral support for this mystifying behaviour, I had to admit defeat. I grabbed some clothes and took myself off to stay once more with my pal Ed.

I spent the next few days in a daze. Denise had said one thing that really hurt me; she didn't trust me anymore. She did not say why, and since I knew for certain that I hadn't done anything to warrant this, I had to conclude that she had misinterpreted or misconstrued some fragment of conversation or some other type of information. All I had was a whirligig of speculation, full of 'if's' and 'buts'; and 'maybes'.

Eventually she called and said in a small and despairing voice, "I can't cope".

I said I'd be there immediately. She had not said she loved me or even that she missed me, but the important thing was that she and Quinlan needed me, and that was enough to be going on with. Whatever demons had got into her, seemed to recede and we returned to our family life.

In March we went, my mother driving, to get Quinlan checked out at Harefield hospital. When we came to speak to the doctor, he told us that Quinlan had not one, but two holes in his heart. The blood was pounding in my ears as I asked, in a strangulated voice, what this would mean. He said that it had been as a result of his premature birth, and that both the holes should heal of their own accord. I noted the use of the conditional, and after making another appointment for six months' time, we left on wobbly legs.

The bag with all the baby stuff that we'd brought with us, a store-bought item, was not where we'd left it and Denise launched into a tirade against whoever had taken it. The fact that an identical bag lay nearby, with no one in attendance, did not stop the verbal onslaught against everyone there, and it wasn't until we'd got out to the car park where my mother was sitting in her car, silently meditating, that Denise quietened down a bit. It was obviously a simple mistake, easily made, but her reaction clearly had far deeper causes. There was a well of anger, frustration, resentment and fear in her now, and I began to fear in my turn, for all of us.

When occupied with Quinlan, Denise was happy and contented, but the good times were becoming less frequent. I never knew which would appear, Jekyll or Hyde. Our boy's first birthday was a really good day. All our affection for each other and of course our love for our son came to the fore, and we fell asleep that night content. It was not to last.

A fortnight later, I was back in Ed's spare room, and this time I had no store of hope to draw on. Denise had failed to make it to work again. By some convoluted logic, she decided that she had to quit the job, there and then, over the phone. I begged her to reconsider. If her boss – it was a small office, about eight employees – who had stood up for her through her accident and her pregnancy, had wanted her gone, he could have fired her. From the point of view of employment and other state benefits, it was essential that she be let go, rather than resign.

Her mother had been invited over, which I thought might help the situation. Denise disappeared into the bathroom at the back of the house, past our boy sleeping in his crib. She was in there for ages. Then I heard banging doors and saw her striding down the garden to the back gate hugging a carrier bag. Alarmed, I hunted frantically for house keys and went out the front door to try and intercept her. To my amazement and further alarm, she was already ahead of me and accelerating, and deaf to my pleas for her to stop, to come back to me and our son, that we loved her and needed her. I was agonised by the knowledge that I had left our infant son alone, unattended in the house, and could see besides that I wasn't going to catch her up. Defeated, I returned to the house, where Quinlan slept on, undisturbed and unknowing.

I was paralysed by fear. I sat with Quin and washed and fed him when he woke. Eventually Denise's mother arrived and I told her what had happened. I finally told her of my greatest fear, that she would do something to herself, maybe even suicide. Maureen said she knew her daughter would never do that. I just looked at her, thinking how little we truly knew each other. When she had been gone some hours, I reluctantly phoned the cops and told them to be on the lookout for Denise, that she was distraught and liable to do herself harm.

The doorbell rand that evening. Two cops, one a WPC, stood there and my heart began to race. They checked that they were at the right address and then the WPC said, "Well, she made her suicide attempt." I half-leaned, half-fell against the wall of the hallway.

I'd wanted to go but Maureen trumped me with the mother card. I sat and waited. I knew what was coming. I wasn't wrong.

She had been found by a passer-by in a park, some way distant, unconscious. An empty whisky bottle was next to her and I'd found an almost empty bottle of port outside the bathroom. She was back in the West Middlesex Hospital again.

There is often talk of the 'cry for help' when suicide is the topic, but only if the attempt is unsuccessful. I'd read that only 15% of women are successful in their first attempt, but that 65% of men manage it. I could not fathom her reasoning, but I could hazard a guess as to what her next move would be. A reason would have to be provided, a cause that somehow had pushed her into it. It did not take much to realise that the face that fit the bill was the one I saw in the mirror.

Sure enough, Maureen came back from the hospital with a strange expression on her face. She started asking questions about me, and what I thought about drugs, about work and about the baby. I could see she was checking the script that Denise had given her, and also what was missing. No mention of Denise's troubled past, nor of the prodigious intake of booze that day. No mention of her previous encounter with pregnancy, nor indeed any of her history prior to the attempt. But I didn't think that bringing this up would have been helpful – mind you, nothing else would have been either. My heart sank as I realised that it was all over bar the shouting.

The shouting began two days after the attempt, when Denise was discharged and came home. She demanded that I leave. When I asked why, she said I was responsible for her actions. This was monstrous and plainly untrue, but that did not matter. I pleaded for a while but there was no help for it. Finally I packed up most of my stuff and took a cab over to Ed's place again. Before I left, I hugged and kissed my son goodbye. I didn't know it then but I wasn't to see him again for sixteen years.

I thought that I had been the reasonable one, that it was I who saw clearly, but from the moment of our sundering, I began to slide into depression and lassitude. I couldn't work, barely ate, spent most my waking hours staring at the walls. When I rang the day-care centre where we had been sending Quinlan, I found he no longer went there. I'd agreed not to contact Denise directly, certainly not to go to the house. When I rang there, I found the number had been disconnected. I wrote letters, many of them, but she did not reply.

I sank deeper into depression, into lethargy and, not to put too fine a point on it, into self-pity. I would find myself weeping uncontrollably in the middle of the afternoon, or crying myself to sleep. The day I heard, third hand, that she had taken up with another man, saw me sick further still. 'When I realised who it was, disbelief took over. It was Terry who had once bought smack for my friend Kay, a recovering heroin addict, with the express intent of getting into her knickers. He was perhaps the only person I knew for whom I had an active, visceral dislike, and what's more Denise knew this.

The final nail in the coffin of my shattered hopes came with the news that she was pregnant again. We had spoken of having another child, back in happier times, with luck a baby sister for Quinlan. Now his sibling would not be my child but another's. I was bumping along at the bottom of an abyss. I could see no way out.

My horizons shrank. I had my motorcycle stolen and then wrecked by joyriders when they were being chased by cops. I got a replacement and had that nicked off the concrete forecourt in front of Ed's place, never to be seen again. I got a third, one which needed work to be roadworthy. Before I'd even insured it, this too went missing again and I gave up in disgust.

Ed had put up with a lot for friendship's sake, but eventually he issued me with an ultimatum: find somewhere else by the first of December. So I tried to rouse myself from the long torpor, and actually began to look for accommodation, something which, in hindsight, I should have done immediately. In my defence I plead emotional breakdown.

I must also add the mitigating circumstance of poverty. What money I'd had a couple of years before, had ebbed away from me along with my self-confidence and peace of mind. I now actually owed money, a position I was unused to and uncomfortable with. I was on meagre state benefits and had been getting three-monthly medical certificates, my physical condition compounded by my mental state. I'd even gone to a shrink with indifferent results. I did not have the wherewithal to put down a deposit. In any case, a distressingly high proportion of those prospective studio flats that I liked the look of (and were not outrageously priced) had gone when I made my inquiry.

I became more depressed still. It was now late November, 1998. With a week or so to go, I lost the plot entirely. I jumped on a cheap flight from City Airport to Amsterdam with the last of my money. I thought I would go out with a flourish and then throw myself off the ferry on the way back. It was there that I was approached with an offer of a cash job, the straw which a drowning man will always grab. I would go to Thailand.

*

I have just finished reading Andy's final piece. He has never spoken or written about the break up with Denise until now. He has had the courage after all and it is I who feel mean spirited. I find him downstairs and hug him. I can find no words.

*

Who is this woman Vicky? How has she managed to get me to pour my guts onto the page when I swore at the beginning of this so-called memoir that I would only write about my time inside?

She insisted in her letters that she was a middle-aged, middle-class housewife from Putney and yet what woman middle-aged and middle class would write to an old con in a South-East Asian prison for seven years and then on his release offer to share her home with him until he got back on his feet?

We are entirely dissimilar, yet I do see points of commonality. We are only a year apart in age. We were both raised as Catholics, both boarding school educated, at least in part, by religious orders. We were each the eldest of four: sisters in her case, brothers in mine. We each have a love of the English language, written or spoken, and found the output of BBC Radio 4 to be the best of soundscapes. [49]

We would both have liked to be born a decade earlier, to have experienced the sixties, the flower power, translucent hippie lifestyle, as adults. She admires the clothes – well, most of them – and would certainly have been on board with the spiritual aspects of the counter-culture. And both of us still have the music of the sixties and early seventies as the soundtrack to our youthful memories.

However even as children during this time, our attitudes were already significantly different, particularly when it came to religion: Vicky liked going to church and was an active member in her parish, though she would be the first to moan if the sermon was boring. She particularly enjoyed singing in the choir. Her belief in the existence of God, angels and spirits, remains undiminished, whereas I cannot even remember a time when I had any such belief.

Vicky's enthusiasm for sports and games has never ebbed. She is an expert skier, a 17-handicap golfer and good doubles tennis player. She runs every other day, and will walk for hours, in any weather. My involvement in participatory sports ceased almost entirely on a curling rink in eastern Switzerland in the winter of 63/64. Even as an observer, I get little pleasure from it, football excepted. Snooker doesn't count, as it is more a pastime than a sport, and conducted in the absence of daylight to boot.

So the clean-living, healthy life was always the one that Vicky would lead. She doesn't smoke and, perhaps as a result, was not tempted in her teenage and university years to try recreational drugs. Her alcohol intake is limited to the occasional glass of wine, or perhaps champagne. Her strong opinions on alcohol, as a result of exposure to the effects of alcohol excess in her own family, has caused me no end of grief. But, that aside, I think we get on quite well.

Indeed the positive aspects of her character are always the most striking thing about her. She is effusive, ebullient, energised, emphatic and full of empathy, and that's just stuff beginning with E. She has a way of engaging your entire attention and of drawing you into a sudden enthusiasm of her own.

Perhaps the best illustration of this are her children. From the beginning she devoted herself utterly to their happiness, as any good mother would, but she consciously made the effort to engage their minds as well as looking after their physical well-being. The force of this enthusiasm was made real to me one evening in Vicky's kitchen. Sam has some notion that I'm an absolute sponge for knowledge, and suddenly conceived the idea that I should apply to enter *Mastermind* on BBC television. My refusal made no difference. Along with Emma, they used the laptop to enter my name, badgered me into giving up a series of 'specialist subjects' and, hey presto, I'm in the computer.

That's not all. After a brief gestation, and once again after steamrollering my objections, I'm back in the damned computer. Vicky has decided, on the flimsiest of evidence, that I'm a natural actor, and with the assistance of Sam, contrives to get my details onto a form applying to be an extra. One question gives me pause: would I do nudity?! What the hell am I being let in for? "Body on a mortuary slab," says Vicky, which utterly fails to reassure me. So far nothing much has come of either of these moves, much to my relief.

All this still leaves me wondering what it is that keeps me here. I should have been away long since but for Vicky. Is it that she needs my support or is it that I am reluctant to be parted from her, even though I occasionally find her utterly impossible? The world would be a more colourless place without her in it, or with me elsewhere. Is this love? I believe it is. God help me.

I'm like a rogue asteroid, steadily being drawn in by the gravity well of this huge bright star, Will I whiplash around her and back out into space, will I smash into her surface? Or will I manage to get into a stable orbit, hopefully not so close that I get burned nor so far out that I freeze. But in the 'Goldilocks zone' where life is possible? I shall have to wait and see how this one pans out.

2014

The Third Discovery

August

I had just arrived in Edinburgh for the festival and was waiting in the rented flat for Suzie, Tom's mother-in-law. An email came through from Nick:

Dear Vicky

I am writing to let you know that (Anna and I have another child,) a boy, born in November 2012.

I very much regret not telling you of this before but for reasons that were misguided and no longer relevant I decided not to disclose it.

[...]

I realise that I have failed you and the children terribly with everything I have done and I am truly sorry I took the path I did. Whatever our problems were, I should have dealt with it there and then. I betrayed your trust and do not expect to be forgiven.'

I felt sick. Hardly able to dial, my hands were shaking so much, I rang Samantha. She told me Nick had sent the four of them a similar email but with a postscript that he was excited to introduce them to the boys. Poor Suzie turned up, to be greeted by me in tears.

I thought that Nick had honoured us by telling us the truth and we could start to heal and build bridges on a solid foundation of honesty. Now I wondered when we would ever be able to find closure? As I rang each of the children in turn, I realised that, for all of us, the ground had shifted once again. We were devastated.

Final Hearing – Family Crown Court, Blackfriars

November

It was rush-hour and I was crammed into the Waterloo train. Today it was my turn to be cross-examined and I could feel the panic rising. I closed my eyes and tried to slow my breathing. I felt a tap on my arm, and a woman asked if she could pray over me. Gratefully I acquiesced and, as she spoke out loud, with her hand on my shoulder, in the full hearing of a packed carriage, I began to relax.

Under two hours later I was in the courtroom, being asked to place my hand on the Bible. I had been prepared by Isabella in her unique way. She told me I wasn't going to be alone. My Indian great-grandfather would be standing on my right side and Archangel Michael on my left. She told me to tilt my head up to open my third eye and pause before answering, for inspiration to come.

I was cross-examined for five hours by Nick's barrister: a florid, belligerent, Old Etonian, in a suit two sizes too small, greasy dark hair and glasses. He accused me of being a 'gold digger', and when that didn't wash, a 'Catholic' and finally 'charming' (I think he meant as in 'witch'). To keep going, I kept muttering in my head, "I'm my mother's daughter, I'm my mother's daughter," for the first time fully realizing how vital for my survival Mum's tough love had been.

If I was a suspected criminal, my barrister could step in with, "Objection your Honour!" Not so in the family courts. The barrage was relentless. After two hours, I began to crack. Suddenly I had this vivid image of William and his struggle with the divorce and drugs. I blurted out, against all protocol, "You don't know what it's like, feeling like a single parent. Walking your youngest son round Richmond Park because his paranoia is making his eyes wander, his words incoherent and you complete one circuit and he's still out of it, another circuit, and he's still all over the place and then finally, after three hours, he begins to be himself and you hug him – you've got your son back." I break down in tears. The courtroom is silent. Eventually the judge clears his throat and suggests it's a good moment to break for lunch. I am escorted out of a side door, as, being under oath, I'm not allowed to talk with my team.

It's as if I'd been holding back these tears for months and now, I couldn't stop. I crossed the road to 'Prêt à Manger,' got to the front of the queue, and then couldn't speak for the sobs. The kind lady serving, came round to my side of the counter, put her arm round me and led me to a quiet table and then offered me anything I'd like on the house. I know I ordered miso soup and a smoked salmon sandwich but I can't for the life of me remember eating them. Still blubbing, I stumbled out and walking blindly, found myself in Lincoln's Inn Fields. It could have been anywhere for all I knew. The tears would not stop, and I had to be in court for further cross-questioning in twenty minutes. How I got from there to the right building, let alone the right corridor, I don't know. I stood there like a pariah. Nick's team were huddled in a corner while I wasn't allowed to approach mine. In the afternoon session, I refused to look at Nick's barrister.

When it was finally over, I got out sharpish, changed round the corner into jeans and trainers, and headed for Waterloo station. I went into another 'Prêt' and blurted out to the young man serving that I'd come from the family courts. I must have looked a sight because he refused my money when I went to pay for the hot chocolate. I thanked him, feeling the tears well up at this kindness.

Exhaustion filled my whole body. I couldn't find my oyster card, queued for another and then found I'd lost that one when I got to the barrier. I emptied the contents of my bag on the ground and was scrabbling round, tears streaming down my face. A couple squatted beside me, asked if there was anything they could do and offered to take me for a coffee.

Thank you to all those people who stepped forward to help me. I have never had so much support shown me in a single day, by complete strangers, when I was at such a low ebb. I try and pay your kindness forward whenever I can. God bless you!

*

It is 2015. As I come round from an operation to remove polyps from both of my nasal passages, I have a dream of being joined to Nick by an umbilical cord. We are tumbling in an infinite abyss for what seems like eternity. I begin to shake convulsively but I can only open my eyes a fraction and much worse, I CANNOT BREATHE. All the nurses are running round trying to find warm blankets to throw on me and as a result they have no idea I am about to die because no air is coming into my lungs and I'm unable to speak to warn anyone. In desperation I scream a silent, "I forgive you Nick." and instantly the shaking stops. Air floods my lungs and the room becomes very peaceful as I at last open my eyes.

I leave the hospital on a mission, namely to work on this forgiveness so that the umbilical cord between Nick and myself is cut for good. My sister Boozy tells me to go and see a healer in Kent who helped her with pent-up anger. After talking to me for 45 minutes, the healer, John Boulderstone,[50] writes on a bit of paper, "I forgive you Nick." He lies me on a couch, lays the paper on my stomach, then puts his hands under my head and as I feel the faintest impulse to move, he runs with that motion until he is shaking my head in an infinity movement. He stops and asks me to read from the sheet. The most insincere "I forgive you" comes out of my mouth. Even I'm shocked. After over an hour of repeating this process, I sound like Meryl Streep. It's an Oscar-winning performance but still doesn't come from the heart. He tells me to return in 10 days' time but to keep a diary of my emotional behaviour in the meantime.

I head for the motorway back to London, stopping at a petrol station en route. Suddenly, just as I'm removing the petrol gun, blind rage fills me. If it had been a Kalashnikov, I would have mown down everyone in the vicinity. I DEMAND justice and revenge. Luckily, because of the session I'd had with John, I am able to detach and wait until these murderous feelings subside and I am safe to drive.

Our next session only lasts ten minutes. I am sincere straight away. At the deepest level, I have forgiven Nick, but I still have to deal with the anger and the grief.

In the following three years I practise Korean qi gong, yoga and meditation at 'The Body and Brain Centre.' Their worldwide philosophy is Tao-based, to become master rather than victim. I attend their courses both at home and in America and New Zealand.[51]

I travel to 'The Temple' in the Peruvian jungle to work with Shamans through their Ayahuasca programme, something I had always promised myself to do following the divorce.[52]

That leads me to attend a course called 'The Shaman in me,' led by the South African healer, Vernon Frost. Through exercises and deep meditation, he works with the group to release trauma and discharge limiting belief systems. He got me to release anger at such a primordial level, I was seeing black![53]

I am now having regular five element acupuncture treatments with Jack, Emma's boyfriend and as a result my sense of smell has begun to return after sixteen years.[54]

I realise now that Nick was in a committed relationship with Anna and may have seen being with me as cheating on her. In the courtroom he declared that at least he had shown, by being with Anna for sixteen years, that he could sustain a steady relationship. Having lived through multiple marriages with his parents, I am certain he didn't want our children to go through the same pain. Nick and I had always worked as a team when it came to bringing up our children. He had given me financial security which freed me up to do voluntary work and pursue my own interests, but still have the time to spend with them. He did not beat me up or arrive home drunk. He was not argumentative and, when at home, was a hands-on parent. Our children loved him, and still do.

It may take me the rest of this lifetime to process all the grief and anger and instead see the bigger picture. I have met so many inspiring people on this journey of self-discovery and gone to so many remarkable places. Best of all, I've learnt to forgive myself.

2017

Poppit Sands

27 August

We're just in time. The sun is an hour from setting, pink only just beginning to streak the underbelly of grey clouds collecting on the horizon. Andy had booked a table on the terrace of the Cliff Hotel, to treat us to this panoramic vista of Poppit Sands and the sea beyond.

A waiter brings us each a glass of champagne, and we toast Andy's 60th birthday. I've driven from London to St Dogmael's on the Pembrokeshire coast, where Andy now lives. His friend Jill had got wind of a semi-detached bungalow for rent. Andy keeps the one-bedroom property in shipshape condition. He had said the first time I met him, that all he longed for was a key to his own front door. He now has it. I can see in his choice of furniture, his attention to detail, from the kitchenware to the Buddha painting and antique world maps decorating his walls, that he is rightly house-proud.

The sea air suits him. He has colour in his cheeks and the old sparkle is back. I give him his present. It's a new scrabble book and board. In the end though, he returns it, preferring to keep my old board for memory's sake.

Vicky hands me my present. I make to tear off the wrapper and realise it's actually a map, it's from Stanford's on Long Acre, an inter-war world map with lots and lots of it coloured pink for the Empire and I later pin it up in my bedroom. I remember to thank Vicky for the 'actual' gift, a scrabble board.

While we wait for our food to arrive, I tell him my news. The Putney house has finally sold, after being two and a half years on the market. It heralds the end of the divorce proceedings. After five years of hanging on, I now have a monthly maintenance and am two weeks away from completion on a terraced cottage in Barnes.

While Andy tucks into a venison pie, I linger over my sea bass. A week ago it had broken my heart to hand over the keys to an eager couple with two bright-eyed and fresh-faced children. Nick and I had been that couple 30 years earlier. I held it together until I'd driven round the corner and then pulled over and bawled my eyes out. I cried for most of the day and, for the next week, kept driving back on automatic pilot. I had been both very happy and very sad in that house. It was all my children had known, and it was gone.

However, now sitting here with Andy, I feel an enormous sense of relief. I cannot take my eyes off the seascape stretching away before us. Bands of cerise, gold and aubergine are crosshatched with rays of white light. It reminds us both of the stunning sunsets we had seen in Portugal. I give Andy news of the family; that Samantha's boy Jack is nine months old now. I tell him how I had pushed this little angel in the pram when he was six months old, down to the beach near the villa at 5:30am every morning, to give his parents a much-needed lie-in. We would sit side by side on a towel, like an old couple, watching the sunrise reflect on the water, the waves lapping a few metres from our feet. Once, I felt a little arm tuck around mine and a tousled head lean in to rest against me.

The food is excellent, the setting glorious, sea, cliffs, sands, the sunset and the quarter moon in the sky with a skein of geese flying past to their night-time stretch of the river. Vicky seems as happy as I've ever seen her, eyes shining, a permanent grin on her face and a wave of deep affection surges through me. We've both come a long way and I'm glad that she seems so engaged with life again. A weight is off her shoulders. Since the divorce proceedings are finally over, her feet are on solid ground and the dynamo inside her is in full working order.

As the sun sinks below the horizon, pink floods the sky. Andy lights up a cigarette as I sip my mint tea. Suddenly we are deafened by the sound of Canada geese as hundreds appear to our right and fly across the water in front of us. We rejoice in this precious moment, knowing that our friendship has been rekindled, that life is easier for both of us, that our love for each other will always be there. Our sentences are over. We have been released.

*

11:56 Saturday 15 September

> *Phone being fixed*
> *Speak to you soon x*

> Ok hun. News quiz on at 12.30, radio 4 x

08:53 Friday 26 October

> Good morning flower! Has Sam had the baby yet?

08:23 Saturday 27 October

> Looking at a rainbow thinking of you x

> Lumme, hail now!

Hail came down
yesterday x

15:46 Wednesday 31 October

Still no
granddaughter?!? X

Yes, Sunday early am.
Girl, GEORGIA WILLOW
Nearly 8lbs. 5 hour
labour. I'm now in
Portugal in pouring rain
back on the book,
attempting a big cull,
cutting lots of people
out of my sections and
aiming to take the
whinging out of yours!
Xxx

11:15 Tuesday 12 February

I'm editing in Portugal.
Read some lovely words
you wrote about me just
now. You are the only
man who has 'got' me.
All emotional I looked at
the time 11.11am!! Xxx

I love you too xxx

16:21 Thursday 14 February

Can you believe they're
showing fifty shades of

grey on valentines
day?! (ITV 2, 9pm if you
are interested!) ps I love

you xxx

*What? do you want me
to watch it?! X*

Ha ha! I shan't, your
call! X

18:30 Wednesday 28 August

*What does redoubtable
mean?*

Obdurate in defence

What the f does that mean?

Que? Utterly cloudless
evening sky, wish you
were here xxx

AFTERWORD

I am now a stranger to the woman who began reading Andy's letters out of curiosity thirteen years ago. I am still moved to help others but I've learnt not to solve or fix, but rather support where I can. I read somewhere of a man staring at a silkworm in a cocoon, struggling for hours to get out. Finally, unable to bear watching any longer, he grabbed some scissors and snipped open one end. Out crawled a half-formed butterfly, wings misshapen, legs deformed. He was horrified at what he'd done.

There has always been help for me at every stage of my life but thankfully I have still had to 'struggle' for myself. I am happier now than I have ever been and I never want to go back to the 'poor me' victim mentality again – a mindset I had for so long, it became an irritating habit for the people around me. Who must I thank the most? Nick of course, for challenging me the most. His actions forced me to dig deep and find a strength I didn't even know I had. He more than anyone else, taught me who I am.

I am no longer desperate to meet 'the right man.' I have learnt to enjoy my own company and to value the little things. I am now a grandmother to Jack, Luna, Georgia and Coco, who teach me to live in the moment. They fill my life with joy. Every time I feel any anxiety, I start to say thank you for everything around me and gradually the feeling subsides. I no longer need to people-please or change anyone's mind as I had done in the past. Everybody is entitled to their opinion and they are not obliged to like me.

Nick and I have no problem communicating by email and chatting at christenings and weddings. He's actively involved with the children's lives, and I am eternally grateful for the help and support that he gives them, especially William.

I spent just under two weeks in Wales last year nursing Andy after his hip operation. Bossy, exacting, and cranky – is that him or me? – we still get on as well as we used to.

*

I've a decent little place with views of fields with occasional herds of cattle or sheep on the far side of the river. A bus will stop for my raised hand and take me a mile and a half into Cardigan. For months at a time I go no further and that suits me. I leave a tiny carbon footprint now. My travelling days are done. I don't need to go anywhere to find myself. I was right here all the time. I too am happy, both to see Vicky happy and because I've found a place I can be. Perhaps, as an ex-prisoner, I will never feel truly free. But I am content.

APPENDIX

(1) *Nick and I encouraged our children to have a 'Gap year' before going to university. It was a chance for them to work, travel, make their own decisions, have adventures and become independent. We agreed that whatever they earned in the months before their travels we would double. Our unwritten rule was that they do some voluntary work so they didn't just bungee jump around the world.*

(2) Putney, a leafy suburb of South-west London.

PRISON

(3) Krap – in Thai this word has multiple uses. First and foremost it identifies the speaker as male, the female being 'Kaah'. It can mean assent, or that one understands, or do you understand or agree; most often it's just used as a filler to end a clause and bring extra thinking time, as punctuation even.

(4) In his book *'The Damage Done'*, the Australian Warren Fellows describes an old-time version of this punishment. The unfortunate idiot would be placed in an open-work metal ball, small enough to make even an average height Thai scrunch up on being locked in. Say four feet in diameter or so Then an elephant would push the ball using its feet or its trunk, around the yard in the yellow-white glare of the tropical sun, until the equally captive Lachyderm got bored. Years later discovered, that the chief medical officer at Bank Kwang had actually acquired said fretwork metal elephant ball, as well as

thumbscrews, pincers, tongs and even an Iron Maiden made of Bamboo Slivers, a creepy hobby indeed.

(5) A character from *Treasure Island* by Robert Louis Stevenson

(6) I developed this childhood disease at six years old. It caused severe malformation of my left femur, particularly the ball-joint at the top. My left leg was put in callipers for roughly two years. Pain came in spasms, sometimes for hours, sometimes for years. While in Bang Kwang I suffered pain in my hip all the time.

(7) My hip condition, bought on by Perthes disease in childhood, was not being helped by the floor level living. I was having trouble walking and the five kilogram of chain was definitely doing me in. After three weeks I managed to get a note from the prison doctor and the shackles were removed for the remainder of my time.

(8) Dieter, Hans and I convene an emergency session. I've caught the tail end of Johan's deliberate slide into being a full-time, pain-in-the-arse junkie. It's time to read the riot act because he's worn out his welcome everywhere and the bullshit and excuses are coming back on the group from all his creditors. Dieter and Hans do the talking once he has been cornered; I'm just additional weight. Hans in particular is peeved at Johan's crap, while Dieter is more re-assuring – he himself was a major user of crystal meth in his base in Manila, and has also done some smack here in prison. He quit cold turkey and urges the big Swede to do likewise, proclaiming that the dope is so heavily cut that he'll hardly notice the withdrawal symptoms. When it's pointed out that he'll be chucked out of our mess group, that he'll have to make shift for himself regarding food and everything else, he agrees to pack it in. He can hardly do otherwise and it only remains to be seen whether or not he can reverse his bloody-minded stubbornness. We have to hope for the best. In the end it's up to him.

(9) *Midnight's Children.*

(10) Reincarnation was a widely held belief among the Christians until the 4th century.

(11) *Quote by Moi!!*

(12) *Keith's story is fascinating. He was raised in the mid-west in a small town so inbred that his relations were either nutters or geniuses. If you were to chop your finger off in the thresher, the family would get down on their knees and pray rather than get you and the finger to hospital. When he turned fifteen Keith could take no more and left home on a bike, cycling to the coast where he joined the navy. With his remarkable brain he learnt both Arabic & Electronics and so became a spy in the six-day war, intercepting enemy data.*

(13) *Goodness! How does a parent today manage with the temptations of iphones and computers?*

(14) *Monika named her first son after William*

(15) The only other case that I've heard of like this is the abdication of Edward the eighth, where his signature in effect put an end to its existence.

CONNECTION

(16) The names were put up by the visitors themselves, to encourage other backpackers to visit.

(17) The Thai monarchy's power to overturn a conviction. The Thais have a word, 'Apai' which can mean forgiveness, pardon or clemency.

(18) *What was I thinking of? Andy's sleeping cheek by jowl in a room with nothing in it!*

(19) One of my earliest memories was riding my little tricycle, whose pedals were on the front wheel straight down the hill.

The pedals were spinning so fast that I could no longer keep my feet on them. The runaway trike was still accelerating when it came to the T-junction at the bottom, flew across the mercifully traffic free main road, hit the opposite kerb and sent me somersaulting into the fence bordering the church. After a few moments I got up and dragged the wretched trike home. Dropping the vehicle outside the kitchen door I stepped inside. My mother took one look at me and fainted. When she came to she took me into the bathroom and there I saw in the mirror the cause of her distress. I was covered in blood; a scalp wound I hadn't even noticed was leaking copious claret all over my face and neck. I had thought it was just sweat from the exertion.

(20) Coincidentally or not, this corresponds to the maximum grouping of individuals in which each person can be expected to know every other by name as well as by face; larger schools break up into houses in order to maintain these groupings within the whole. I am told the same is true in the services, and the number of kids in the school plus the number of staff was roughly equivalent to a full company in the army.

(21) A hot stew of cabbage and Polish sausage with some side bacon added.

(22) *On asking Andy "What were you doing instead?" (of studying)*

"Bugger off!"

"Wine, women and song?"

"Not the wine."

(23) *Samantha was working as one of the beach water-front staff for the season.*

(24) DP – displaced person.

(25) The literal translation is "Amply rich."

(26) *In the sixth form Itsy would sneak out of boarding school on a Friday night, catch the train into London, hitting the nightclubs with friends doing the same thing. She'd return to school the next day, hiding her disco gear in a bag in the bushes.*

(27) *Lauren's deceased mother-in-law asked John to tell Lauren to please not scream every time she and one of her two friends visited her bedside. It was scaring THEM half to death.*

(28) This maximum had been raised from 25 years in the mid-1960's; we were pretty sure that this was due to pressure from the US (during the Vietnam war). The Thais also discovered from the Yanks the exciting possibilities of the consecutive sentence, so that an individual might end up with a total sentence in excess of a hundred years.

(29) Vicky saw <u>one</u> photo of me not smiling, the <u>only</u> one in existence! I'd just had a row with my dad. Somehow this becomes ALL later photos. Go figure.

(30) I kept the glasses I was arrested with until my release: cracked, but decidedly better than the government-issued pair I was eventually given.

(31) *As we walked back down the mountain, I told this lad that he could do what he felt was the honourable thing and stay with her and the baby but that I couldn't see him lasting more than two years. His grandfather was an explorer, his father a captain of freight ships. Wanderlust was clearly in his make-up. I said walking out from a young child's life, having been a daily presence would be traumatic. Better that he establish a pattern of regular visits and calls from the beginning, vowing in his heart to maintain them until his child was an adult. I met him many years later. He became a marine and has a great relationship with his daughter.*

(32) *The French resistance took their name from this impenetrable terrain and it was easy to see why.*

(33) *No shit Sherlock!*

(34) *Inside Time* - a monthly free newspaper for prisoners in the UK

(35) *There are strict rules on visitor dress-code. Tom should have been wearing trousers and shoes. As it was his only chance to visit Andy, he charmed the wardens into finding appropriate attire for him from the pile of confiscated clothes that had been worn by inmates on arrival.*

(36) *My mother had been desperate for a boy. Itsy Bitsy was a temporary name that stuck, while Elizabeth Josephine didn't. Itsy eventually changed her name by deed poll.*

(37) Short for Madgorzata or Margaret in English

(38) After six months of my sentence, I was moved to cell no. 25, because, as a rule, it housed foreigners, and remained there for the rest of my sentence. We all agreed that new incumbents needed to speak English.

(39) The figure is 80-85% drug offenses, rising to 95% for foreigners within these walls.

(40) *A term used for skiing outside the usual ski areas marked by piste signs and poles.*

(41) *These are strips of artificial seal skin, sticky on one side. When attached to the skis, it's possible to slide one foot in front of the other and so ascend a mountain slope without sliding backwards.*

CHANGE

(42) *I had asked the angels to give me the right words. The next morning, I told Gail to keep his friends walking and talking, to give us space. Eventually we found ourselves alone. I told him that I believe we choose our life before we come into it, that his son's soul only needed three years to get all the love and lessons from the family. He himself had taken on the toughest role because he*

knew he had the inner strength. The rest of his family had taken on the role of forgiveness. I asked him if he could imagine forgiving them had the roles been reversed.

(43) Andy had at this point, decided to transfer to a UK prison.

(44) *Symbol of both transformation and good fortune in eastern cultures. The first Arc represents the material world, the second, the spiritual realm)*

(45) *"God created man in his own image; in the image of God He created him." (Isaiah 53:2)*

RELEASE

(46) Thailand's tourist industry slogan – an in-joke amongst the prisoners.

(47) *We have come to this island in our ski boat since the year 2000. The children have dived off the wharf, fished by the lighthouses and collected cockles in the shallows. We have watched from the old restaurant in horror as our speedboat, having come away from its mooring, has drifted towards the rocks on the far side of the estuary and then in relief as a water taxi rushed to rescue it.*

(48) Cape St. Vincent – the place used to be used by King Henry the Navigator in the days when the Portuguese were the foremost exponents of exploration and exploitation in Europe, perhaps the world.

(49) To that I used to add the World Service, but sadly that has now degenerated into a rolling news programme, like CNN with no pictures.

(50) *John Boulderstone*

(51) *'Body & Brain', a wellness, yoga and qi gong centre in London. Bodynbrain.co.uk*

(52) *'Temple of the way of the light; Ayahuasca retreat centre in the Peruvian amazon. templeofthewayofthelight.org*

(53) *Vernon Frost, International metaphysical teacher and healer. Vernonfrost.co.za*

(54) *Jack Jewell, five element acupuncturist working in London. jjacupucture.co.uk*